A Comprehensive
Guide to

Parenting
On Your Own

A Comprehensive
Guide to

Parenting
On Your Own

Lynda Hunter, Ed.D.
Editor of Single-Parent Family Magazine

ZondervanPublishingHouse
Grand Rapids, Michigan

A Division of HarperCollinsPublishers

Parenting on Your Own
Copyright © 1997 by Lynda Hunter

Requests for information should be addressed to:

ZondervanPublishingHouse
Grand Rapids, Michigan 49530

Library of Congress Cataloging-in-Publication Data

Hunter, Lynda.
    Parenting on your own / Lynda Hunter.
      p. cm.
    Includes bibliographical references.
    ISBN: 0-310-21309-6 (softcover : acid-free paper)
    1. Single parents—United States—Life skills guides. 2. Single mothers—United States—
Life skills guides. 3. Single-parent family—United States. I. Title.
HQ759.915.H85 1997
649'.1'0243—dc21   97-30616
                                                              CIP

Interior design by Sue Vandenberg Koppenol

Printed in the United States of America

02 03 04 /❖ DC/ 10 9 8 7 6

*To moms and dads everywhere
courageous enough to singlehandedly
do the job that God designed for two*

10″

A Road Map for Single Parents

5 What Roadblocks Do You Face?

6 What Are You Learning?

Acknowledgments

When I go to museums to view works of art, I feel awed by the composition, perspective, and harmony that hang within the frames. I can't help but wonder, what were the artists' inspirations? Where did their encouragements come from? What individuals helped them achieve their designs?

My writing has been born out of the everyday, unpredictable experiences of my life. Like an artist, the quality of the strokes has largely depended on those who provided the inspiration:

friends and family who encouraged me through the experiences—both good and bad;

my children—Ashley, Courtney, and Clint—who provided many of the experiences;

my editor, Sandy Vander Zicht, who saw the value of sharing these experiences with others;

and most importantly, God, who has used each one of these experiences to teach me valuable lessons.

To all of you, thank you. Thank you for seeing the artist in me. Thank you for helping me frame *Parenting on Your Own*.

Introduction

I sat with my head against the window in the backseat of the car, watching as dry August winds whipped swirls of dust across the road. Tumbleweeds rambled aimlessly. It was late afternoon. We were on our way home.

I had been visiting my mother in southern Arizona with Aunt Joan—Mom's sister. Our stay was brief, but fulfilling and eventful. My husband was holding down the fort in Indiana. Our lives were comfortable, his business was secure, and in another six months, we would give birth to our first child.

These events were tucked warmly in my mind as I closed my eyes to rest for my turn at the wheel. I would take over when we got to the southwestern part of New Mexico. Soon, I was sleeping soundly.

How much time passed, I do not know. But I opened my eyes to a voice from the front. The car had pulled to a stop. I sat up in the darkness. Bright streetlights shone into our car.

"Where are we?" I asked, still groggy.

Aunt Joan turned slowly. "I think I made a wrong turn."

"Where are we?"

"El Paso. By the stockyards in El Paso."

"El Paso?" I asked. "Why El Paso? That's two hundred miles from where we need to be!"

I climbed out of the car and grabbed the map from Joan, thinking, *Some rest that turned out to be.*

Later I apologized for my grumpiness. But it was much, much later before I stopped feeling those emotions crawling around inside of me—anger, bitterness, confusion, disappointment. We were in a foreign place, far from where I had planned or wanted to be. I looked at the map to try to find my way back. The long journey had begun.

On Down the Road

Four years later, I was pregnant again in August—this time with our third child. Once more I was lost in a foreign place where I had never wanted or planned to be. My husband had decided he didn't want to be married and was gone. I was alone with one- and three-year-old daughters and had a son on the way. What would I do?

I felt shrouded in gloom, reminded of the darkness that had surrounded me in the car years before. And just like then, it seemed ominous lights streamed in around me, reminding me I had to move on. But how? And where?

I've now been driving down this single-parenting road for nearly twelve years. At first I could only think about finding my way back to a familiar place. But as the pavement of our journey stretched on endlessly, the description and location of our home was redefined.

With every mile I drove in the beginning, I felt the same anger, bitterness, confusion, and disappointment at someone I thought had knocked me off my path. I struggled to find my way. Tears blinded me as I looked to the thousand miles that lay ahead. *What about emergencies? The unforeseen? The breakdowns? The blowouts?* Most of these crises I imagined never happened. The ones that did I handled as they occurred. And I kept on driving.

As I got a little further on, I began to take some new turns. I found myself in unexpected places, and I actually enjoyed my stay and the scenery along the way. I met other single moms and dads driving around me and beside me and coming up from behind. I had the privilege of looking at the map with those new to the journey to help them plot their own routes. Different roads brought us together. Different emotions awaited us. Different roadblocks confronted us. Different skills were required of us. Different side roads were presented to us. Different destinations were being reached by each of us. But we all drive on by ourselves, with our children riding along.

I haven't yet arrived, but it's been some ride. The road continues to be bumpy, and I still take some wrong turns. I've had to make many decisions on my own and trust for the best. Other times I have asked for directions and sought help from those who knew the terrain. During the trip, I have passed on what I learned to my children. We have discovered that the impossible can be possible, that hopelessness can turn to hope, and we can always, always make our home from wherever we are.

While I don't know what my final destination is, I am headed for places where I can drop off each of my children—as mature and grown, to discover their own way. My goal is to finish raising them into the lives they were created by God to live. Beyond that, I don't know, and that is okay for now.

I keep driving—mile after mile. One difficulty and then one more breathtaking stretch of scenery at a time.

I open the window to draw in some fresh air and my foot dips a little deeper on the pedal. I'm not sure how or when or where, but I know I will make it safely on this journey of parenting on my own, and so can you.

1

What
Route
Brings
You Here?

Marital Status

It was a Wednesday, the middle of May. I pulled to a stop in front of a hotel in Colorado. Twenty-eight hours across country in a van with three kids and three animals—we smelled like Noah's ark. My job as editor of *Single-Parent Family* magazine would begin on Monday.

I had been divorced and raising my children on my own for nine years. I assumed that experience had earned me a badge that read, "I'm a single parent, know what I mean?"

But as I look back, I'm not sure even I knew what that meant. Every day, through my work, I find new friends—friends who bond to me through our common experience of raising kids alone. They come from everywhere, represent every background, and some have experienced every atrocity one can imagine:

Jerry lives in Washington State. He lost his wife, mother, and daughter in an automobile accident several years ago. He parents his remaining two children, alone.

Sue is from Georgia. She has been divorced twice. Her two daughters lived together in an apartment with their two children. The father of one of Sue's grandchildren came into the apartment and killed both of Sue's daughters and one grandchild before turning the gun on himself. For five years, Sue has been raising the remaining grandson by herself.

Dick lived in Iowa with his wife, Janet, and daughter. They were expecting twins when Janet had a stroke and became an invalid. Dick is now a single parent to three children and his wife.

Adrienne parents her daughter alone while her husband serves time in prison.

Dot was a teen who had no idea that an innocent night out with the girls would result in rape and the daughter she now raises alone.

At fifteen, a pregnancy and physical abuse changed Stephanie's life.

Deanna is finding what it means to be a single parent to a child from China.

P.J. lost her husband to Iraqi gunfire on the day of the cease-fire in Operation Desert Storm.

Statistics Change; People Remain the Same—Hopeful

Single parents come in all shapes and sizes and from all kinds of backgrounds. Some of us have experienced death of the ones we loved, others have suffered through death of another kind through divorce or abandonment. Some of us are moms, others dads. Some custodial, others noncustodial. Some of us are teens raising kids alone, others are grandparents. We represent every ethnic, socio-economic, and geographic category.

We hear much about our large numbers and possible effects our single-parent status could have on our children. But the statistics fail to reflect the tenacity, dedication, and hope most of us single parents have. We are sinking our lives into the lives of our children. We have determined that regardless of the statistics, the circumstances, or the forecast, where there is life, there is hope.

Hope makes the difference between those who are making it and those who are not. Hope drives people toward their goals, regardless of the obstacles. Hope says that everything is going to turn out okay. The deepest instinct of all human beings is hope, the desire to survive. And the Bible says, "Hope does not disappoint us."[1]

I received a letter recently from a woman named Christine from New South Wales, Australia. She reflected hope from across the globe as she wrote:

> For the last three years, my family and I have been making our way through the pain of divorce. When I was at my lowest point, I went for a walk in my garden and felt sad that as friends mowed my lawn, they would mow down my little freesia flowers.
>
> But God let me know that no matter how the lawnmower or hail or anything else destroys the leaves of the freesia, the bulb is safe from harm, buried in the soil. It will only miss a season of blooming, and then it will be back.
>
> So, too, the most precious parts of my personality and my soul and spirit are kept safe in God's loving care—and after a season, I will bloom again.

That's a single parent who's going to make it. That's a single parent with hope.

1

The Divorced

I touched the box leaning against the wall. Plastic covered the contents and preserved them, protecting them against dust and damage. My mind flashed back to our elegant November wedding and the till-death-do-us-part promises we had made to each other. I found myself wondering why someone could not have preserved my marriage as well as they did my marriage gown.

What You Should Know

Divorce in the United States has changed the home life of 12.2 million women-headed homes and 1.2 million men-headed homes. Since the introduction of no-fault divorce in 1970, the number of single-parent homes is up 122 percent for women and 163 percent for men. Over the same period, the number of married-couple families grew by only 20 percent.[1]

More than half of American children are expected to spend time in a single-parent home before they reach age eighteen. A Gallup survey found the major reasons for these large numbers are incompatibility (52 percent); drug or alcohol problems (16 percent); disputes about money, family, or children (10 percent); and physical abuse (5 percent).[2]

Questions You Ask

My divorce will be final next week. Can I expect things to really be that final?

Divorces are never final when children are involved. The problems do not necessarily disappear once the marriage is dissolved. Many times the alcoholism or abuse is transferred to a different setting in which one parent takes primary charge of the children. How ongoing the issues are depends on the number of changes that take place, how old your children are, whether either of you remarries, and the amount of conflict that persists between you.

I can't afford an attorney, but my husband and I can't work anything out together. What are our alternatives?

Mediators can help you find creative solutions to your problems. Impartial men and women are appointed to hear your case and decide on things such as who will be responsible for health insurance, how college expenses will be paid, and what information is shared. Your county courthouse can tell you how to contact a mediator.

Never give up, however, trying to improve your relationship with your ex. You *and* your children will benefit by these attempts.

I'm new to divorce. What is the main problem I'll have to deal with?

Probably the most important psychological challenge for former partners involves redefining power and intimacy boundaries. For many families, visitation represents the only remaining link between ex-spouses. That is why it often becomes a major battleground. But it also can provide an ideal place for redefining these needed boundaries and for sorting out the continuing roles as parents from the past roles as spouses.

The People Involved

As a dad, how can I minimize the impact of divorce on my children?

Stay involved and keep your responses toward your ex-wife under control.

When you are a part of your children's lives, they will likely have fewer psychological problems. When custodial mothers and noncustodial fathers get along better, the children usually exhibit higher self-concepts and get better grades in school.

These children, especially daughters, are often more popular with their peers. This may be because the children learn how to get along well with others from parents who are working hard to get along with each other.

If you remain involved with your children and get along decently with your ex-wife, it tells the children that they are still loved, will not be abandoned, and will be okay. Furthermore, you will teach your children discipline, respect, and how to remain in control of their lives and the choices they make.

I am a single mom. Things seem to be going pretty well for us except in the area of money. Can you help?

Leslie N. Richards and Cynthia J. Schmiege conducted a study in which sixty mothers and eleven fathers participated in a telephone interview about their single-parenting experiences. Four issues were targeted: problems, strengths, ease of pulling parenting off, and the differences between men- and women-headed households. They found:

- Mothers reported problems with money, 79 percent; role/task overload, 58 percent; social life, 30 percent; problems with ex-spouse, 10 percent; and other, 30 percent.
- Fathers reported problems with money, 19 percent; role/task overload, 38 percent; social life, 18 percent; problems with ex-spouse, 38 percent; and other, 28 percent.

In this study, money appeared to be the most pervasive problem for single mothers. Fathers reported more problems with ex-spouses, including the desire of an ex-spouse for more child support, manipulation of the children, improper treatment of the children as a means of revenge, rejection of children in favor of a new significant other, and denial of visitation by the ex-spouse who was awarded custody.[3]

Money could represent the biggest problem for you while your ex-husband sees problems in other areas. Keep the lines of communication open and work through issues as they arise.

Meanwhile, budgeting, buying within your means, cutting out non-essentials—these are all things you will need to continue to do. It's not fair but it's doable. And you can find creative ways of celebrating life with your family in spite of your meager financial means.

Does single parenting get easier as time goes on?

For most of the single parents I talk to, single parenting does seem to get easier, probably because of increased experience and organizational skills. The difficulties that persist are often linked to challenges of adolescents and/or continued strife with the former mate.

I've been divorced for almost seven years. My ex-husband and I have forgiven each other for the hurts we caused. As a result, our daughter has two parents who are always there for her and never fight over inconsequential things. Is there a way other divorced parents can put aside their anger and hurt and realize what they do to the children?

Barb Schiller writes, "The time spent [healing] depends on how many losses the child has suffered and how much continued strife occurs between the parents."[4]

Parents work hard to put the right food into their children, but sometimes forget the ramifications of their behavior. Though every situation is different, it is in the best interests of all children to have their parents get along—married or not. Hard work and a determination to swallow one's pride at times are involved. But getting along is one effort well worth the trouble.

My ex-wife and I struggle to get along with each other. How can I best parent my children in light of my relationship with their mother?

The effort to get along for the children's sakes is an important decision to make. Living in a home full of conflict is often worse for parents and children than experiencing the challenges of a single-parent family. Improvements can sometimes be gained by the determination of both you and your ex-spouse to make it happen. Other times, mediation or family practitioners may be needed. Whether you get help or do it alone, the most success will be had when you both determine to make the situation work. Start in these areas:

- Examine every aspect of interdependence the two of you still share: How many children do you have? How much financial interdependence is there? How much hostility or self-blame still exists?
- Work through feelings of blame as well as ways to make the

custody arrangements benefit all concerned.
- Redefine roles and expectations to accommodate the changes.
- Allow input from both of you about things that are and are not working in the divorced arrangement. Then get together either by yourselves or with an impartial mediator and generate give-and-take solutions to the problems.

You don't have to like your ex-spouse. But you do need to get along for the sake of your children. It sounds as though you have taken the first steps toward doing that.

Besides the obvious of getting along well with each other, how can my ex-husband and I prepare our children for their futures?

You sound as though you already understand the importance of always putting the kids first. While doing that, consider the following:

- Assure the children that the divorce was not their fault. Let them know that while you may be separating from their other parent, you are not parting company with them.
- Explain scheduling—when they will be staying at home and when they will get to visit the other parent.
- Accept that your children will feel bewildered and helpless.

They can experience difficulty expressing their confusion and fears. Be available. Treat every question seriously. Listen and talk.

- Honestly share your feelings. Admit to being frustrated, lonely, sad, angry, and afraid. Your candor will help your children to be more open about their feelings.
- Allow your children to grieve. Assure them that you will always be there for them.
- Realize that a child's healing process will be slow. Be tolerant of unique grief reactions and unusual behavior. Get help if necessary.
- Communicate effectively with the child's other parent regarding concerns you may have. Work together toward solutions.
- Pray with your children. Ask God to guide you in your new family circumstances.

Our single-parent home is doing well. The children and I have developed a good life for ourselves since the divorce. Should I feel guilty that their dad is gone?

I feel the same way most of the time, but our good home has taken many years to build. The strengths I observe in successful single-parent homes include:

- A sense of honesty and trust and conveying ideas clearly to family and friends.
- Personal growth despite the circumstances.
- Pride in the parent's ability to provide for the family.
- Support of the children—remaining patient, helping children cope, and fostering independence.
- Skills to become well organized, dependable, and able to coordinate schedules.
- Higher levels of autonomy and responsibility in children.
- The assurance that despite the changing circumstances, you are still a family.

While celebrating the strengths in your home, never minimize the importance of your childrens' father. Do everything you can to keep him involved in their lives.

Sometimes in the evening all I can do is crash with my son. We snuggle on the couch and sometimes don't even talk. Is this enough?

Don't neglect talking and doing with your son as well, but never stop touching. As he grows, your touches will change to different settings—on the way to his football game and at home after he returns from a date.

My family and I have found creative ways to cram multiple bodies together on the couch as well. In church, my shoulders have supported heads on both sides through many Sunday morning sermons.

One day at the beginning of a school year, Courtney came home from her third-grade class and handed me a crumpled lunch bag as I prepared dinner. I opened it to some strange contents and a scrap of paper bearing this message written by her teacher:

"In this bag you will find—rubber bands to remind you of hugging and those times when you want to give a hug or when you just want to receive one. Tissue to remind you to dry someone's tears away. Toothpick to pick out all the good qualities of someone. Candy kisses to remind you that people need a treat once in a while. Eraser to remind you that everyone makes mistakes, and that's okay."

I read the reminder through my tears and looked up at a young girl who was already on the run through the house. I put down the spoon I was holding and picked up a little boy with eyes full of adventure. I ruffled Courtney's hair and tickled her, realizing again how tall she was going to be. I winked at Ashley and gave her a quick hug as she did her usual thing on the phone. I had been reminded one more time of the most special way to stay in touch with my kids— even though I am parenting on my own.

2

The Never-Married

When I was a child in Ohio, we had some old clotheslines in our backyard. With the benefit of two poles secure in the ground and in close proximity to each other, these poles were able to support everything we hung on those lines — even the still-wet towels from the old ringer washer, towels that froze solid in the winter.

But when one of those poles was removed, there was no physical way the remaining one could support all the lines. One by one, the lines fell to the ground.

Never-married moms and dads find themselves in positions of being the only pole available to hold up the many lines involved in parenting. They need help doing that.

That help comes from others— not to become that other pole (their lives are busy enough with their own things), but to pick up individual lines. Coaches, church members, family, and friends can assist the never-married parent in accomplishing their impossible tasks. But how does the never-married parent find that help?

What You Should Know

Single parents who never married before the birth of at least their first child are no longer a minority. From 1970 to 1992, the numbers have increased from 11 to 30 percent.[1] Today the percentage of mothers who never married is about equal to the percentage of mothers who are divorced.

Those numbers are still growing at a rapid rate. Percentages of never-married mothers with their own children aged six to seventeen were 40 percent of blacks, 21 percent of Hispanics, and 12 percent of whites.[2] Among mothers with their own children under six, the percentages of mothers who have never married are 78 percent of blacks, 65 percent of Hispanics, and 55 percent of whites.

In spite of the growing number, society often still frowns on the never-married mom. Many adoption agencies will not assist an unmarried woman in finding children to adopt. Those who become parents through artificial insemination, sperm banks, or surrogate individuals may face disapproval from others. Those who make wrong choices and, as a result, get pregnant sometimes face unforgiveness and rejection by those who could help the most to hold up the lines for a single parent.

Questions You Ask

I chose to give birth, even when others advised me to abort. My son is three months old, and I still can't get over the stares and whispers about me not having a husband. Isn't my choice better than killing my unborn child?

You bet it is. Many of the decisions we make in life, however, require courage, conviction, and the need to take a lonely stand. But giving birth and raising your child has to mean more to you than the disapproval it brings. Your decision may continue to bring whispers from people, but God will forgive any mistake we make. We just have to ask. "If we confess our sins, he is faithful and just and will forgive us our sins."[3] Once you do, your past is behind you and your future is before you. God will help you find your way and bring along people to help you do that.

Stand tall in your decision. Become a good mom in spite of the adverse circumstances that surround you. That lucky little boy in your home is worth that stand.

The father of my child and I do not have a solid enough relationship to marry. Our daughter is now two months old, and her father's lack of interest in seeing her reinforces my decision to let the relationship go. Should I force him to help with child support?

Both mom and dad are responsible to help rear their child. Fortunately, the courts can help with the financial responsibility. Unfortunately, it doesn't work all the time. And the courts can do nothing toward forcing either parent to take an emotional interest in a child.

The best thing for your daughter is to have both parents involved in her life in a healthy way—married or not. Try to work out all you can between the two of you. If the man is genuinely not interested in his child, I would probably let it go. Some legal things can be done to try to enforce financial contribution by the father. But going to court to pursue money from the father that he doesn't have costs money that you probably don't have. And while these court procedures drag on, you can begin to feel bitter and angry toward your child's father.

If your ex-husband is self-employed, collection is more difficult. Garnishing his wages is the only reliable way to get the money he owes. I have often found it easier to find ways to press on independently than to stay behind trying to find justice when child support remains uncollected. Believe me, you and your daughter can make it. Find people you can rely on to help you. Then become the best mom in the whole world for your daughter.

I'm an unmarried single dad who is trying to see his four-month-old son. The child does not have my last name on the birth certificate, but he is definitely my son. What can I do legally to see my child? Do I have the right to just take him from her? Would that be considered kidnapping?

The first thing that both you and your son's mother need to ask yourselves is, *What is best for our son?*

You are without legal rights concerning your son's welfare until you establish your paternity. If your former girlfriend is unwilling to admit that you are his father, you need to take your own measures, keeping your son's welfare in mind. Establishing paternity will help your son financially as well as furnish him with important medical history and benefits from the government. In most states the child support enforcement office can help you go through the right channels to do this. State laws will differ, but many require laboratory blood tests. The cost is minimal. Your son's mother cannot prevent this.

Once you have established your paternity, go through the proper channels (county court) to pay your child support. The courts keep good records that can be used in the future. If you continue to meet resistance concerning visitation with your son, contact a mediator in your county who can help with your visitation rights. You may, in fact, have to consult an attorney and hope the mother will cooperate to avoid further conflict.

Again, think and do what is best for your son and never act outside the law. No, it would not be good to take your son from his mother, and yes, it would be considered kidnapping. In addition, you would be alienating your son as he grows older, and that's exactly what you do not want to do.

My mother and my grandmother were both never-married moms. I am now the third generation in my family to bring a child into the world without being married. What can I do to keep my daughter from making the same mistake?

Researcher Barbara Dafoe Whitehead says, "Difficulties associated with family breakup often continue into adulthood. Children who grow up in single-parent or blended families are often less successful as adults, particularly in areas of love and work. Research shows that many children from disrupted families have a harder time achieving intimacy in relationships or in holding steady jobs."[4]

Author Gary Sprague grew up in a single-parent home and now is head of Kids Hope, an organization that works with single-parent children to help them heal from the pain of loss. Sprague writes, "For children to break the cycle of single parenting, they must face the unhealthy patterns that existed before them." He suggests the following steps:

- *Maintain honesty*. It creates an environment where love, forgiveness, and restoration can take place.
- *Allow talk about uncomfortable matters*. Kids need to see

their parents talking to each other and working through conflict.

- *Let kids share deep feelings*. They will respond positively when we acknowledge their emotions and this will set them on the road toward effective communication.
- *Help kids to know why their parents split up*. This will help them avoid the same patterns in their own marriages— adultery, abandonment, abuse, addiction. Gary Sprague says, "While not blaming the parents, individuals can examine their shortcomings and discover ways to change these in their own lives."[5]

I'm having trouble adjusting to my new role as a never-married mom. What should I do?

Parenthood, even in the best of circumstances, is a major adjustment. But remembering a few things may help you in your transition:

- Get rid of any guilt or shame that may surround the circumstances of your parenting.
- Decide on the father's role. Legal counsel may become necessary, or you might need to draw up a contract delineating the responsibilities of both parents. In other cases, the father may not be around at all. Work your situation out and move on.

- Don't marry the father just to give your baby a name.
- Never refuse the father access. However, in cases of abuse, seek assistance immediately. Don't put your child in danger.
- Never bad-mouth the child's other parent. Find ways to resolve any conflicts privately.

By Example

With so many unplanned pregnancies and so many children without parents all over the world, why is it so hard for a single mom to adopt? I finally found an agency that would, and I will become Mom to a girl from Cambodia in July. But I have a friend who is meeting with the same deadends as I did in the beginning. Can you help?

Research shows that the best way for a child to grow up is with a healthy relationship between a mom and dad. This is the reason many agencies are hesitant to offer adoptions to single men and women. Your decision will involve sacrifices that will reap benefits long after you are gone.

Make sure you have a support system in place before the child comes and that you have covered the bases of child care, financial needs, and so on. You will experience all kinds of emotions after the child arrives. Like all parents, you will have good days and bad.

You and your friend can find support with other single adoptive parents through a handbook and newsletter by contacting the Committee for Single Adoptive Parents. A resource list and support information can be obtained by calling (202) 966-6367 or Single Mothers by Choice (212) 988-0993. One conference takes place in the fall through the National Conference on Single Parent Adoption (508) 655-5426.

Several international adoption agencies are open to finding children for single individuals like your friend. They include:

- Children's Hope International, 7536 Forsyth Blvd., Suite 140, St. Louis, MO 63105.
- Family Connections Adoptions, P.O. Box 576035, Modesto, CA 95357-6035.
- Holt International, P.O. Box 2880, Eugene, OR 97402.
- New Hope Child and Family Agency, 2611 NE 125th St., Suite 146, Seattle, WA 98125.
- Adoptive Families of America, Inc., 333 Highway 100 North, Minneapolis, MN 55422.

When should I tell my daughter she is adopted?

From your child's earliest years, be honest at levels she can understand. That might mean one day describing some unfortunate details such as her birth parent's abandonment. Always find something good to tell her about her birth parents, even when it's a stretch. Don't project any disapproving feelings about the birth parents onto your child. I would also tell her only as much as she needs to know for the time. Go into more detail as she asks for it.

If you have laid a secure foundation in your home and your daughter is absolutely certain of your unconditional love for her, things should go well. Be sure she knows that she was a gift from God to you.

Because my daughter has seen hardly any solid marital relationships, has never met her father, and has had few other men in her life, how can she learn anything about selecting the right kind of husband herself?

It's up to you. You have honed in on a real need that will take some hard work from you to provide. But it can be done. I would do the following, starting today:

- Be sure your own life models the decisions you would like for her to make. You may have to seek help and accountability in this area by connecting with other adults at church or in the community who mirror the values you want your family to uphold.
- Convince your daughter she has the power to draw lines, erect boundaries, and make her own choices in life.
- Expose her to some two-parent families in your extended family, neighborhood, or church. Let her see the role a man plays in the home. You might become fortunate enough to find a man who will take a personal interest in your child. Be sure, though, to always solicit this help through the other person's wife. You want to avoid problems down the way.
- Together read some books that can help you discover qualities to look for in a friend as well as a mate. Two I recommend are *Safe People: How to Find Relationships That Are Good for You and Avoid Those That Aren't*[6] by Henry Cloud and John Townsend and *Finding the Love of Your Life*[7] by Neil Clark Warren. Sharing this information together in a relaxed setting will bond the two of you, allow you to have some fun, and instill some common principles for which you can hold each other responsible in future choices.

It's not going to be easy, but you can do it, Mom.

How can I tell my child not to have sex before marriage when I did?

Kelly Martindale addresses this topic. She says:

- *Don't fear confrontation.* Martindale's own concern over the children throwing her past in her face prevented her from doing what she needed to do.
- *Answer questions honestly* as they come up.
- *Teach consequences.* Martindale teaches the advantages of saving sex for marriage, and she shows examples of disasters resulting from poor decisions, such as a neighbor who contracted AIDS due to a promiscuous lifestyle.
- *Give affection* regularly and unconditionally.
- *Get the kids involved.* Martindale arranged volunteer work to help her children be less inwardly focused. She says, "The one thing happy people have in common is they each help someone else."
- *Model.* Practice what you preach.
- *Teach the kids.* Martindale got the children involved in an active church youth group that reinforced the principles she wanted to pass on.[8]

My daughter is six and has seen me date a lot of different men. I have had sexual relationships with only a few of them, but never in my daughter's presence. As long as I remain private about this, is it okay to go on with my life and still be a good mom?

No doubt you are a good mom, but ask yourself, *Do I want my daughter to become promiscuous?* I presume the answer is no. And yet, the person who matters most to your daughter and is in the position of showing the greatest example—you—is doing just that.

Don't delude yourself. Your daughter will soon know exactly what is going on if she doesn't already. Going to bed with a man will become as natural to her as a kiss on the cheek if this is what she sees her mother do.

I believe we should not take anything away from our children without putting something better in its place. Involve her with extended family and two-parent families through church, sports, and school activities. Allow others to help you raise your daughter by endorsing the principles you believe in. Don't just tell her no! Give her a reason not to do it and get her involved with things she will stay busy with—sports, 4-H, or a church youth group.

Above all, you must make an important decision. What's good for the goslings is good for the goose. Give yourself a reason not to become sexually involved outside of a solid marital relationship. Like your daughter, become an integral part of other groups and communities, and stay busy with sports, clubs, school, work, or church activities. This will be one change you will be glad you made. And you can hold your head high and say to your daughter, "Do as I say *and* as I do."

3

The Widowed

Of all the routes to single parenting, widows and widowers find perhaps the most unique circumstances. They comprise about 5 percent of the total single-parent population.

One widow from Indiana wrote: "Loss of a spouse due to death versus divorce is a very different experience indeed. There is no 'ex' mate, no treachery, no deceit, no fights, or betrayal. Only deafening silence, an empty place at the table, and a cold lonely bed."

What You Should Know

The Shock

Shock occurs when a person experiences a sudden or violent physical, emotional, spiritual, or mental disturbance. I had my first experience with shock a number of years ago.

I was pregnant with our first child. Seated over the left back wheel of the tractor, I rode with my husband who was going to mow horse trails for a trail ride the following week. When we hit a pile of hidden debris on the path, I was thrown from the tractor. The wheel grabbed a pair of jeans that was tied around my waist and pinned me underneath the rotating wheel. I lay lodged under the tractor, looking at the brush hog still operating behind, gasoline dripping in front, and my husband above me as he frantically moved gears back and forth.

Finally the tractor rolled forward, freeing me, and I rolled to the side of the path. Lying in my blood, I wondered how badly my baby and I were hurt.

My husband carried me to our van and later into our home and onto our bed. I drifted off but woke up convulsing, crying, throwing up, and passing out. A doctor's examination revealed a broken ankle, lacerated hip, and delayed shock, but my baby was okay.

That shock bolted me from a physical equilibrium. The shock I experienced four years later when my husband suddenly left us, however, once again turned everything in my world upside down. Like those who have lost a loved one through death, the permanence and safe places of my life were shaken, and I searched for tranquillity once more.

Questions You Ask

"I can't believe it!"

I feel numb since my husband died. Nothing registers. Will this feeling ever end?

This "numbness" that you describe may actually dull your pain and help you get through the turmoil going on around you. Everyone needs you for everything, from burial arrangements to the children's concerns, to the estate.

Lower your expectations for a while. Allow others to do for you while you attend only to the essentials. Don't say yes to anything right away—including buying or selling. Delay all decisions possible. Go with how you feel. You'll need your energy for what lies ahead.

It's been several months now. How can I get past denying my husband is dead?

Draw the curtains on life as you knew it and try to move on. Giving his clothes away may help. Change the decor of your house. Alter some of the routines and places you used to enjoy together.

This time of your life is both a time to remember and a time to forget. Take lots of time alone and recall all the special things you enjoyed together. Remember, too, those faults your loved one had. But forget the things that hold you back—the plans you had for traveling or building, for example. Draw from the things inside you that are prodding you to move on.

All this will help you get a vision for a new life without your husband. In the meantime, remember to:

- *Find a relationship with God.* Let him help you make sense of your pain.
- *Keep things as normal as possible* to provide structure, routine, purpose, and accomplishment.
- *Talk through your feelings* with someone safe who can help you discover what to do.
- *Learn to express your emotions* and not hold them in.
- *Talk and listen to your children.*
- *Consider professional help.*

- *Read books on grieving.* See the Recommended Reading Section in the back of this book.
- *Sing.* When you feel least like it, sing. Hymns. Funny songs. Songs with a beat. One day I had a serious problem to handle concerning one of my children. My heart was cracked in two. I did everything I knew to do, then I went into my bathroom, sat down on the floor, put my head against the wall, and I sang. It wasn't pretty, and the tears kept flowing, but it was liberating. It freed me to move past the problem and go on about my day.

I don't think I've accepted my wife's death yet. How do I know, and how can I move on?

Denial hides itself in many places. But if it is not dealt with properly, it will poke out its ugly head when you least expect it. Try looking in these corners to see if your denial is lodging there:

- Getting overly involved with work, family, or other commitments
- Claiming that you have things that need to be worked through
- Denying the truth about someone's death
- Refusing to establish new traditions.
- Forgetting the bad parts of the marriage, the deceased, and so on
- Overly relying on others

- Reluctance to move on with life

Once you've recognized that you are still denying your wife's death, work through the emotions you are feeling, such as anger and loneliness. The following may help you do that: talking to a professional counselor, participating in grief counseling, reading some excellent books on grieving, or dialoguing with others who have lost mates. Recognizing your denial is a healthy place to start.

I have cried every day since my husband died. How can I stop crying and start living again?

Some people express their grief through tears. Sometimes we cry when our grief is immature, sometimes we cry because the loss has not yet gained closure. Some do not cry at all but choose instead to express their grief through anger, and they find a constructive way to do this, like beating a pillow. Others distract themselves by getting involved in worthwhile endeavors where they can use their own pain to help someone else.

If you still need to cry, then do it. Be sure to find safe places in which to express this emotion and safe people with whom you can share. Also, be careful about what kind of grief and how much grief you exhibit in front of your children. It may upset them greatly to see you cry.

Give yourself permission. Find private places to look at pictures or touch items that belonged to your husband—and cry, cry, cry. You should find yourself needing to do this less as time goes on.

Some tell me that I should get over my husband's death and move on. I can't do that yet. Is there something wrong with me?

Your friends are right in that you do need to move on, but you are right in that you need to do it in your own timing. Immediately after my husband left, a friend of mine handed me a book by Dr. James Dobson called *Tough Love*. In the book, he called the person who had been hurt "the victim."

I put the book down, hurriedly. I wasn't ready to be called the victim. It wasn't until several months later that I opened the book again. By then I found myself underlining some important parts and finding strength and direction from its contents.

How soon should you be where? Only you know. Be strong enough to pull away from others when they urge you to move on before you are ready or when they try to heap guilt on you. Likewise, don't hang on to those who hold you back and keep you from healing and handling your loss. As long as you can measure growth in some areas,

you probably will be okay—in your own time.

The Emotions

I feel so angry at God for taking my husband. I even feel angry at my husband for leaving me. Will I ever work past it?

Anger is a natural part of the grieving process—if you handle it the right way. Your plans have been drastically altered. You feel lonely, insecure, and betrayed. Hurt is usually behind it all. Perhaps you blame someone for not taking good enough care of your husband.

Vent your anger in constructive ways. Run. Punch a bag. Exercise. If you must voice your anger, allow someone who is neutral to listen. The Bible tells us that when we feel angry, we must refrain from sinning.[1]

There were things I didn't say to my husband, issues we didn't resolve before he died. If only I had. Will I ever overcome these regrets?

Regrets are not unusual in the grieving process. We are human and make mistakes and misjudge from time to time. *If only I had told him more that I loved him. If only I had not prayed for the end to come to end his suffering. If only I had not yelled at him that way. If only our marriage had been stronger. If only I had fed him better, he would never have contracted the disease.*

Guilt may be a part of the grieving process, but move past it as soon as you can. Seek forgiveness from God.[2] Learn from the mistakes you feel you made and strengthen your areas of weakness. Then leave the guilt and regrets behind or they will eat you alive.

How do I know if I'm grieving in a healthy way?

According to Elisabeth Kubler-Ross, acceptance is the final stage of the grieving process.[3] Just be sure that what you feel is acceptance, not submission. Submission means you give in against your will, often shaking your fist at God in the process. This can bring about harmful emotions in the long run. Guard against them by trusting that God knows best and then resting your issues with him.

Acceptance sometimes happens over time. Other times, we need a miracle from God to make acceptance occur. One woman from Virginia found her source in God.

This Virginia mom was backing out of her driveway to take her oldest child to kindergarten. The other two—ages one and three—were strapped in their car seats. The car got stuck in the muddy driveway, and she got out to push the car while leaving the gear in drive. The car rolled forward, gaining momentum as it moved down the driveway. The car splashed into a pond at the end of the driveway and the force of the water closed the door. The car filled with water, and all three children drowned. About ten years later, the woman's husband committed suicide.

How can this woman ever come to the acceptance stage without help from God? There is no way. Her question of "Why?" will never be answered in this life. Her survival has involved a day-by-day decision to come to acceptance and then move on. Without surrendering it to God, however, bitterness and rage can take over her life.

My wife and I had a terrible marriage. We were on the verge of calling it quits many times. Then she was suddenly killed in an auto accident. Others have shown much sympathy, and I feel like a hypocrite. What can I do?

Loss through death is compounded when we feel we have failed at life. It's easy to concentrate on the weaknesses you may have had in your marriage. But this is a new day. You have children who are waiting for you to be a good dad.

I suggest sharing your concerns only with a select few. That may involve a counselor. Turn your regrets into energy that can help you make a new life for youself and your family.

The Children

My children are still grieving from the loss of their mom. What are the chances of them turning out okay?

This will be a constant challenge as you parent on your own. Generally, children who lose a parent to death have an easier time of coping than those dealing with divorce or abandonment. Your children probably had a good relationship with their mom and experienced minimal conflict in the home. Because death is final, they can feel closure to the relationship. Divorce and abandonment don't allow that.

Allow your children to talk, cry, and heal. Read everything you can find on this subject to keep you wise. Involve counselors if necessary. Pray for your children. Then model how to move on with life.

How do I explain death to my children?

Your question doesn't have easy answers. If you avoid the topic, your children will come up with their own explanations. They need to have death explained by someone who loves them and has their best interests at heart.

When my children were small, their great-grandfather died. Ashley was four, and she asked lots of questions. In the yard one afternoon, I got an opportunity to explain.

We were trimming a rosebush, and I pointed out the dying blossoms as well as the buds—how one dies and another is born.[4] I explained that death was an inevitable part of life for all of us.[5] And I explained that if we belong to God, life *and* death are in his hands.[6]

My daughters are four and ten. Their mother died a short time ago. Should I handle their grief the same?

Kids deal with grief differently at different ages. From three to five years of age, they do not understand the finality and think the missing person will return. They deny what has happened. You might try allowing your four-year-old to work out her emotions through things like art or play.

From ages five to nine, your child will have a clearer picture of death and will tend to personify its reality by saying things such as, "Jesus took Mommy to heaven." Your ten-year-old can understand more concrete explanations. Be available to answer every question she asks.

I feel like my children and I have died a hundred deaths since we

found out about my husband's illness. He is supposed to die any day. How should I handle this with our children?

My heart goes out to all of you. While you have had more time to prepare for death than those who lose someone suddenly, the agony is being prolonged. Allow your children to be around their father until the end. If they need to pull back some, let this happen as well without criticism. When possible, permit the children to minister to the needs of their father. This will allow them to have ownership in the event as well as develop their own sense of closure. Finally, remember the words of the Bible in Matthew 5:4: "Blessed are those who mourn, for they will be comforted." Lean on God and on other people through these times.

For every single mom or dad who has lost a mate to death, may I encourage you to accept new challenges. Find meaning in your work. Search out new relationships and enrich the old. Create ways of helping others.

Finally, become the best parent you can be, because life is moving on and needs for you to move along with it. Edna St. Vincent Millay wrote:

> *Life must go on,*
> *And the dead be forgotten.*
> *Life must go on,*
> *Though good men die.*
>
> *Anne, eat your breakfast;*
> *Dan, take your medicine;*
> *Life must go on,*
> *I forget just why.*

Your children are the reason life must go on.

2

What
Legalities
Are
Involved?

Issues

In more than a decade as a single mom, the relationship between my ex-husband and me has never been easy. We have had to go back to court numerous times, mostly for non-payment of child support.

One such occasion occurred on a humid Indiana summer day. I went to court physically prepared with all the documents I would need and thought I was emotionally prepared as well. Bruce and his attorney sat at a table across from my attorney and me. They presented his issues, and my attorney presented mine.

When business was finished, everyone left. I climbed into my car to drive back to the airport, but I had to pull my car to the side of the road. I was crying uncontrollably. Sadness gripped me from deep inside. Things had gone the way my attorney and I had hoped, but I realized in the car that day that I would never be equipped to handle the emotional toll that events such as these exact. If I remained in this role as a single mom for another decade, these things would still not be easy. I would never be jaded to the accusations and hurts hurled at me by the person I once loved.

Most people don't know about legal issues until they are forced to put them to work. In the breakdown of a relationship, two once-intimate parties go their separate ways, but only for a short distance. When children are involved, the parents' lives continue to intersect. That point of intersection is governed by legalities that dictate the rules of the game. These rules, as well as how they are carried out, set the stage for heated debates and high emotions. Individuals become painfully aware of life and reality and cold, hard facts.

I hope the worst of your emotional intersections are behind you. If they aren't, realize that ignoring the issues won't make them go away. Choosing to remain ignorant of the laws rather than dealing with them won't erase the conflicts.

You and I would be wise to remember the words from the Bible: "Be as shrewd as snakes and as innocent as doves."[1] In single-parent talk, that could mean stay informed, know what you're doing, watch out for yourself—but don't hurt others.

I've chosen to handle the legalities that have governed our lives in just that way. The months and years ahead probably will bring more trips to the courthouse for me. I'll never be good at it. I'll never be happy about it. But I will always be informed concerning it as I do my best to stay shrewd as a snake and innocent as a dove.

4

Custody

"While driving home with my kids one night," noncustodial dad William Larson from Minnesota writes, "I told my children it was the best Christmas I'd had since the divorce."

"Why, Dad?" one of the children asked.

"I've been on good terms with your mother lately, and I just got a new job," he explained. "What more could I ask for?"

"A little more hair?" his twelve-year-old blurted out.

Unfortunately, the issues for custodial or noncustodial parents are never as insignificant as the desire for more hair. Most custodial parents are stretched so thin, one more added duty can send them over the edge. Many noncustodial parents are working their way through the loss of relationships *and* of their children. Reduced to parenting from the sidelines, nothing can appear more frustrating and unfulfilling.

For every single parent who struggles to raise a child alone, there are other single parents watching from afar and participating to varying degrees. The issues are real and the needs are great for both custodial and noncustodial parents.

What You Should Know

In divorce as well as in never-married situations, the primary care of the children must be determined. That primary care might go to the child's parents, guardians, or the state. The courts call it "custody." The children's day-to-day welfare is entrusted to one parent, who becomes the primary caregiver. Sometimes an arrangement is made where both parents in different homes share equal control of decision-making and responsibility for minor children. This is called "joint custody."

Traditionally, two models have been used by courts and mental health professionals to determine custody of children: the "best interest" of the child (usually the mother is appointed as the custodial parent) and a "family systems" approach (both parents remain involved in raising the child). These two theories share some common goals—providing for the security and development of children, maintaining continuity, and reducing loyalty conflicts.

In early England, divorces didn't occur often. When they did, fathers usually got custody of the children. This practice spread to the United States during the first seventy years after the United States gained its independence from England. By the late 1800s, either parent could receive custody. Eventually the courts assumed that the care of young children should remain with the mother. This practice became known as the "tender years doctrine."

The tender years doctrine is not universally endorsed by the courts, and it is often contested. Both mothers and fathers are supposed to be considered equal candidates for custody in divorce proceedings. But almost 90 percent of custody arrangements, whether contested or uncontested, result in mothers receiving custody of their children.

This probably is because the mothers spend the most time and effort caring for the children in their early years, and the courts decide that the primary caregiver should continue having primary care of the children. The "best interest of the child" standard is not spelled out clearly and does not acknowledge that a child's interests are not the only things to be taken into consideration when determining his or her care.

Almost everyone agrees that the continued involvement of both parents is important. Several areas are directly affected by this involvement—or lack of it:

- Most mothers are overwhelmed with financial and emotional problems when the father leaves.
- The absence of the father is especially devastating for boys.
- The long-term results are sometimes greatest if the separation of the father from the family unit occurs when the children are less than five years old.
- The presence of the father fosters a sense of self-esteem and well-being unless that father has mental or substance-abuse problems.
- More frequent contact from the noncustodial parent and that parent's greater involvement

in a child's life is associated with better academic performance for boys, greater popularity for girls, and fewer psychological problems for both boys and girls.

Security comes to children when they realize both of their parents will continue to be there to help and guide them, even though their home situation has changed.

Questions You Ask

Custodial

My daughter saw her dad much more when she was younger. Now she's involved in many outside activities that interfere with dad. Is this okay?

Noncustodial fathers seem to spend more time with younger children. The older the children get, the more social contacts they have. Adolescent boys and girls are especially prone to becoming involved in many relationships and activities, and they have fewer hours to spend with family members, especially the noncustodial parent. In the later years, noncustodial moms are more likely to maintain visitation with a child than noncustodial dads are.

If your child's father still wants to see your daughter, help make that happen. If she can't see him during her scheduled time because of outside activities, find time on the weekend. Be flexible. Your daughter needs to spend time with and feel loved by both of you. If you keep that from happening, it could come back to haunt you.

My husband walked out on us and hasn't been in contact with the children. I wonder, does he even think about his kids?

It is hard to imagine a justifiable reason for your husband to sever his relationship with the children. His decisions have created pain and hardship for everyone. For the majority of divorced dads, however, research shows that the children are constantly on their minds, probably more than if they were actually living with the children. If a dad does nothing about it, though, his concern matters little.

In your case, just continue to be the best mom you can be and expose your child to as many good male influences as you can. Get a lot of outside support for yourself as well. Once you've done all you can, stop worrying. Anxiety weakens you and reduces your effectiveness as a mom.

What are my ex-husband's responsibilities toward his children as a noncustodial father?

I wish the question could be answered in a brief list, but unfortunately no such list exists.

Nowhere is the role of the non-custodial father clearly defined. That lack of definition may play an important role in why non-custodial fathers do not stay more involved in their children's lives. Getting fathers to participate when they live apart is difficult—especially if the fathers were not directly involved with their children while the family was intact.

I would probably list the following as basic expectations for noncustodial parents:

- Pay child support on time
- Stay in weekly touch with the children.
- Remember special days of the children.
- Support discipline in the custodial home.
- Stay involved with school and extracurricular activities.

My ex-husband has not contacted the children for four years. Now he wants visitation rights. Do I have to comply?

In most states, a parent's rights can be terminated if that parent hasn't been in touch for a certain period of time. In Virginia, this happens automatically. Most likely, however, you will have to petition the courts to get the father's rights taken away. Just having an attorney sign it won't do anything. Both parents probably have to sign, and the contract signing should be witnessed by an impartial third party. Sugges-

tion: A less expensive way is to draw up a contract between the two of you that relinquishes his rights. Have an impartial third party as a witness when you both sign and date that contract.

Before you decide to take such action, however, be sure you think through a couple of things: If you terminate his parental rights, you can never expect to receive child support from him, and your children may one day blame you for keeping them away from their father. If your husband is not involved with drugs, alcohol, or abuse of any kind, perhaps it would be good to let him back into your children's lives. If the reasons that brought about his lengthy absence from the children still exist, however, he probably will again wean himself away. Then, after the children see that you've encouraged and not prohibited a relationship with their dad, and he still doesn't visit, you can have his parental rights terminated. Be sure you have carefully considered everything before you make your decision.

A counselor told me once that parents fight for custody for many reasons. I want my children so badly, it's hard to imagine any other motives. What other reasons could there be?

You'd be surprised. I know of a father who had abandoned his children after a series of affairs then tried to get custody to be able to tell the children he had fought for them. Other parents fight for primary care of the children so they can hold on to the primary amount of child support.

Still others, like you, just want what's best for their kids and believe they are the parent who can provide those needs best. Whether or not you get custody, keep your kids as your most important motive. It will make all the difference in their worlds.

I have sole custody of our two children. Their dad shows up every now and then to be with them, but the responsibilities are all mine. How can I make everything work for my kids?

You can only make the parts work that involve you. Your husband obviously can't handle financial or physical responsibility for his children. He may still be a decent dad and offer extended family opportunities that are beneficial to your children. Allow that to occur, but don't permit him to make important decisions that affect your children. You sound like the stable one. Remain faithful to your mothering role.

I read a Bible verse during my early days of single parenting that said, "The Lord has chosen you to build a house for a sanctuary. Be strong and do it."[1]

Situations have been tough and unfair at times and, like you, I have felt frustrated and wanted to give up. But I keep being strong and I keep building my sanctuary—for the sake of my kids.

I need to move out of state to work on my degree, but the divorce isn't final yet. Will this prevent me from going?

The same situation happened with me. I had my attorney set a court date to meet with the judge. They had me make a list of the furniture and other things we would need to live. The judge granted me temporary custody and the okay to take what I requested, less the things Bruce had contested. Among the things that had to stay behind, was my one-year-old's antique iron crib. A week after we moved, Clint rolled off the bed he slept on, and he had to get stitches in his forehead.

The decision to get the stitches was mine without consultation because I had temporary custody. A future date had been set to decide permanent custody, which I was also granted, but for that time I was free to do what needed to be done to move on. You can do the same.

I never married my child's father. Do I even need to establish custody for my son?

By all means, yes. In most states, biological fathers—even

when unmarried—have rights. Your child's father can come back later and sue for custody. It's best to have that taken care of from the beginning.

Noncustodial

I fought for joint custody of my children and lost. I was devastated as this decision seemed to assume I was an inferior father, when I have always made my kids a priority. How do I put this all in perspective?

The court's decision to award custody to your ex-wife does not negate the influence you have on your children. Both "best interest" and "family systems" approaches recognize that continuous relationships with all primary figures—both parents, grandparents, relatives, and friends—are necessary for the healthy development of children's identities.

The family systems perspective does not assume the mother is the best caretaker of the children. Rather, that approach maintains that the needs of the whole family as a system will continue to bring about cohesion after separation or divorce. It emphasizes the importance of continued access to the children among all family members.

Your job as a dad is not terminated because you lost custody. It is possible to still be an excel-

lent father from afar. It just takes more work.

How can I as a noncustodial father parent my children more effectively?

Good books on the market can suggest ways of staying involved. I recommend *101 Ways To Be a Long-Distance Super Dad ... or Mom, Too.*[2] In addition, here are a few ideas you might try:

- Let the children know in words and actions that you are there for them at all times. Invite them to visit, call, or write at any time.
- Send cards for all or no occasions.
- Call the children often.
- Model your values in your daily life.
- Talk, talk, talk.
- Pray with the children every time they are with you.
- Decide together on house rules and display them for all to see.
- Discipline consistently once everyone understands the rules and their consequences.
- Keep track of important events. Photograph everything and keep an album listing names and places. Pass this album on to them when they're older.
- Visit their schools. Make appointments with teachers and principals directly. Establish your own rapport with school

personnel. You might even chaperone class parties or field trips.

- Attend every activity possible—sports, school events, and extracurricular activities.
- Coach or help direct activities. Helping to lead one of your child's activities will go far in your bonding.
- Plan the unplanned. Check ahead of time with the custodial parent and pick up the kids. Buy them a hamburger or take them to the park to feed the ducks.
- Read every good parenting book you can find.

Joint Custody

I am a noncustodial father who fought for joint custody of my daughter and lost. Why do many courts not see the importance of constant exposure to both parents?

Joint custody provides children with the benefit of living with their mom *and* dad. It also helps both parents more easily manage their other responsibilities—including time for themselves. In addition, joint custody sets the stage for quality time from both parents. Each of you knows your time is limited, so you probably develop some pretty solid self-discipline and organization. Then when the kids are with you, you can devote your full attention to them.

Statistics show that 90 percent of the fathers who share joint custody pay their child support in a timely fashion. Because this rate is so much higher than the national average, this could mean these men contribute more money because they feel they are contributing more in the other areas of the children's lives.

Joint custody can be a rewarding experience if both parents agree on most child-rearing decisions. It does not work well when you and your ex do not get along. When children of joint custody are caught in the middle of hostility, they are forced to take sides and sometimes fear they have betrayed the other parent.

The decision has been made. Your child will live with her mother. You will need to work extra hard to keep an awesome relationship going with your child.

Someone recommended that I go back to court and try to get shared physical custody of our son. Is this wise?

Did you ever travel a lot and have to live out of a suitcase? Remember how tiring that got and how much you looked forward to getting home? Shared physical custody means both you and your son's mom have equal responsibility and access to your child. Neither party pays child support because both of you are sharing equally in the upbringing of your child.

This type of arrangement upsets the normal routine that helps a child feel secure in a stable and predictable home. I do not recommend this type of arrangement, and most judges will not grant it.

My ex-wife and I have just started joint parenting. What are some pitfalls we can avoid?

The goal of everything you do should be what's best for your child. That includes:

- Resolving conflicts with your ex in private.

- Respecting each other in the way you talk and the manner in which you consider each other's needs.
- Providing for the child emotionally and financially without argument.
- Consulting with each other.
- Showing flexibility with schedules.
- Being honest about all your shared issues.

In all you do, remember that the common love you share for your child is more important than the differences you have with each other. Keep that in mind, and you'll make it through.

5

Visitation

A divorced dad from Virginia wrote about having joint custody of his daughter and what a privilege that was. But when she grew to an age when she needed her mom more, Dad wrote this letter to his daughter:

> It's been a year and a half since we talked that night in your bedroom [about the daughter wanting to live with Mom].
>
> When I first held you on the third-floor corridor of St. Mary's, you were pink and wrinkled and sooo cute with that tight pullover knit cap. I felt part of my heart leave me as it poured into you. Adults call that bonding. Who would have guessed back then that today you would need two bedrooms?
>
> Today is uncertain. Anything can happen. But I feel peaceful. I am confident. I can rest again. God has given me some special promises concerning you. They

are as real to me as all the bedrooms in the world. The most important thing is about where you will spend eternity, not where you will spend the night. I love you.
> Always, Your Daddy[1]

This dad has learned that some things are more important than winning his legal rights. He's learned that the one vital issue involved in custody cases is the child. He's learned how essential it is that he make the abnormal situation of living in two houses as normal as can be. And he's learned how to make his relationship with his daughter grow to include the changing circumstances. What should you learn?

What You Should Know

Visitation is not a reward for a noncustodial parent's faithfulness in paying child support. The two

53

are unconnected. The custodial parent cannot withhold visitation for nonpayment, and while the state can mandate child support, it cannot force a parent to see his or her child. Except for special or dangerous circumstances, all parents are awarded some kind of visitation. And a large percentage of those who see their kids regularly also pay timely child support.

Many fathers of young children are uncertain about what to do during visitation and about their role as disciplinarian versus weekend friend. Maintaining contact with children usually means maintaining a connection with one's ex-mate—a link that was already strained enough to lead to the breakup of the relationship. Promoting visitation with the other parent will place less responsibility on the custodial parent for explaining the other parent's actions, and the child should benefit in some way from interaction with the other parent.

Questions You Ask

My ex-husband has often gotten verbally and even physically abusive while dropping off the children. What can I do?

Once when meeting my ex-husband at our usual drive-through restaurant, he yelled at me about something. His words were so loud and caustic that a man from the gas station next door came over to see if I was okay.

It is not uncommon after a divorce or the breakup of a relationship to have certain things and places be trigger points. It sounds as though visitation drop-offs and pickups have become triggers for you. You should make every effort to make this experience safe once again. You might:

- Be sure someone else is around.
- Find a public place to meet.
- Put communications into written form.
- Have the children ready on time.
- Make your schedule flexible for late drop-offs or pickups.
- Try to not provoke the other parent.

I am still nursing my daughter. Do I have to let her visit her dad?

Talk to your ex. Maybe the inconvenience of it all will deter him for a while. Breast-fed children are often irritable when Mom's not around and usually won't take bottles. I was pregnant with our son when my ex left, and I nursed him for about ten months. During this time, Clint's dad took the girls on a three-day trip to Disney World and left Clint behind with me. This allowed me time for my son and to visit my parents in Arizona for a few days.

If your ex won't cooperate, there may be nothing you can do. Consult your attorney if the problem continues.

My ex and I do not get along, but I am interested in co-parenting for the sake of our child. Can we do this?

When two people co-parent, they decide that they *will* cooperate in raising their child even though it isn't easy. It will require everything you can muster in the areas of compromise, flexibility, and respect. Laying aside your differences, showing respect to the other parent, and communicating openly with both the other parent and the child are musts when it comes to parenting your child together. Co-parenting means that one of you is the primary parent. Decide who that is.

This arrangement will take much work. Hang in there.

My granddaughter is a toddler. I am a nurse and suspect sexual molestation of my granddaughter by her dad when she goes for visitation. What can I do?

I know a grandmother who had the same experience. She began by having the child checked by a pediatrician and a psychologist to see if her suspicions were true. When nothing could be proven, she kept a close eye on the little girl and the pediatrician apprised. In addition, this grandmother let her former son-in-law know that she suspected something and made it clear to him the consequences of such a crime. Unfortunately, that's about all she could do unless something could be proven.

If you do discover evidence of foul play, get the courts to order supervised visitation. You will need solid evidence to prove this. Even with supervised visitation, your granddaughter may still not be safe. I heard recently of a child who goes with her mother to visit the child's father in prison. The mother removes the panties from the little girl, and the father secretly fondles her after she arrives.

Stay on this one. You may be the only hope this child has.

What are the most common difficulties encountered during visitation that I can try to prevent?

We probably hear the most on this subject from nonresidential parents. Check out these common complaints and plug them in to where they fit in your situation:

- *More time.* Noncustodial parents often want more frequent visitation.
- *Interference.* The residential parent sometimes sabotages visitation.
- *Denial of visitation.* The kids are frequently prohibited from

going to the other parent's house.

- *Impeding relationships.* Directly, custodial parents interfere with visitation arrangements. Indirectly, they say negative things to the children about the other parent and visitation.
- *Inconsistency by the parents.* Such issues as noncustodial parents being late, canceling at the last minute, or failing to show up for a scheduled visit are common complaints.
- *Non-compliance.* Some spouses do not comply with child-related issues of their decree.
- *Child-rearing practices.* Dad and Mom disagree about how to raise the kids.
- *Emotional involvement.* The process of divorce is a volatile period characterized by fighting, guilt, anger, and hurt about the divorce as well as ambivalence about one's ex-spouse.

An informed parent is a parent who is on the way to improving things. My hat's off to you for wanting to put the welfare of your child above everything else.

When my daughter turned fourteen, she left her mother's house and came to live with me. Should I have custody transferred legally?

Yes. That way you have the legal right to make any and all decisions regarding your daugh-ter. Otherwise, your ex-wife's custody arrangement is all that's on file, and if an emergency arose, your hands would be tied.

Because I see my children for only a few days a month, have I lost my influence in their lives?

The frequency of visitation is not all that creates an impact on your children. A father who is in the house all the time may not be spending quality time with his child. On the other hand, count-less noncustodial fathers invest everything they have into contin-ued influence on their children. Successful parenting from a dis-tance is less dependent on fre-quency of visits than it is on the quality of interaction through telephone calls, cards, e-mail, and actual visits.

Frequency does matter in that it provides an opportunity for the father-child connection to develop. Whatever amount of time you have with your children, you should make the most of every opportunity to stay involved.

I worry about a lot of stuff when my kids go to visit their dad. Is this normal?

You are not alone. Many other primary caregivers also worry about things such as

- Children being spoiled from the Disneyland-dad activities.
- Children displaying behavioral problems after a visitation.

- The noncustodial parent being a poor role model for the children.

Noncustodial parents also have problems with visitation, most having to do with the unwillingness of the custodial parent to change visitation schedules. Most single parents report that visitation the first year after the divorce is moderately to severely stressful.

Stability can occur if both parents work at it. But the role of the noncustodial parent must be redefined in the context of co-parenting. This change in role is probably what causes your ex-husband to be unreliable. It might help if you get your kids into a certain routine when they return. Have a special snack prepared and talk about what happened that weekend. You should also talk to your ex about setting up mutual expectations in the areas of responsibilities and personal care.

My ex has been absent from our child's life for three years. Suddenly he is interested in seeing his son and wants to take him on a week's vacation. He has threatened to kidnap our son if I don't let him go. I have never legally terminated his parenting rights, and my son is begging me to let him spend time with his dad. What do I do?

You face a real dilemma. An incredibly large number of the children who are kidnapped in the United States are taken by the estranged parent. Kids are often snatched to scare the custodial parent into relenting on child support or other legal issues. If you are presently trying to get money from your ex, it is possible that this tragedy could occur.

What can you do?

- Find out if he has recently cut any ties—quit his job or sold his house.
- Have a police officer warn him about the consequences of kidnapping.
- Contact your child's school or day care telling them never to release your son to his dad.
- Be sure a copy of the custody decree is on file in your ex-husband's county.
- Be wise and keep your eyes and ears open.

Your ex-husband might have trouble getting legal backing to take your son on a week's trip—especially after his threats. If you find no reliable evidence your son would be in danger with his dad, I would let him go on shorter excursions (out for ice cream) and under guarded circumstances (a family reunion or church picnic). Just stay on your toes regarding this situation.

My ex-husband lives in another country. He wanted to get joint custody, but I insisted on sole

guardianship. He's a good dad. Did I make the right choice?

You certainly did. If your ex takes your son and a joint-custody decree is on file, officials might take this to mean your son can stay there. If you are the custodial parent and the decree specifies that the child can't leave the country, be sure a copy of this decree is registered with the Office of Passport Services in Washington, D.C. Also prepare your child to take good safety precautions: name, phone number, address; who to talk to; when to run from danger, and so on. Some parents even get 800 numbers, pagers, or cell phones so they can be reached by their children at all times. You can never play it too safe when it comes to international exchanges in custody.

I want to draw up a visitation agreement for my ex-husband and me to sign. What should I include?

A visitation agreement is worthwhile if both parties live by it. But even if your ex-husband does not cooperate with your efforts, you can make the situation better by yourself and raise his awareness of what you are working on. Perhaps these principles will sink in at some point as he realizes your own attempts to improve the situation. Here are some things you might try:

- Be courteous.
- Never say negative things about the other parent to your kids.
- Don't argue during pickup or drop-off times.
- Send all the things the kids will need.
- Honor rules in the other home.
- Save important discussions with your ex-mate for private times.
- Share important information and concerns.
- Alter plans only when necessary and give plenty of notice.
- Don't milk the children for information about the other home.
- Accommodate the other parent whenever possible.

6

Child Support

The day I went to court to finalize our divorce, I didn't know what to expect. I sat alone in the courtroom with my attorney, staring at my ex-husband and his attorney. At eight that morning, his attorney handed my attorney an offer. My attorney handed one back. This went on all day, with offers and questions and discussions and compromises. We didn't even take time for a lunch break. Could I let go of the flatware? What about the nativity set he had gotten me for our last Christmas that he now wanted? More offers, questions, discussions, compromise. I just wanted the day to end.

At eight that night, a settlement was reached out of court. We stood for the judge's entry. We sat. Sweat popped out on my forehead. I grew weak as I realized, *This decision will affect my children and me for the rest of our lives.* I felt faint.

Finally, the day was over. I went to bed in a nearby hotel wondering what the day's events would mean to me and my little family. Yet somewhere inside of me, I had a peace. I had prayed every day for God to give me wisdom to do and choose the right things. I had pondered each step carefully. Now it was time to trust that that wisdom had come and would do its work in the days ahead.

I never discussed the terms of my divorce with anyone. I didn't want anyone to say "you got too much" or "you got too little" or "you should have . . ."

No, I determined that what's past was past, and it was time to move on. We would make it with or without involvement from the children's dad or his financial help.

What You Should Know

All minor children are entitled by law to receive financial support from both parents unless one of the individuals has had his or her parental rights terminated. The amount to be paid is determined by the child support guidelines in each state. These guidelines are based on the incomes of the parents, cost of living in that state, and the needs of the child. In 1992, President George Bush signed a bill making it a crime for a noncustodial parent to move out of state to avoid paying child support.

Yet the major reason that more than half of single moms live below the poverty level is because of unpaid child support. In 1992, the U.S. Department of Health and Human Services reported that 25 percent of custodial parents never get any child support, and 25 percent get only some of the amount due. In all, 23 percent of all child support awarded is never collected. About $22 billion goes uncollected each year.[1]

Questions You Ask

I am a never-married mom. My son is two months old, and his father has not paid any child support. He assured me he would take care of me and the baby, but I can see he has no intention of doing so. What can I do?

First, you have to prove that this man is the father. Then you need to contact your local IV-D agency (named after Title IV-D of the Social Security Act) under the Department of Social Services and Human Resources and tell them that child-support collection is still problematic. They will tell you what to do. This agency is federally funded in every state to help you collect support for dependent children.

I have been after my ex-husband for more than ten years trying to collect. Is anything being done to improve this frustrating situation?

With passage of the Child Support Enforcement Amendment of 1984, states were required to establish, by 1987, guidelines to be followed in the calculation of child support. Nevertheless, while perhaps an increased number of women and men have received reasonable awards, enforcement still remains problematic.

Some believe a national system of wage withholding would ensure that all children would be financially supported by both parents. Oftentimes noncustodial parents view child support as an optional expense. Such a national system would guarantee payment to offset the escalating cost of raising children. Because of the inequities faced by women in the labor market, the calculation of the amount of child support should take into account the respective earnings of each parent. This proposal would not solve the problem of mothers or fathers who do not work or those parents who disguise their actual income.

I am so tired of hassling with child support, I have just about decided to give up and do it on my own. Am I right?

I see two extremes from those who are owed back child support: Those who blame all their ills on the ex-spouse's nonpayment, and those who get tired of the frustrations and let the ex-spouse get off scot-free.

Your children have a right to the best standard of living you can provide for them—and that includes child support. Men who pay child support are also more likely to remain involved with their children. For these reasons, I suggest you do everything you can to collect what is owed to your children. You are right, however, in believing that you will make it, with or without these funds.

I could certainly use the child support, but my former husband is a drug addict and is going downhill fast. He has disappointed the children time and again. I know children need their fathers, but isn't this one of those extenuating circumstances?

You are probably right. Only you can assess the circumstances. It may be in the best interests of the children to have him relinquish his parental rights, particularly if he is willing to do so. Contact an attorney to find out how this is done.

I don't know where my ex-husband is. He is behind more than $20,000 in child support. How can I find him?

Begin by trying to find his whereabouts through someone who knows him well: business associates, family, placement offices of schools he attended, credit unions, professional affiliations, voter registration lists, and so on.

If you are unsuccessful with these attempts, contact the State Parent Locator Service (SPLS). For searching out of state, get in touch with the Federal Parent Locator Service (FPLS). These organizations go after only child support, not alimony or other expenses. Call your local clerk of courts office to get telephone numbers for these services.

You can also get in touch with the Internal Revenue Service. Give them your ex-husband's social security number if you know it. If he owes more than $750, the IRS can go after him with its collection services just as it does with back taxes.

My ex-husband lives out of state. He told me he would move to a different state, and I would never

get a dime. Is there anything I can do?

All states in the U.S. have adopted the Uniform Child Custody Jurisdiction Act (UCCJA). No matter where a parent resides, the laws on child support apply. This avoids conflicting ruling by two states on the same issue. If some kind of litigation is pending in your state, have your attorney contact the state and county in which your husband resides. Be aware, however, that only about one quarter of unpaid child support is successfully collected from out of state.

If you can prove your husband moved out of state to avoid paying child support, he can be charged with a felony.

My ex-husband is paying child support, but the amount is not sufficient for his son. How can I get a more fair amount?

Every state has some kind of guideline for the amount of child support to be paid by each parent. Though this amount is based on incomes of both parents, cost of living, and needs of the child, you can also make a case for needing more.

Do some research and make a list of what it costs you to raise your child. Include education, food, clothing, housing, social, recreational, and any special needs he may have. You can even include the cost of basketball camps or that family vacation.

My ex-husband told me he would quit his job so he wouldn't have to pay child support, and he did. What can I do?

Request a judgment with the local IV-D agency to attach his federal and state income tax refunds for nonpayment of child support. If he were still working, you could request a wage withholding order.

My ex-husband earns money he doesn't report to the IRS. How can I prove this?

Your local IV-D can do a credit check and find out what his assets are. If he has no wages to collect, they can go after his house, car, or other assets.

When my husband left, he put everything he owned in his mother's name. On record, he doesn't own anything. What can I do?

If you can prove that he is purposely hiding assets, you can get him for fraud.

I haven't had any luck from any of my local agencies in collecting child support. Can I get a private agency to help me?

You can, and you will probably get faster, more successful results. But it will cost you quite a bit.

Expenses in raising my daughter have gone up since the original decree was granted. How can I get more child support? And can you recommend any good books to help me know more about collecting child support?

Attorneys Nancy Palmer and Ana Rodriguez from Florida wrote a book called *When Your Ex Won't Pay*.[2] The book is written in easy language that any of us can understand. As for getting more child support, you will need to have the original decree modified. For that to be successful, you must prove that there has been a substantial change in circumstances since the original support decree was granted. It isn't enough to just say, "We need more money." List all expenses required to live.

Palmer and Rodriguez recommend that you gather totals in the following areas to see if your statement of greater need can be substantiated:

- Household
- Automobile
- Child's expenses
- Payments to creditors
- Insurance
- Other: Personal (dry cleaning, clothing, medical, and dental); pets; membership dues; church and charitable contributions

7

The Ex

When I found out about the extramarital affairs my husband was having, he never said, "I'm sorry." He did try to talk me into sharing custody and settling our divorce out of court. "I'll take care of you and the children all your lives," he said. His parents told me that if I ever needed anything, they would be there to help.

Not much time went by before I realized that neither would happen. My greatest advocates had become my adversaries. The father of my children had moved into the enemy camp.

I kept people around me who had my best interests at heart and advised me on decisions I should make. I held them close. I determined from the beginning not to get back at my husband. But I also learned to stand in a defensive posture. Anything could happen, and I needed to be prepared.

What You Should Know

No matter what conditions brought you to single parenting, the person with whom you once shared intimacy is gone. Life is moving on for both of you, independent of each other. You can proceed grudgingly and not enjoy the scenery along the way. You can try to move forward while holding on to the past. You can hate the person responsible for causing this to happen. Or, you can let go of what lies behind and get going to what lies ahead.

An ex is particularly hard to deal with after a breakup because of the intensity of emotions that were shared before. When sexual intimacy occurred, one more connection was created between the two of you. You try hard to undo those ties, but even if you successfully put your emotions behind you, physical intimacy can never be undone. You have children to remind you of that fact every day.

So, in one way or another, our ex-spouses are here to stay, whether they visit often or seldom. Whether they are creeps or nice people. Whether they are near or far, living or dead, they exist through the lives of your children. So how do we make the best of this ex-factor?

Questions You Ask

The In-the-Flesh Ex

My ex and I have settled our disputes reasonably well. We can even talk together pretty well. I don't have any romantic feelings for him anymore, but we created a beautiful son together, and we both love him very much. Are we alone in the way we feel?

Alone, no. Rare, yes. Other than offering your child a two-parent, intact home, what you are doing is next best. Your child is seeing you model good conflict resolution skills, and he probably is secure in your love for him.

But be careful. The issues that brought about your divorce have a way of creeping back up in places you least expect. Many find that getting apart from one another does not solve the problems. Instead, after the divorce, the problems often get worse. Parents who were emotionally distant before the divorce will probably continue to be distant.

If a parent was irresponsible with money before, you can probably count on not getting child support.

Keep an eye on these and other issues. Circumstances change— remarriage, relocation, and so on. Your need to resolve difficulties in a divorce situation is ongoing, and you already know the reason to keep on trying.

Sometimes I want to kill my ex-husband. He does see the kids, but his child support is irregular. He undermines me any way he can, and he still wants to control us. He left us for another woman when the children were babies. Since he appears to not be leaving any time soon and murder really isn't an option, what can I do?

You don't have control over him, but you do have control over your responses to him. Find out what's causing the problems. Ask yourself: *What do I do that sets him off? What can I do to communicate with him better?*

Your husband sounds very controlling. He probably put himself in charge of everything while you were married. I was married to a man like this. Once I bought and hung a picture in our new house without getting his "permission." He blew up. I walked away from the situation with my head bowed, but the longer I thought about it the madder I got. Finally, I walked up to him and stood my ground—for the first time. "You go to work every day and make decisions there. I work at home, and I make the decisions while I'm here. If I decide a picture should be hung, I will hang it."

My ex-husband stopped challenging me on things like that after I drew some clear boundaries. It sounds as though your husband, while he was messing around and monopolizing your marriage, thought he could maintain control. Today he is still trying to maintain control over the family. He is probably still dealing with his guilt by trying to keep your home close to his way of doing things.

Define the areas where he violates your responsibility as a single mom. Then draw some clear boundaries in ways such as the following:

- Contacting you before coming to your house.
- Calling the children at appropriate times.
- Relinquishing any say in your household decisions.

My ex walked out of our children's lives last November—both physically and financially. He told them he is moving to Alaska with his oldest daughter by a first marriage. He doesn't support them at all, but thinks he can find time to drop off their bikes before he leaves. The courts are involved to collect the support, but what can I do about the way I feel about him and what he is doing to our children? I would just love to find someone else to be a father to my kids.

It sounds as though your husband lacks emotional connection to anyone. He probably finds his fulfillment in other ways besides being a good dad. It doesn't bother him to live extravagantly while his children barely get their needs met because they aren't connected emotionally to him.

You probably will never be able to change your ex. Find as much support as you can from family, friends, and church. Remain informed by your attorney. And be the best mom you can be for your children. Act as though you will never have another individual to share the load again and learn the coping skills you need to survive and even thrive. The time to act is now. You can't wait until something better comes along.

I wish a book were available that talked about an ex and what to do with them and how to respond. Are there any rules I should follow?

You're right, there is no one book or easy formula for doing everything right, but these commonsense suggestions might help:

- Keep the kids your priority.
- Understand the kind of person your ex is.

- Get on top of your emotions against your ex—hatred, anger, unforgiveness.
- Don't let him or her control your life.

My ex left us and now he undermines and bad-mouths me to the kids. Can I do anything about this?

Maybe not, but you can work on how you respond. Remember, your children will be watching.

- *Don't return bad for bad.* When the children tell you what your ex said, respond with something such as, "I'm sorry he feels that way. He must not feel too good about himself."
- *Don't react.* If your kids tell you something and get no response, they stop telling you, and your ex-husband has lost his reason to do what he's doing.
- *Do talk with your ex.* Tell him his words are hurting the kids, not you.

I have tried to not say bad things about my two teenage boys' father. But they get discouraged because we don't have enough money to buy their clothes or participate in the activities they want. Should I tell them how long it has been since their dad paid any child support?

It's one thing not to bad-mouth your ex. It's another to withhold truth from your children. People told me when I was a new single mom not to say bad things about their dad. Eventually they would know the truth.

Those words have proven to be true, hard as they have been to uphold at times. Your boys should know the truth. Tell them what is happening by going after what the ex is doing, not the ex himself.

I suspect my ex is taking drugs, even when the children are visiting him. We have had conversations about it, but it ends up with both of us screaming. What can I do?

Any time your children are in danger, act quickly. You will need proof of or witnesses to his drug use. When you get this, take it to court. Your ex probably will get a warning. If these actions continue, he may have to endure supervised visitation with his children. Taking away his visiting rights would be the last move. To stay on top of this situation, be sure to:

- Instruct the children to call if they are frightened or confused. Be accessible at all times, perhaps with a beeper, 800 number, or collect calls.
- Use a mediator to help you with the heated discussions.
- Call the police if you suspect he is under the influence anytime he is with the children.

The Ex's Family

My wife's family totally sided with their daughter after she took our son and left me for another man. "He should have been home more," they said. I get so angry when I think about things, I don't want to see them again. What can I do?

Many have been through what you are experiencing. Your children, however, need to maintain a relationship with these individuals. Why? Because they are blood relatives. Part of a child's sense of self comes through understanding who he is and where he came from. He will be intrigued to hear about his roots. The car is always quiet when I tell my children a story about something one of their granddads did or how I felt when a certain thing happened when they were small. The children are especially interested in the things involving them: "What time of day was I born?" "Where did we live when I was a baby?"

Allow the extended family to help build that sense of self. If you do, your child will uncover information and develop his own opinions. If you don't, your child may blame you for keeping him from the others. This sets the stage for either/or choices the child must make later. You don't want that to happen.

I just wish I had some relatives to contend with. Not only is my child from a single-parent home, he has no extended family to connect to. Is there anything I can do?

When my children were young, we lived next door to my in-laws. This arrangement had its drawbacks, but my children established warm relationships with their grandmother and granddad. Even though much has happened, I will never forget grandmother's cooking—custard, macaroni and cheese, banana bread. Granddad was always a tease, and he snorted when he laughed with the children.

When I was pregnant and found out about my husband's involvement with another woman, I told my mother-in-law about it first. She and her husband embraced me—for a while. I wasn't interested in them taking sides but rather helping me save my marriage. But that's not how it turned out.

For most families, blood is thicker than water. Though they didn't condone his acts, they did stand by their son. It hurt more deeply than I have words to describe. I was thrilled when the children and I eventually moved from the house, eighteen months after their father left.

Future contacts with family in cases like this are difficult. It takes a determination on your part to let the hurt go and an understanding that you need to do what's best for the kids. We moved to another state where we knew no one. My parents lived two thousand miles away, and my father died a couple of months after the divorce was final. My husband's mother had a stroke and died later.

Aunts and uncles lived so far away, only occasional visits were possible. One of my sisters became a single mom after I did. Though we lived far from each other, it was within driving distance. We agreed to celebrate Christmas together and become family for each other. We exchanged birthday presents and found ways to get together occasionally.

It won't be easy physically or emotionally to keep a relationship going. But on down the line it will be worth your efforts.

I'm going to see my ex-husband's family next month for the first time since the divorce. What do I say?

My ex and I met for one of the first times since the divorce at the funeral home after my mother-in-law died. I deliberated whether I should go, then remembered I loved my in-laws and had had a relationship with them. I needed to pay my respects. So I contacted my ex-husband, extended my condolences, and told him I would like to visit the funeral home. He had done the same when my father died.

I considered several things during this visit:

- *I imagined different scenarios and what I would do to handle them.* This made me somewhat prepared.
- *I put myself in the family's shoes.* This was easy since I had another brother-in-law whom I loved much, but I had not known what to say or do around him after my sister and he were divorced.
- *I tried to be my best.* I dressed and talked in good taste without going overboard. Overcompensation was something I had to guard against when others asked me what we were doing these days and how the children were getting along.
- *I asked myself what I wanted from this family.* We needed them to be family to my kids. Whatever they chose to do wouldn't make or break my children and me, but the invitation had been extended.

Should I contact my husband's family and tell them I want us to stay involved?

I wish I had done so. It was long after the divorce that I sent Christmas cards to the children's paternal aunts and uncles. They lived all over the world, and we had lost touch before the divorce ever took place. I never found a way to mend those lost relationships completely.

My children and I have no extended family to rely on. This makes me sad for my kids. What can I do?

Families usually offer support and encouragement. I got involved in our church right away. Much of the support and encouragement we missed from family came through our church. School and sports activities also offered this.

My former husband has just remarried. How can I help my children adjust to this new situation?

You will need to establish open communication with your children about things they are feeling about the new wife. I suggest:

- *Listening without judgment.* Let your children say what they feel.
- *Reinforcing respect.* Guide your children's description of the new stepmother to be respectful. This sometimes means helping to rephrase a statement.
- *Letting your children know how to continue to love you while also loving the new stepmom.* They have love enough for both of you.
- *Not allowing name-calling.* Permitting descriptions such as the "wicked stepmother" gives the children the okay to call you and other adults names as well.

- *Trying to coordinate with your ex* on working with your kids through the transition. Compare notes when possible.
- *Congratulating the stepmom* when appropriate and tell her not to take the children's actions too seriously. Encourage her to establish her own relationship with the kids.
- *Considering the new wife's feelings.* She might hear: "Mom does it this way," "That's not the way we do it." Let the kids know that she is now part of their lives. Help them feel safe and free to love in this new environment.
- *Working with her.* Communicate everything you can on behalf of the children. Coordinate discipline. Remember that her addition into your children's lives creates a new position; it doesn't replace yours.

I became the villain to my husband's family after we divorced. I keep wanting to defend myself. What can I do?

Divorce was not a common thing in my ex-husband's family. I think it was easier for them to blame me for things than it was to look at reality or possible ways they might have contributed.

All kinds of dynamics can be involved. Many unsure things and unexplained responses are in the past. The future for you and your family is ahead. Go there and leave the ill feelings behind. It will free you like nothing you can imagine, and your decision will affect all your decisions to come.

This is my first holiday season as a single parent. The children are scheduled to spend the time with their dad. I keep thinking about the festivities that used to be, and now my chair will be empty. How can I cope?

It sounds as though you haven't let go of the past. Your life has taken some new turns. Make the most of them. Plan something you really want to do. Treat yourself to something special. Get some rest. Read a good book. Eat what you want. Exercise. See a play or a movie you've been wanting to see.

It's a time to establish some new traditions. A couple of Christmases ago, I stayed in my robe and didn't wash my face all day. It was weird, but I found myself enjoying the day in spite of myself. Other times we got together with friends in the afternoon after their own family had celebrated the event. Through the years, when my children have gotten home from being gone on the holidays, I have tried to have a gift waiting for them, something for each one that tells them I know them intimately. The biggest gift of all, I find, is to be a healthy, happy, rested, adjusted, not-angry-at-the-in-laws-anymore mom. I'm glad I made that choice.

3

How
Do
You
Feel?

Emotions

One spring brought few signs of new life for me but many old reminders of severe trials my family and I had just gone through with one of my children. I had prayed, strategized, and agonized over how to respond to every detail of the challenge, but it seemed I had failed. Not only were the few successes hard to measure, but I had no strength left to try.

In March all my children went to visit their dad for a week. Exhausted and depleted, I arranged to borrow the empty apartment of a friend and made my way into the mountains. I stopped for lunch and a trip through an outdoor mall. I arrived at my destination in the early evening.

After unloading my luggage, my real time of unloading began. I was an emotional wreck. I sat on the living room couch, after putting a chair in front of me across the room, and imagined God sitting there. I needed for him to feel tangible to me that night. One by one I asked, "Why have you allowed all this to happen?" "Why don't you help us in these circumstances?" "Why?"

But I felt like he didn't hear. My questions and explanations seemed to bounce off the wall much as they did for C. S. Lewis in his book *A Grief Observed*. "But go to Him when your need is desperate, when all other help is vain, and what do you find? A door slammed in your face, and a sound of bolting and double bolting on the inside. After that, silence. You may as well turn away.... What can this mean? Why is He so present a commander in our time of prosperity and so very absent help in time of trouble?"[1]

I finished every desperate prayer I could think of. Then I began to thank him. I lay on the couch and wrote out many of the good things that had happened in our home. The problems were not lessened, but I became convinced that I could do nothing more about them, and they were in God's hands. This realization went with me the next morning onto a ski slope where I spent the day doing something I loved.

I was home by 6:30. Exhausted, I lay across my bed and read more of the words of C. S. Lewis, "Aren't all these notes the senseless writhings of a man who won't accept the fact that there is nothing we can do with suffering except to suffer it? Who still thinks there is some device (if only he could find it) which will make pain not be pain. It doesn't really matter whether you grip the arms of the dentist's chair or let your hands lie in your lap. The drill drills on."[2]

I closed my eyes to sleep as the drill drilled on, but this time with my hands in my lap. I would be okay because that chair would never be empty. God would always be there for me.

8

Grief

"I don't know why people get so uptight about things that happen to them," I remember telling my mom when life seemed to be going as planned. With my education behind me, I had married, was financially comfortable, and had two sweet little girls.

It was a few months after I had spoken those words that my husband and I were in Toronto at a convention. In the middle of the night, the phone rang: My dad had been in an automobile accident and had ruptured his spleen. Two hours later, we heard from home again: The doctor had discovered pancreatic cancer during the operation. "He doesn't offer us much hope," my mother said.

The weeks that followed demanded responsibilities for Dad from all of us. Meanwhile, my husband's behavior had changed, and he was leaving the house more. My perfect life had now been turned upside down. I had become one of those people who gets uptight about things happening, and I didn't find much courage or strength to go on.

Weeks passed. Dad got worse. Bruce walked out. I woke up one night and slid my hand to the empty side of the bed. I thought about my two little girls and the son growing inside me. The course of history was being changed for my family. *I can't let my children grow up without their dad*, I thought. *Surely there is something I can do about all this madness.* I fell into fitful sleep as I touched the wedding ring I still wore on my left hand.

What You Should Know

A single parent's trip through the emotional maze often starts with grief—the sense of loss that comes with the death of a spouse or the failure of a relationship.

One way individuals deal with grief is not to deal with it at all. They deny its existence, saying, "Boys don't cry." Other people think it's wrong to grieve, that it takes away from their belief in God's power. But the shortest verse in the Bible, "Jesus wept,"[1] tells us that Jesus also grieved.

When we find ourselves in the middle of loss that involves a consequence of our own choosing, it's easier to accept because we maintain our sense of personal power. But when losses out of our control grip our lives, we feel powerless to stop the pain.

The more quickly and more efficiently we handle our grief, the sooner we reestablish our equilibrium. But if we don't deal well with our grief, we cripple ourselves for handling the changes occurring around us. Rather than accepting our losses, we use our emotions to grasp onto the person or situation that is now gone. Instead of using our efforts to move past the event, we often spend those energies holding on to our sadness and mismanaging our grief for the rest of our lives. Individuals managing their grief well ask questions such as, "Where do I go from here?" "Who and what do I need to help me get through?"

One of the most famous researchers to study grief is Elisabeth Kubler-Ross.[2] She identified a pattern of grieving with five stages: denial, anger, bargaining, depression, and acceptance. Not everyone goes through all of the stages in order, and once someone passes through a phase, it does not mean he or she may not go back and experience it again. But grieving individuals generally experience these emotions in one form or another. And as they work through these feelings, they move one step closer to accepting their loss and to healing their deep wounds.

Questions You Ask

My husband left me about the same time my friend's husband was killed. Though others see my friend as the one grieving, my grief seems more intense. Is this unusual?

If relationships are insecure before the loss, the result is more woundedness and pain afterward. If your friend had a strong and healthy relationship with her husband during their marriage, it may be easier for her to grieve. If things were turbulent, she may be dealing with similar issues as the ones you face in the breakdown of your own marriage.

Relationships with strong attachments build self-esteem. When two people grow in a healthy way together, they encourage development both separately and together—how to be alone and how to combine. They develop strong boundaries and share in each other's efforts as individuals and as a couple. Healthy grief expresses a mourning for the loss: It does not attempt to hold on to it.

Grieving will probably be harder for you to do than it will be for your friend because your situation lacks closure. In addition, you are most likely dealing with other complicated emotions to soothe your hurt.

Give yourself time and permission to grieve. You have lost something you wanted to keep. That deserves careful handling.

I grieved so much over the death of my husband, I feel like I have lost my hope. How can I get my life back?

Begin by determining why you are feeing as you do. Are you depressed or in despair? We often encounter depression and despair while we grieve. Depression is an anger we feel on the inside; depression causes us to dwell on the past. Despair is what we feel when we lose our hope. When in despair, we see a bleak future.

Sometimes we allow so much of our identity to be defined through our mates that when they are gone, our foundations are pulled out from under us, which shakes our self-esteem, purpose, and plans for the future.

To help with these emotions, start with the basics—eat well, exercise, and rest. Pay special attention to your grooming. Bad days can become better with a good hairstyle and makeup. Find new friends and explore new interests. If depression persists or runs very deep, seek professional counseling.

My divorce is not final yet, but I have met someone who makes me feel good about myself again. Am I rushing things?

Taking your time before you explore a new relationship can only be to your benefit. I would not trust my emotions or my choices with such a fresh wound. A support group may help you work through your losses. You can't control the things that are happening to you, but you can control the ongoing power they have over you.

Developing close relationships with friends and family members will help you heal. You can never replicate your former relationship, but if you build other supportive, secure connections, the loss will be more tolerable.

One woman in Canada told me that her husband had died more than a year before, leaving her to raise her son alone. She missed her wonderful marital relationship so much, she immediately became involved with another man—a married one. She said he filled her emotional and intellectual voids and was good to her child. Sadness overwhelmed this beautiful young woman's face, illustrating that there is no substitute for grieving your own losses, remaining in control, and then moving on to the next phases of life. This woman had never taken time to grieve properly.

Go slowly. Grieving losses takes time that nothing can circumvent. If you don't take the time you need, you can make some dreadful mistakes.

When I first went through my divorce, I wanted to be alone much of the time. I don't need that so much anymore. Is that normal?

Embracing aloneness prepares us for intimacy with others. A death must occur (loss, sadness, aloneness) before we can enjoy new life.

A few days after my husband walked out, I took my aloneness to a private spot, and I looked up to God. I asked him to take not just this situation but my whole life and make things right. Though I had lost the most important relationship I had had, that afternoon surrender brought new fellowship with the one who would never leave me during the many hard and lonely days to come.

Other new friendships developed as time when on that will always be dear to me, and God used those individuals to help

me heal. But those initial times of aloneness brought clarity and rest, commitment and strength from sources that would not fade away.

My children's dad left two months ago. How can I help us through this difficult time?

Cry. Ask questions. Look honestly at what might have gone wrong. Reevaluate your beliefs and your options. Face your new status and your aloneness. This is a time to gather your children in close to you and minister to one another's needs. Try not to take on any more changes than are necessary. Start some new traditions. Assess and strengthen your relationships, especially those that are the most important to you. Develop healthier, more empowered relationships in your life. These kinds of choices will help you put some joy back in your home.

I'm a single mom who is handling my own difficulties, but I know a recent single mom who leans on me to help her work through her pain. It's draining me, and I wonder if I'm really helping her. What should I do?

One good way of helping your own healing along is to help others. But you need to keep your helping role in balance and help in a healthy way. You want to provide assistance to your friend so that after each inter-action with you, she needs you a little less. Help her work her own way to wholeness.

I taught Sunday school when we lived in Ohio. One of the women in my class was a single mom who felt extremely victim-ized. She asked if she could come over one afternoon and talk about some of her problems. I had been up late doing another job for the church and desperately needed some rest. In addition, I had interacted with this woman many times before and felt the futility of trying to give her advice. So I asked her to call me.

I took a nap that afternoon, and when she called, we agreed to meet at a park where I liked to run and walk on a path around the lake. I needed to spend some time with this woman, but I also had personal and family needs to attend to that afternoon.

I loaded my son and his bicycle into the car and headed for the park. We started our brisk walk, with my son on his bicycle taking the lead. I asked her to introduce her first topic of concern. She talked. I listened. I offered some advice, then I modeled a prayer for this issue—with my eyes open as I walked the trail.

Before the three-mile trek was over, we had covered about six problems. Back at my car, I reviewed what we had talked about and wrote them on the back of a bank deposit slip. Then I handed it to her and told her to do the same thing day after day with these and other issues and to keep track of the ones that worked out.

My goal that day was to help her apply healing to her own wounds and remove part of her dependency on someone else.

My church and neighborhood don't seem to know what to do with me now that I'm a single parent. I don't belong with the married couples because I have no spouse, and I don't belong with the singles because I have children. Why can't they understand?

Single parent and author Barbara Schiller[3] says four stereotypical reasons exist for this type of omission. Single parents are perceived as a:

- *Threatener.* "They could break up our relationships."
- *Failure.* "They couldn't even keep themselves in a rela-tionship."
- *Alienator.* "They just don't fit."
- *Parasite.* "They are so needy—time, money, energy."

Until these individuals realize the stereotypes are not fair or accurate, they will probably not fulfill your needs. I suggest help-ing to clarify this misunder-standing or looking for help someplace else. Attend another church. Find relationships at your work, neighborhood, and with those involved in your children's activities. Eventually you should find someone who understands your needs and is willing to lend a hand.

Helping Others Grieve

How can I help my 9-year-old daughter deal with the death of her father?

Barbara Schiller[4] quotes Claudia L. Jewett[5] as she answers this question:

Phase 1: Early Grief. Use flannel bedsheets, play radio softly at bedtime, and serve food with mushy, milky texture and high potassium content. Jewett also suggests buying a watch to give a sense of control and providing your daughter with a house key to alleviate fears of abandonment. Then watch for evidence of these phases as your child:

Shock. Becomes sullen and withdrawn.

Alarm. Has looked to her parents to keep her safe, and the loss of a family member heightens her sense of vulnerability. Insomnia, loss of appetite, or food binges sometimes result.

Denial. Thinks parent will come back.

Hyperactivity. Displays high impulsivity, intensity, and physical activity.

Phase 2: Acute Grief. The child should be kept close as much as possible. Further changes should be kept to a minimum. Parents should go easy on responding to incidents of acting out. Assurance of love and security become paramount in this phase. Counseling may be necessary.

Yearning, pining, and searching. Looks for something good in the past to help her cope with the present and future.

Strong emotions. Becomes angry, scared, sad.

Disorganized or disoriented. Sits with blank stares.

Despair or depression. Feels profound sadness.

Phase 3: Integration of Loss and Grief. This should happen over time. Keep stability wherever you can. Don't fight with another adult in front of the child.

Talking about the loss. Life appears to offer hope again, in spite of what has happened. The big picture becomes clearer.

Getting involved again. Laughter and involvement return to the child's life.

Caring about others. The child becomes less inwardly focused and learns to look past her own hurts to life in general.

Be sure to communicate with your child's teachers about any of these phases. Share telltale signs of stress your child may manifest. Let teachers know the behaviors that may continue through the year and how important it is that the child not be isolated for misbehavior.

Most important, keep at it. Your daughter's grief is healthy. It's up to you to help her grieve in healthy ways. Allow her to talk about things she feels without interrupting or judging what she says. Permit as much time as your daughter needs to integrate her losses. If she wants to hold on to or turn loose of possessions or friendships, understand and work with her.

As I am working through my own losses, I encounter others going through similar experiences. How can I help them and myself?

Psychologist Greg Cynaumon recommends getting and giving help as soon as possible. He describes it this way:

The Window of Opportunity Time Line

The window of opportunity for preventing crisis with children and teens following divorce is approximately 24 months. If symptoms are not recognized and treated during this period, they are likely to become more ingrained and serious. The earlier the treatment, the more effective and successful it will be. The starting point is the divorce, death, breakup, or the point in the marriage when it entered a crisis and divorce seemed inevitable to the children.[6]

If warning signs exist during the first 24-month period but go untreated beyond two years, there is greater resistance to intervention and the problems

Window of Opportunity Time Line				
Start	6 months	12 months	18 months	24 months
Up to 6 months Begin by looking for warning signs during the first 6 months. They are more hidden at this stage so they need to be watched especially closely.				
	6 to 24 months This is the stage when post-traumatic stress disorders, depression, acting out, etc. are most likely to occur and easiest to recognize.			
		12 to 24 months During the latter part of the window, warning signs become easier to find but harder to diagnose and treat.		

become more ingrained and serious. Helpers should see these 24 months as a window of opportunity to single-parent families. Single parents look much different coming out of this period than they did going in if they are getting the help they need.

How can I explain to others what I and other single parents are going through? How can I make them understand?

Life is a series of developmental stages through which we move. We complete one task or stage before moving on to the next. When a family experiences death or divorce or other relationship breakup, the life cycle stops.

For your family to get back on track, you must adjust to the losses that have occurred. Completing that loop means going through the grief stages. If you or others are new to single parenting, you are very needy. Your family unit will need to reestablish itself in ways that meet the needs of the members. The minimum time for single-parent families to recover from such losses is two years, but the average readjustment time is usually between three to five years.

Most families searching for help are going through the loop of healing stages. Assist those in helping roles to understand that the early stages of healing involve a front-load investment. But single-parent families don't stay in the loop forever. Help others see valuable talents and gifts you all can offer after healing.

Where are you on the loop? Where are each of your children? Some are still in the loop and will have different needs than the more stable ones who have lived this way for a while.

Help for moms or dads parenting on their own is born out of a thorough understanding of the needs. Counselor and speaker on single-parent issues Carmen Hoffman says: "Single parents are not necessarily more needy than others, they just bring an authenticity of need, stripped of pretense and honed true by their daily dependence on God and other people. They know they need others."

Help people you know understand that, too.

9

Fear

One of my children's favorite books when they were younger was *Harry and the Terrible Watzit.*[1] It is about a boy named Harry who is afraid of what lurks down in his cellar. When his mother goes down for a jar of pickles and does not return, Harry reluctantly goes down in search of her with a broom in hand. There he discovers a double-headed, three-toed, long-horned Watzit. Harry is afraid of the monster, but he is more afraid of what will happen to his mother if he doesn't find her.

When I became a single mom, I was afraid of what lay ahead. How would I handle everything? Where would I turn? But much like Harry, the fear I felt for the future was overcome by the greater fear of what would happen to my children if I did not take charge. That fear helped me decide to muster courage and move on. What is this terrible but awesome emotion that caused you and me to take on our single-parenting responsibilities?

What You Should Know

The meaning of the word *fear* comes from the Old English word meaning "sudden calamity or danger." The Hebrew word for fear can also be translated as "dread," a heavy oppressive sensation of anxiety. *Worry* comes from a root word meaning "to strangle or to choke." Worry is the uneasy, suffocating feeling we often experience in times of fear, trouble, or problems.

Many single parents who have experienced a lot of hurt believe that anything that is bad will happen to them. As a result, they fear everything: their kids won't turn out right, their bills won't be paid, their friends and family will reject them.

Some fear is good and necessary for survival; other fear is destructive. Author Carol Kent defines three different fears:

- *Holy fear.* This involves a reverence for God. The Bible says: "The fear of the LORD is the beginning of knowledge, but fools despise wisdom and discipline."[2] The absence of this fear is the cause of many of the problems we face with our children. I opened a teen magazine recently to see these ads: "Live life as you see it"; "Play with fire. Skate on thin ice"; "Be good, be bad, just be." I see T-shirts and other paraphernalia with these words branded across them: "No Fear." If our society convinces us—adults and children alike—that we are godlike and have nothing or no one to fear, we start to believe that there also are no consequences, that we are not accountable. And if we have no consequences, we have no need for boundaries or rules or codes of conduct. Holy fear keeps that from happening because it puts God in charge of all things.

- *Self-preserving fear.* This allows us to protect ourselves and those we love from danger. When I was a teenager, I baby-sat for a family in our hometown. Their youngest son, Randy, was barely walking when I joined him and his family one afternoon around their grandparents' pool. My job was to watch Randy while I enjoyed the day. He toddled near the water. Bravery and boldness marked his immature steps. Suddenly Randy plunged into the deep end of the pool. I jumped into the water, fully clothed, and pulled him out. Randy sobbed in his mother's arms for a while, then he took his bucket, truck, and newly found respect for the water close to the safety of the chain-link fence and played there the rest of the afternoon. Randy was learning about self-preserving fear.

- *Slavish fear.* Carol Kent describes this as the negative fear "that kills expressions of love, plugs lines of communication, imprisons victims of abuse, taunts with ridiculous phobias, controls by manipulation, erodes all confidence and security. Wise, self-preserving fear shifts into slavish fear when it becomes obsessive and controlling."[3]

Whether real or imagined, slavish fear is our response when our safety or control is threatened. We mismanage this fear in one of two ways: by running from our fear and blaming others or by fighting the perceived enemy with unsure weapons.

For single parents, both of these mismanagements come easily. We avoid doing something to combat financial ruin and blame our ex when it happens. Other times, we face head-on our fear of being alone by reaching out to someone, only to be met with rejection. For this, our former mate might also get the blame.

In both cases, we see ourselves as victims—out of control of what is happening in our lives. This can happen to us when we define ourselves by our single-parent status and the events that brought us to this point. We sometimes glorify life before the breakup or the death of our mate and refuse to do what we need to do to move on.

Managed fear, on the other hand, alerts us to the need to be courageous and to take charge of the situation in spite of the circumstances that caused our fear. Courage is never about ourselves in isolation. Single parents who exhibit courage do so because of the important people at stake— their children. Courage causes an individual life to connect to something or someone bigger than itself and become more. Courage appears when single moms and dads keep going when they want to quit or run away or when they face another big challenge. True courage is found in one difficult situation after another when we determine we are going to make it through.

Questions You Ask

I've changed since I became a single parent. I've been more aggressive, and I am impatient with those who are inefficient. Is this masking fear I feel?

When individuals become single parents through death, divorce, or abandonment, life changes. These changes may also bring about alterations in personality characteristics. I became overly ambitious and a perfectionist after my husband left. Some become workaholics. Others become so fearful that they don't want their kids out of their sight. All these can be over-compensations for fears we have about further changes.

Since my wife died, I have felt gripped with fear about things that have nothing to do with my loss. Why?

C. S. Lewis felt similar emotions after his wife died. He wrote: "No one ever told me that grief felt so like fear. I am not afraid, but the sensation is like being afraid; the same fluttering in the stomach, the same restlessness, the yawning. I keep on swallowing."[4]

When death brushes our lives, it exposes our humanity and our vulnerability. The helplessness we feel in doing anything to fight the intrusion takes away the power we feel in life. That's enough to make anyone afraid. But time and acceptance of things you cannot change should help you regain your footing on the things you can change.

How can I know when to retreat and when to muster courage and advance?

You need to be good at both fight and flight responses. If you are a fighter, learn how to pick your battles carefully. Walk away to deflate volatile situations. Sometimes silence is the best response if someone is accusing, blaming, or threatening you.

If you are a fleer (one who runs away from the challenge), you need to develop assertiveness skills. You may benefit from self-defense training or from taking a speech class to learn how to speak up. Standing your ground, especially when being blamed for someone else's feelings, can be invaluable in protecting a single parent from harm. With the proper support, even the most timid of us can speak the truth and defend our space. Fear, then, becomes a friend rather than an emotion to dread.

I fear everything: things that happen and things that don't. What can I do?

Carol Kent distinguishes several ways we fear.[5] These fears can especially affect single parents:

- *Fear of things that haven't happened yet.* It's easy to imagine the worst for the future. With the busyness and the dismal statistics we face each day, we shudder at what could happen in our families.
- *Fear of being vulnerable.* When we realize life for our kids depends on the decisions we make, we fear losing control. Because we have often been betrayed or greatly disappointed in life, we become afraid of revealing who we are.
- *Fear of abandonment.* Most single parents have been abandoned in some way. Now we find it frightening to risk being rejected one more time.
- *Fear of truth.* Sometimes we are afraid to face where we went wrong or made mistakes, especially when we have been severely wronged. Also, life gets going at such a fast pace, we don't have time to search the past. It's easy to let the truth slide.
- *Fear of making wrong choices.* Because many of our single-parenting experiences have been the result of one or more wrong choices, we often hesitate about making future decisions. We are afraid what one more failure will mean to us or to our children.

No matter what fear you face, recognize that you still have control over your response to it. Take one fear at a time and determine what type it is. If you are afraid of what might happen, do all you can to prevent the occurrence, then surrender the rest to God. Combat your fears of being vulnerable and being abandoned by learning to trust again. Develop new relationships with those who will not betray you or leave you—in your family, at church, and through activities you enjoy. Realize that some bad things do happen, but that lots of good things happen, too. If you keep this in mind, learning the truth of new challenges will not affect you so deeply. Finally, do not let the fear of making wrong choices immobilize you. Start with small decisions. Weigh all the choices and possible consequences. Pray about your decision. Then make your decision and stand by it. The Bible says, "The steps of a good man [or woman] are ordered by the LORD."[6] Pray and find out what those steps are.

Anxiety

I feel so anxious all the time, and it has begun to take a toll on my health. How can I overcome these feelings?

Author Karen Randau tells us that anxiety produces a feeling of being out of control and can easily accelerate into panic. Symptoms include shaking, a racing heart, sweaty palms, ringing ears, dizziness, nausea, a feeling of losing sanity, chills, heat waves, choking, and intense loneliness. More than three panic attacks a month are an indication of what psychiatrists call a "panic disorder" that requires professional treatment.[7]

For a single parent, anxiety is a symptom of emotional overload. It is an indication that you are not dealing with your own feelings. You learn to deny them by either concealing them or disguising them as something else. Until your emotions are exposed and put into perspective, they will continue to haunt you.

I am petrified about what may happen to me and my family. How can I use these fears to motivate me rather than immobilize me?

Author Gary Oliver says that fear is a healthy reaction to harm. He describes it as a smoke signal that alerts us to danger and the need for action. While fear focuses on impending danger, Oliver tells us that anxiety is a constant level of internal tension over something that may or may not occur.[8]

According to Edmund J. Bourne, Ph.D., anxiety is "vague, distant, or even unrecognized danger . . . about losing control

... about something bad happening."[9] Some people permit their anxieties to excuse them from responsibility and moving forward with life.

In your situation, I would lay out all the possible outcomes before me to see what's the best and the worst that could happen. Next I would list all the things I can do something about. Finally I would make an action plan with the steps I can take, and let the others go. I have often found a great sense of relief once I have done all I know to do. Then I pray and hope for the best.

When I feel anxious about things, I don't always know what I am anxious about. I even feel guilty sometimes if I'm not worrying about something. What's going on?

Bourne defines four types of anxiety:

- *Free-floating anxiety*. This kind of anxiety is prompted by no specific event. It often leaves as quickly as it comes.
- *Situational anxiety*. This involves an uneasiness over an upcoming situation, such as a court hearing or an uncomfortable confrontation.
- *Phobia*. This type of anxiety causes the individual to avoid specific situations out of fear.
- *Anticipatory anxiety*. Single parents worry about what could happen during a phobic situation.

You might need to seek professional help to assist you in pinpointing exactly what is bothering you and how to work the best with it. Once you determine what is causing your anxiety, you are better equipped to deal with it and draw boundaries around those things that are within or outside of your control.

How can I overcome my anxiety?

You can begin by discovering the negative emotions that are driving you. Forgive the person who hurt you. Honestly face the ways you are feeling and how you are responding. Then seek balance in your lifestyle.

Don't try to avoid or deny your anxieties by jumping from one relationship to another, staying busy, or even masking the problem by becoming dependent on things such as drugs or alcohol. This can easily happen.

When I am anxious about things, I pray about what concerns me, and what a reliable source that has proven to be: "Do not be anxious about anything, but in everything, by prayer and petition, with thanksgiving, present your requests to God. And the peace of God, which transcends all understanding, will guard your hearts and your minds ...."[10]

How do I keep from feeling like a victim again?

Recognize yourself as a powerful individual who impacts the

lives of those around you—especially your children's. Use your fear to hold others accountable for their actions and take responsibility for yourself.

Holding others accountable means setting clear boundaries in your relationships. Get help from others you trust, such as a counselor, friend, church, or support group. Feeling protected in a geographical location, in relationships, or within a community is something the single parent needs. With the assistance of others helping you, you can decide if your boundaries should allow a particular person to come close. They can also help you stand up to others when you need to. If your boundaries are violated, be bold. Explain how amends could be made. Protect yourself from future misuse.

Don't play the blame game. Pick your battles carefully. Some are worth confronting, others are not.

No one response is correct in every situation. For some, it is better to walk away. For others, you need to take a stand. The same danger may require fighting one time and fleeing the next. There are no easy answers to effectively managing your fear, but it can be done.

The first time I read *Harry and the Terrible Watzit* to my children, I realized I, too, could face my monster with weapon in hand. I have even used the letters in the word *fear* to help me conquer my slavish fears:

F—Face the monster. Meet what I'm afraid of head-on.

E— Engage in battle. Do what needs to be done.

A—Abide. Stick with it until I'm not afraid anymore.

R—Reflect. Look back on my conquered monsters and get courage to face the next one.

More than once I have found myself reaching for God's gift of courage when fear squeezed me in its iron grip. I have found that fear preceded victory. And I have found God faithful to help me with all my monsters.

10

Anger

I had been a single mom for about seven years. I was finishing my doctorate and was stretched about as far as one can imagine.

One Friday morning in the summer, I woke the children. I was taking them with me to the university where I had an appointment regarding my dissertation. I was braiding my oldest daughter's hair when I saw she had picked up lice. I spent the day canceling my appointment, talking with the pediatrician, making a run to the drugstore, showering each of the children, washing all bed linens, and vacuuming from stem to stern. I was one exhausted mom when I dropped the children off for the weekend with their dad.

I pulled my used van up next to his new Porsche. His girlfriend waited a short distance away. He sashayed to the van with his tanned arms outstretched to the children. "Daddy, Daddy," they called in unison. He hugged them one by one, and they were off to their newest adventures, barely turning to say good-bye.

I pulled away, recounting every treacherous, deceitful, and dishonest thing Bruce had ever done to me—and the dates he did them. Anger had made its appearance once again.

What You Should Know

Author Neil Clark Warren defines anger as "a physical state of readiness or preparedness to act."[1] Anger makes the adrenaline flow, the heart beat faster, and the blood pressure rise. We can cause permanent physical damage to ourselves if we remain angry or don't deal with the anger we feel.

Frederick Buechner says: "Of the Seven Deadly Sins, anger is possibly the most fun. To lick your wounds, to smack your lips over grievances long past, to roll over your tongue the prospect of bitter confrontations still to come, to savor to the last toothsome morsel both the pain you are given and the pain you are giving back—in many ways it is a feast fit for a king. The chief drawback is that what you are wolfing down is yourself. The skeleton at the feast is you."[2]

With the anger I felt that day, I had several choices of ways to respond. I could:

- *Deal with it* (use it to help change what needs to be changed). "I'm angry, but I'm not going to let it ruin our lives."
- *Hold it in* (self-criticism, guilt, depression, bitterness). "It's all my fault."
- *Handle it indirectly* (nagging, being sarcastic, withdrawing). "You are always on my case."
- *Blame and focus outside myself* (finding fault with others, having angry outbursts). "It's all your fault."
- *Act out* (drinking, taking drugs). "I'm going to find someone better than he was anyway."
- *Do violence to myself* (psychosomatic problems, suicide, or other physical abuse).

We often experience anger as a result of circumstances we cannot control. But what we do with that anger is an everyday choice. So how do we conquer our anger before it conquers us?

Questions You Ask

I get so angry when I have to deal with visitation problems. Shouldn't this be getting easier?

Visitation should become less of a problem over time as both of you learn to work together better and get more experience in your redefined relationship. You should also learn how to separate your role as co-parent from your relationship with each other. But this doesn't always happen.

If conflict persists between the two of you, counseling or mediation could help achieve a more harmonious visitation. These interventions can help redefine your roles and help your ex accept a reduced say over the children. If the emotions settle with the passage of time, so should the conflicts. Both of you should want that to happen to get the best results. Even if you work at this alone, however, you should see some positive results.

Is my anger toward my ex-husband really that detrimental to the children?

The more hostility a custodial parent shows toward the ex-mate, the less chance there is of building a peaceful family framework. Closure on the old life and moving forward with the new is invariably delayed or prevented altogether when prolonged anger is involved. As long as hostility exists, the ex-spouse is psychologically present with the family.

As long as I don't fly off the handle, is it okay to be angry?

Anger isn't okay when aggression occurs. The Bible says to "be angry, and do not sin."[3] Aggression happens when the angry person threatens someone with words or weapons. Revenge motivates negative responses, and destructive consequences result.

Anger can cause real problems if it is not managed correctly. But without anger, we would become vulnerable to everyone who could hurt us. So use it to make you better, not bitter.

Sometimes people just make me so mad that I feel no control over my responses. Is this normal?

The events that cause your anger and your response to them are independent of one another. You can never gain control over someone else's affronts toward you, but you can get control over how you respond.

Anger can distort perceptions. Failure to manage our emotions keeps us from resolving the problem. We choose our responses, according to Dr. Albert Ellis's model of the ABCs of emotion:

A—*Activating event.* Your son fails to come home when he is supposed to after being told repeatedly to do so.
B—*Belief system.* You think he's being willfully disobedient.
C—*Consequence* (resultant emotional response). You get angry.[4]

A does *not* make C happen. B causes C to happen. We choose our own responses based on our interpretation or belief system about the activating event. Any reactions you might have had—ignoring, yelling, grounding, or discussing—will result from how you perceive the initiating event. Never again should you use the excuse that someone causes you to lose control. No one has that kind of power over you.

What are some things I can say to defuse angry situations toward my children or their other parent?

You need to be empathetic whenever possible. Force yourself to grow in this area by stepping back from the situation long enough to step into the other person's shoes. You might find yourself looking at the situation from a whole new perspective. When verbal responses become necessary, use nondefensive statements, regardless of how angry you feel. Try:

"I understand."

"I can see that there's a problem."

"I am aware that you are concerned."

Responding angrily to an angry person will only perpetuate the problem. Nondefensive statements such as the ones listed will quickly reduce the intensity of the situation.

When I get angry, is it really indicating a deeper problem?

Anger is often a response to fear we feel when something we value is threatened physically or emotionally. It is a God-given response available to help us cope effectively with life's hurts or fears. How we express that anger is an attempt to defend ourselves or those we love. Anger almost always occurs out of some degree of pain.

If anger is a natural response, is there any good that can come out of it?

Let's say your ex-husband tells you he will not be able to visit his children again this weekend because he has to work overtime. But you find out that he has a getaway planned with a new girlfriend. You're angry. Why?

Something that involves your children is wrong and needs to be corrected. Your anger and concern over the best interests of your children provide a powerful source of motivation to move you to positive action and change. It can help you set boundaries and clarify what is best for the children. Work hard to help your ex-husband see that. But managing your anger can contribute to a less threatening relationship with your ex-husband.

In this instance, I would have a talk with your ex-husband. In a non-threatening way, explain the damage he is doing. If verbal communication is difficult, try writing it down. Let him know how much his children need his input, consistency, and example. Numerate how that might happen:

1. Make every effort to carry out visitation.
2. If emergencies arise, give plenty of notice and reschedule at time that can be kept.
3. Model solid values. This means telling the truth and making choices he would like his kids to mimic.

How Others Handle It

My daughter is angry at God for taking her dad. What are some techniques for handling this kind of emotion?

All of us, including your daughter, handle anger in one of four ways:

- Repression (keeping it in)
- Suppression (postponing it)
- Expression (expressing it)
- Aggression (responding with physical and emotional hurt)

If you don't allow your daughter to say how she feels, it will bottle up inside and affect her physically and/or emotionally. If you delay getting her help, it will be harder to fix. You can find a safe place for her to express it—in counseling and in open communication with you. If the anger is not effectively dealt with, it could result in open aggression and hostility toward someone else, in which case physical harm could result.

Anger at individuals is often an anger toward God. Involve your pastor or clergy in helping your daughter work through these emotions. Most of all, read the Bible and pray together. Allow your daughter to get to know the character of God. If she does, she will realize that God is not looming above, waiting to hurt her. Rather, she will find him loving and waiting to hear her tell him her hurts.

Facing It

I find myself resenting my ex-husband, his family, and others who seemed to condone what he did. How do I deal with my resentment?

When we forgive, we stop feeling resentment against an offender. We don't require the offender to pay us back. The Bible tells us: "Get rid of all bitterness, rage and anger, brawling and slander, along with every form of malice. Be kind and compassionate to one another, forgiving each other, just as in Christ God forgave you."[5]

Resentment manifests itself after unresolved anger occurs. Bodies buckle under the strain of a persistent state of anger—being ready to respond to an emotion—and many physical ailments can result, such as headaches, stomach problems, colds, colitis, and hypertension.

I felt much the same way toward those who observed what my husband did. The more I tried to stay behind and convince them he was wrong, the less innocent I felt. My answer was to move on and that meant a physical move for me. I moved to a different place, found different friends, and become involved in different activities. This lessened the control those I left behind had over me.

Deep down, everyone knows right from wrong, including those who observed your husband's choices. It just may not be your role to point that out. Spend your energies building a new life for you and the children. This decision will speak much to those who watch from afar—and to your children who will learn by example to pick up and go on.

I've spent a lifetime apologizing, losing relationships, and undoing damage from my temper tantrums. They had a lot to do with the breakup of my marriage. Is it too late to change?

It's never too late, and you've already taken the first step—deciding to do it. But it won't be easy to undo a lifetime habit.

Neal Clark Warren recommends the following therapy for exploders:

- Spell out in writing the kind of person you want to be while expressing anger.
- Know what causes the provocative events. Catch explosive buildup at first signs.
- Delay responses. Choose an alternate route at critical junctures in the anger process.
- Answer two questions: What do I want from this confrontation? How can I get what I want most effectively?
- Determine your expectations? What do you want to happen as a result of this situation?[6]

By thinking through the situation that prompts your anger, you put yourself back in control of your emotions. These strategies can help you filter your responses. By the time you have finished this routine, your anger is often defused.

Does how I was raised have anything to do with how I am responding to my own children?

My dad was very negative in his approach to disciplining my seven siblings and me. One statement I heard him use over and over again as he was trying to bring about a difference in our behavior was, "As usual you . . ." then he would proceed to name the negatives. I disliked this response.

One day my children and I were driving in the car, and one of my daughters did something she shouldn't have done. Then I heard my dad saying, "Courtney, what's wrong with you?" but it was coming from my mouth.

We should have received good parenting skills from our own parents. Whether we did or not, we should not dwell on past weaknesses. Instead, we should assess them and learn from them.

All of us either raise our children exactly as we were raised or very differently. Reflect on your own upbringing and answer the following questions:

- When my mother became angry, she _____.
- When my father became angry, he _____.
- I respond to my anger by (crying, hiding, hitting, yelling, throwing things, blaming others, pouting, feeling sick, holding feelings in, other) _____.

- Situations that make me most angry are _____.
- I react to these situations by _____.
- Things I need to change are _____.

The beginning steps in managing your own responses is recognizing what motivates them and deciding you do have control over them.

When I feel myself getting angry, what should I do?

You have already begun the process by determining that you want to deal with your anger productively and responsibly. Paying attention to the following will help:

- Be your best physically—proper diet, sufficient sleep, and regular exercise. We sometimes harbor deep resentment for feeling overworked and underappreciated—an easy plight for single parents.
- Take a few minutes to sort out why your temper is flaring up. Ask yourself: What will my anger change or accomplish? What is causing my anger? Am I tired, hungry, or disappointed? Is my anger a result of my own mistakes, demands, or expectations?

- Become aware of the circumstances, people, or places that breed anger in you. Try to avoid these confrontations.
- Strengthen your feelings about yourself. Violations to self-esteem through insults and humiliation cause anger. Surround yourself with people who help you feel good about yourself. Emphasize your strengths and reward yourself.
- Confess your anger as sin when it has hurt others. Read Ephesians 4:17–32.
- Clarify your goals and stay in close touch with your feelings.
- Keep a diary. Catch anger at its first signs. Write down the following:

The anger felt

The time and place

The situation

How you responded

What you actually want but haven't gotten so far

What action you plan to take

Any previous action plans completed today

After several months of keeping a detailed anger diary, you should better understand your anger and move beyond management to solution.

11

Guilt

The year my husband left, our oldest daughter, Ashley, started preschool. I was devastated, alone, embarrassed, and pregnant. Clint was born in the spring, and two months later, I attended Ashley's preschool graduation. I took my place in the front row and watched my sweet little girl with yellow bows in her hair, eyes wide in anticipation for what life had in store. Ashley's dad was in the back of the room filming the ceremony.

When the program ended, the children were instructed to take their diplomas to their parents. Ashley started toward me. Then she moved toward the back of the room. Then she turned and moved again my way. My heart ached as she looked at me with inquiring eyes as if to say, *What should I do?*

I smiled, nodded, and pointed toward her dad. Relief covered her face as she skipped to the back, diploma in hand. But guilt stayed behind.

How could I have married him? How could I have been so blind? I've tried to give my children the best of everything, and now this—a broken home.

Guilt was doing its number on me.

What You Should Know

Psychologist and author James Dobson says, "Few human emotions are as distressing and painful as feelings of guilt and disapproval. . . . Since the voice of the conscience speaks from inside the human mind, we cannot escape its unrelenting abuse for our mistakes, failures, and sins. For some particularly vulnerable individuals, an internal taskmaster is on the job from early morning until late at night—screaming accusations at his tormented victim."[1]

The word *guilt* actually refers to the state of having done a wrong—making a mistake, breaking a law—not just feeling like you did. But guilt has a way of spilling over into our emotions, causing us to feel guilty even when we haven't made a mistake or broken a law. When we can't make the distinction between actually committing the wrong and feeling like we did, we continue to be plagued by guilt.

Ty C. Colbert says, "The only kind of guilt we should feel is a sense of remorse resulting from intentional, harmful, or irresponsible behavior, and we must learn to address it properly for our own benefit." He calls this kind of guilt "true guilt." He defines "false guilt" as "an undesirable emotion that is not caused by any wrongdoing, but is a psychological defense mechanism against pain."[2]

Author Les Parrott III says: "True guilt keeps people in line by acting as an internal alarm that warns us of danger. False guilt, however, keeps the alarm ringing even after we've been notified of the problem or even when there is no danger.

[The] guilt alarm . . .

is based on solid facts.

signals an objective condition.

is heard when the responsibility for wrongdoing is clear.

sounds as a result of a violation of a law, code, or moral value.

The false guilt alarm . . .

is based on personal feelings.

signals a subjective experience.

is heard when responsibility for wrongdoing is not clear.

sounds in the absence of violation of a law, code, or moral value."[3]

Much of the guilt single parents feel is false guilt—especially when we've been treated wrongly. Because what is happening makes no sense—husband dying, mate abandoning—the receiving party decides that it must be his or her fault. Guilt-inducing questions come flooding in: *What did I do wrong? What's the matter with me?* If true guilt is dealt with properly—confess the sin and seek forgiveness—it should become a thing of the past. If not, it becomes false guilt that takes over our lives. We avoid punishment for our wrong choices by becoming the super parent or getting involved in another "better" relationship. But this kind of guilt, authors Carmen Berry and Mark Baker say, "can become a dangerous force by trapping us under a dark cloud that rains on every relationship that could bring us love."[4]

Berry and Baker explain that when based in love, guilt motivates us to take responsibility for our actions, make amends to those we have hurt, and restore mutual power in the relationship. Properly managed, guilt helps us mend a broken relationship.

So how do you know if guilt is a problem for you?

The following questionnaire from *Love's Unseen Enemy* by psychologist and teacher Les Parrott III will help you measure your level of guilt. There are no right or wrong answers. Answer each item as accurately as you can by placing a number beside each of the items as follows:

1 Rarely or none of the time
2 A little of the time
3 Some of the time
4 A good part of the time
5 Most or all of the time

_____ I worry about what others think of me.

_____ I believe I should always be generous.

_____ I feel I should be punished.

_____ I believe I am guilty.

_____ I believe I should not be angry.

_____ I take a hard look at myself.

_____ I feel ashamed.

_____ I punish myself.

_____ I detest myself for my failures.

_____ A guilty conscience bothers me.

_____ I believe I should not lose my temper.

_____ I feel guilty.

_____ I am fretful.

_____ When I feel guilty, it lasts a long time.

_____ I feel I am unforgivable.

_____ I feel I am a reject.

_____ I detest myself for my thoughts.

_____ I feel nervous about others' opinions of me.

_____ I believe I should not hurt another person's feelings.

_____ I fear something bad will happen to me in the future.

_____ I have spells of very intense guilt.

_____ I avoid some places due to my guilt feelings.

_____ I cannot tell the difference between feeling guilty and being guilty.

_____ I avoid some people due to my guilt feelings.

_____ I avoid being alone because of my guilt feelings.

Score yourself by totaling up your points on the items and

subtracting 25. This gives a potential score of 0–100.

_____ TOTAL

_____ minus 25

_____ SCORE

80–100. You are wracked with feelings of guilt and probably need to seek outside help.

60–79. You aren't out of the danger zone.

40–59. You are in a guilt trap that has probably taken its toll on your relationships. You can use some practical tools to help you escape.

20–39. You are not allowing your guilt to get the best of you. You could use some fine tuning, however.

0–19. You have what it takes to lay a solid foundation for healthy relationships. Too low a score indicates an underdeveloped conscience.

Questions You Ask

My son is acting up. He seems to be defying everything I say. But I hesitate to scold him after all he has been through. It's all my fault for what he is going through, isn't it?

We all experience guilt with being and feeling wrong at some time or other. We judge ourselves by internal standards and, when things turn out wrong, we react by adjusting our standards, changing our behavior, or justifying our actions.

We might also feel ashamed when we have violated our moral standards, such as having an affair while we were married (true guilt). Sometimes we feel ashamed when we have not violated them at all (false guilt).

Don't let guilt interfere with your discipline. Now, more than ever before, your son needs boundaries. Determine what they are and then be consistent about upholding them.

My wife abandoned my son and me when he was two. For the last three years, I have felt guilty for whatever I did to cause my wife to leave and guilty for raising my son without his mother. What can I do to get rid of this guilt that's eating me alive?

Ty Colbert recommends five steps to help you eliminate true guilt and avoid false guilt:

• *Recognize the guilt.* Then tell yourself: *I feel guilt over the part I played in my wife's leaving.* Don't let your imagination run rampant over what that behavior might have been.

• *Identify the real source of the guilt or pain.* Do you feel as though you neglected your wife or didn't love enough or understand her? Were you working too many hours to meet her needs?

- *Determine if you are feeling true guilt or false guilt.* Did you love your wife? The answer probably is yes. But perhaps you could have let her know that more often or been there for her—face that reality as well.[5]

If it is true guilt, confess it, ask for forgiveness, change your behavior, forgive yourself, and move on. Let guilt help you recognize wrong for what it is. If you know how to get in touch with your ex-wife, tell her how sorry you are for your neglect and try to rectify the situation where you can. If you do not know how to reach her, your most important confession will be to God, yourself, and your son. Confront it, confess it, learn from it, then get on with life. In this way, you can teach your son more about giving. And, if you have an opportunity to be in a relationship again, you will know how to do it better.

If it is false guilt, feel and release the hurt and correct the violating situation. Place blame where blame is due. Stand up and say, "I'm not going to live this way anymore. What's done is done." Any guilt you feel from then on is not necessary. Put it behind you and make a new life. Be the best dad you can be! And a guilt-free one at that.

I've been a single mom for two years. How do I respond to guilt from my son?

Women, in particular, have heightened sensitivity toward others' needs and problems. Your inability to handle guilt from your son could be a result. As a single mom, you no doubt feel responsible for the emotional health of your child. In doing so, you probably allow him to place the blame for his problems on you because you're the one most accessible. After a while, you start to absorb that guilt.

You need to distinguish between true and false guilt or you will remain hostage to wrongful blame. You will continue to internalize the messages you get and forget whether you are guilty or innocent. You will also continue to buy into others' opinions of what is right or wrong instead of deciding for yourself, based on your own set of values. See guilt for what it is and refuse to be a servant to it.

I had an affair that broke up my marriage. I am so ashamed. Will I always feel this way?

First, you must understand the difference between guilt and shame. Guilt is the internal alarm that tells us we have committed a mistake (I have done something bad), but shame tells us we are a mistake (I *am* bad).

You are a unique individual created by God and subject to mistakes just like the rest of us. Confess your sin to God and to the persons you betrayed. God will forgive you, but even if the person(s) you betrayed will not, you have taken the necessary step toward getting rid of the shame and moving forward with life. So do it and be a wonderful parent to those children.

How do I stop feeling guilty?

To find out where your guilt might be coming from, try asking yourself these questions:

- Is my self-esteem low?
- Are my expectations too high?
- Is my guilt true or false? Deal with true guilt; move past the false one.
- Am I saying no enough? Don't be afraid to say no to requests that need more than you can give.

My heart goes out to every single parent who feels guilt— either true or false. Make this the day that you hang it up for good. You'll sleep a little sounder, see life a little clearer, and parent those kids a little better. It's time to move on—guilt free.

12

Forgiveness

After my husband left, I rehearsed every detail of all he had done to break up our marriage. I could recount times, places, and details—and I did. But as I tried to move on, no matter what successes and new directions I found, I felt like I was tethered to a stake from the past. I pulled to try to loosen its hold, all the while grasping onto the continuing affronts from my husband. While the past and present feelings restrained me, they did nothing to hold my husband back. It finally dawned on me. I had to forgive. Let go. It didn't happen in a day or a week or even a year. Instead, it is still happening every day—as I make the decision to forgive.

I realized that though the cost of forgiveness was high, the cost of unforgiveness for both me and my children was higher and exacted an even greater toll. I chose to forgive.

What You Should Know

Unforgiveness allows who we are to be defined by the hurts we've known, and we develop a victim mentality, expecting to be hurt again. We become negative and defensive, and communication becomes impossible. The offense may be serious or minor and may involve deprivation of property, rights, or honor. Forgiveness means giving up resentment against someone and our right to get even, no matter what's been done to us.

Forgiveness sets us free from past hurt, frustration, and fear. It also equips us to handle new crises we encounter in the present. Forgiveness has brought closure to my relationship with my ex-husband—though while the kids are young, we will still be connected. Forgiveness has reduced my anger. Because I no longer expect anything from my ex-husband, he cannot let me down. I am able to focus on the present and the new lives and relationships the children and I now know.

Questions You Ask

But you don't know what my husband did to me. Must I forgive it all?

The cost of unforgiveness does not affect just you—your health, emotions, and spirit—it affects your children. They see the way you navigate your way through relationship problems and will replicate your strategies. They will also experience the everyday effects of unforgiveness that hang like a cloud over all you attempt to do.

You and only you hold the key that opens the door to a future of forgiveness. But it's worth it—whatever the cost.

I can be having a perfectly good day, but my ex can say one thing and send me into fits of rage. How can he still wield this kind of power over me?

It sounds as though you are still angry with your ex-husband. Think of three situations recently in which he made you angry.

Which of the following happened in each of the situations?

- *Repression.* Your anger was pushed down inside. You may have asked, "Hurt? What hurt?" This leads to dishonesty and to ulcers.
- *Blame.* Anger is pushed outward. You return insults and verbal darts. It causes more pain.
- *Ignoring.* Anger is pushed against a wall. The dishonest conclusion of ignoring is a false sense that you're okay.

If you want to be freed from the hold your relationship with your ex-husband still has on you, you must forgive—again and again and again. Only forgiveness leads to open and honest communication. Only forgiveness leads to freedom and to a relationship of respect and trust.

Does forgiving my ex mean I forget everything that took place in the past?

Many single parents misunderstand forgiveness. Before we look at what forgiveness *is*, let's look at what it is *not*.

- *Forgiveness is not ignoring conflict.* Not dealing with the difficulties you face with your ex is a form of repression. Nothing will be resolved, and your body will pay the price.
- *Forgiveness is not forgetting.* You are not being honest about

what you are feeling. This reaction will keep you from moving on.

- *Forgiveness is not excusing.* We excuse people when we know they were not to blame, and they had to do what they did.

- *Forgiveness is not tolerating everything.* Author Lewis B. Smedes says, "You can forgive someone almost anything. But you cannot tolerate everything. Whenever people try to live or work together, they have to decide on the sorts of things they will put up with. The group that puts up with everything eventually kills itself."[1]

I hate my child's father for abandoning us. Is hate something I can ever get rid of?

If you hate this man, who did the wrong to you, your hatred will live on no matter how many times he says he's sorry. Lewis Smedes says, "We attach our feelings to the moment when we were hurt, endowing it with immortality. And we let it assault us every time it comes to mind. It travels with us, sleeps with us, hovers over us, and broods over us while we die. Our hate does not even have the decency to die when those we hate die."[2]

Separate your child's father from what he did to you. Forgive the wrong and then take a fresh look at the man. He is a human being who makes mistakes like the rest of us. You are probably familiar, too, with many reasons why he could have made those mistakes. Did he learn how to be a good husband and dad from his own father? What weaknesses do you know exist in his life? What hardships do you know he has gone through? What struggles does he have?

My husband has done a lot against me, and he continues to do so. I have had to be on my guard and be wise. At the same time, I realized a couple of years ago that unforgiveness held me in its grip. Once he gave the children skiing lessons for Christmas. I took them to their class and skied on my own while they had their instructions. Bruce came to watch, and I had to ride up on the chairlift with him. I hyperventilated and considered jumping off. That trip up was longer than I ever remembered.

With incidents such as this one, it's easy to see that I needed to forgive. I have been working hard on that. I realize I cannot do it on my own, so daily I pray to God, "Today I choose to forgive Bruce." When instances happen, I give my feelings back to God and give him permission to work in my life. But forgiveness for ongoing misdeeds is a process. So succeeding at it takes continuous surrender.

Recently, I went to court in Indiana with my ex-husband. The facts were clear: He owed back child support—a lot of it. The hearing was long and costly and did not turn out as fairly as I had hoped.

But during that time, I came to a bigger realization. I felt sorry for him and observed that the bigger battle had been won because forgiveness was under way. His life was messed up, and I honestly wanted things to go better for him. I walked away from the courtroom without the money I was owed, but with the assurance that my ex-husband no longer held me captive to hate and unforgiveness. I was on my way to healing.

I just wish my ex-wife would explain to me why she hurt me. I don't understand. Will she ever seek forgiveness?

Unfortunately, it doesn't usually happen that way. You must decide what you are going to do and where you will head in spite of what your former wife does or does not do. Unforgiveness locks you in darkness and shackles you to the person who did you wrong.

Your ex-wife probably doesn't know why she did what she did. She probably has no clue how to forgive herself, much less ask for forgiveness from you. We usually never understand why we were

hurt, but we can forgive without understanding. You need to forgive, no matter what your ex-wife does. Otherwise, you and your children will suffer.

The Decision to Forgive

How do I forgive? Can I forgive too soon?

"You need to forgive your ex-husband." I heard these words over and over. What I didn't hear was that forgiveness takes time, and sometimes it has to happen again and again. Meanwhile, I needed to concentrate on me and my family. I needed time— time to grieve, time to heal, time to regroup. My decision to forgive was the first step toward forgiveness that would take place later on.

Don't try to rush the process. Smedes says, "Sometimes we do it so slowly that we pass over the line without realizing we have crossed it, as children pass from childhood to adulthood, not knowing just when they crossed over. "Sometimes you seem to slide into forgiving, hardly noticing when you began to move or when you arrived. But after a long dry desert of trying, you gradually get a feeling that somewhere along the way you crossed the line between hating and forgiving."[3]

The trick is to keep on trying until it happens.

When I try to forgive, I get so emotional. Why?

Forgiveness is neither easy nor clean-cut. You don't decide you will forgive one night and wake up the next day with the job all done. How deeply you were hurt will affect how hard it is to forgive. And sometimes, long after you have forgiven, the anger remains.

Smedes says, "You cannot erase the past, you can only heal the pain it has left behind.

"When you are wronged, that wrong becomes an indestructible reality of your life. When you forgive, you heal your hate for the person who created that reality. But you do not change the facts. And you do not undo all of their consequences. The dead stay dead; the wounded are often crippled still. The reality of evil and its damage to human beings is not magically undone and it can still make us very mad."[4]

But so much has happened. Where do I begin forgiving my ex-wife?

Begin by deciding to forgive. Then forgive one act at a time. Remember, don't expect anything in return. The person you are forgiving may not change at all. She may continue to inflict pain on you and give you new things on which to practice forgiveness. But the good thing is, once you decide to forgive, something releases you from that prison.

Strategies are learned. Mind-sets are forged.

Forgiveness does not guarantee that life will go easily from there on, but unforgiveness guarantees that nothing will. It's your choice, and you need to make it regardless of what the other person chooses to do.

Can I ever be happy if I don't forgive?

I've never met a person lacking forgiveness who leads a truly happy life. Even his or her pleasant moments are shadowed by bitterness and anger. I don't talk long to a single mom or dad before I can see where they are in the forgiveness department.

Unforgiveness always hurts you more than the person or persons you are infuriated with. Messed-up thinking and physical problems result.

But my children's mother is a creep. She continues to hurt the children and me. Isn't my resentment justified?

No resentment is justified. Countless single parents have withstood atrocities that defy description. But the body and mind don't know the difference between little infractions and big, ongoing ones. The psychological and physical toll that resentment and unforgiveness exact is more than any of us can afford.

Good mental and physical health depends on your capacity to let forgiveness replace resentment in your home in order to make it a happier place.

Trace it back. Talk it out. Turn it over. Make it work.

Kids and Forgiveness

How do I show forgiveness toward my children?

If you blunder, ask the children to forgive you for exploding.

If your children blunder, talk with them and find ways to deal with the issue. Many times, I sit down calmly and ask my child how they could have answered me more respectfully or responded to a certain conflict in a better way. Healthy relationships are built on clear communication, mutual problem solving, love, understanding, and forgiveness. Real forgiveness is conveyed with loving words and actions—reassurances at bedtime, etc.

Recently I found a branch to one of my plants broken off and hidden behind the couch. I asked my son about it. He timidly nodded when asked if he had done it.

I explained that people were more important than things in our house, and that I wanted his honesty with me more than I wanted ten beautiful plants. He smiled, and I found myself hoping he would remember that conversation more than others I hadn't handled as well.

Can my kids pick up on my bitterness?

If you carry around bitterness against those who hurt you, you will make the children think it is okay if they also cling to lingering resentments. This is played out in everyday life from the person who cuts you off in traffic to their dad who lets you down one more time.

Consider how your example of prompt forgiving will foster a sense of peace and enhance self-esteem in your children. If you don't, you could live to regret it down the line as the children later rebel and turn on you. After all, they learned to hold on to resentment from the best of teachers.

I can think of several reasons for not being able to forgive. Is this wrong?

It's normal, but it will keep you from gaining the freedom you are seeking. Jay Carty lists some of the reasons you feel you cannot forgive:

• "I don't feel like forgiving!" You don't have to feel like forgiving to forgive. A guy on the freeway cut me off. I felt like ramming the rear end of his car. I didn't. I don't have to respond to my feelings. Forgiveness is a choice, not a feeling.

- "If forgiveness is forgetting, I'm whipped!" If you forget what was done to you, you have a bigger problem—Alzheimer's. Forgiveness is a choice. You don't have to forget in order to forgive.
- "But I don't trust him anymore."[5] If you loan your car to a friend who drives it recklessly and causes an accident, you can forgive him for wrecking your car, but you would be foolish to loan it to him again. Forgiveness can be granted in an instant, but trust takes time to establish and even longer to reestablish.

Do I have to apologize when I forgive?

If we apologize to some people, they take our apology and move harder against us. More likely than not, it is better to skip the apology and send out a set of positive signals toward the person against whom we have had resentment.

Perhaps you could send a note along when you send your child's report card to his dad. Speaking kind words when you meet to exchange the kids will go a long way, too.

It's better not to write or give a verbal apology if the results in our everyday life will not be apparent. Spend your efforts on just forgiving and making life and daily decisions better for all of you. Your changed attitude will almost always evoke a positive response. But even if it doesn't, you are making a valuable investment in the lives of you and your children.

A new relationship is much more important than a wimpy apology. But if the apology will help give birth to a new and improved relationship, then try it.

Does everyone wrestle with unforgiveness at some time or other?

C. S. Lewis said, "Everyone claims that forgiveness is a wonderful idea, until they have something to forgive."[6] We read in the Bible, "Forgive us the wrong we have done, as we have forgiven those who have wronged us."[7]

I heard a story once about a little girl in Sunday school who said, "Forgiveness is when you step on your dog's foot, but he just licks your hand."

I agree.

13

Sadness or Joy?

Once I was in a restaurant with some fellow teachers from my first teaching job. I had told one of the girls a joke, and she wanted me to share it with the rest of the group. I was a little shy about telling everyone, so my colleagues started chanting, "Lyn-da. Lyn-da."

The chanting continued around the table. We were all laughing. Then suddenly I was no longer laughing, but crying. At that moment I realized what a slim line there is between a smile and a tear.

As I grew older and life began to make its demands, I experienced these emotions again. Life would be going along well—bills paid, family healthy, dreams fulfilled—and I was happy and content. This happened when I was married. Though I have not

forgotten the bad days and non-perfect details, I was where I wanted to be. I had a husband. Wonderful children. A beautiful home. Our health. Life was good. I was happy.

Then BAM! Divorce. Changes everywhere. I was not happy. That slim line between the smile and the tear was drawn with circumstances of my life. I gave people and weather and situations the power to control each of my days. I allowed things to be done *to* me, and I would take them as they came each day and grin (or cry) and bear it.

But as time went on and perfection didn't come, I began to wonder if I could be happy anyway. Could I smile while my world was crashing in? Could I dance on uncertain ground?

Sad: What You Should Know

We all feel normal emotions of sadness from time to time when we experience loss or disappointment. But depression is something deeper and more enduring. Authors Siang-Yang Tan and John Ortberg Jr. describe the following causes of depression:

- *Physical factors.* Poor nutrition, overwork, exhaustion, or lack of regular exercise can contribute to depression.
- *Temperament vulnerability.* Some personality types are more prone to depression.
- *Physical, mental, emotional hardships* that take place in our lives.[1]

Questions You Ask

Do I have certain character flaws that can intensify my depression?

Could be. Ask yourself the following questions:

- *Do I compare?* It's easy to look at others and think they have an easier road in life. You look at what they have and you do not in the areas of things, talents, the future, and so on. Statistics show that only 20 percent of the struggles single parents face are specific to single parenting. The other 80 percent are common to others. Someone will always be richer, brighter, or prettier, and you'll just get depressed

---

Symptoms of Depression

Although serious cases of depression require intensive medical attention, Archibald Hart lists the following symptoms of mild depression:

- *Mood.* An unhappy, sad, "blue," or down mood.
- *Thought.* A negative and pessimistic thinking, often with ideas of guilt and self-blame, lack of motivation, problems with concentration and even memory, and suicidal thoughts in more severe depressions.
- *Behavior.* Energy is usually low, with retardation, sluggishness, neglect of personal appearance at times, or even agitation.
- *Physical.* Several symptoms may occur—loss of appetite and/or sexual drive, poor or excessive sleep, weight reduction.
- *Anxiety.* Although feeling down or sad is the major emotional characteristic of depression, anxiety, fears, tension, uncertainty, and indecisiveness may also be present.[2]

when you compare yourself to him or her.

- *Have I clearly defined who I am?* This includes limitations that make it clear "you've had enough." It also includes guidelines that delineate what you stand for. Both limitations and guidelines help us remain in control of our lives. They also prevent others from wielding undue power over us. If I lose control of my guidelines or limitations, I feel powerless, hopeless, resentful, and depressed.

- *Can I ease up on myself?* Don't be a such a perfectionist. Admit you are fallible and get on with life. Many people make gigantic to-do lists that Superman/woman could not

There is not one profile for those who suffer depression, but Brenda Poinsett lists the following as common factors in those who become severely depressed:

- *A family history of depression.* Find out how members of your family have responded in the past to tragedy or crisis.

- *Chemical imbalance.* This must be determined by blood tests and extensive medical examinations.

- *Personality type.* You can discover how affected your responses are by your demeanor. Tests are available through counselors.

- *Painful experiences in early life.* Has anything happened earlier in your life that triggered depressive responses?

- *Gender.* Women are more prone to depression than men.

- *Tangible or intangible loss.* Death of someone close, divorce; or loss of income, position, or material possessions.

Poinsett says, "Stressful events—the kind that trigger depression—can usually be pinpointed to a specific moment: the night we broke up, the day my mother died, the day the factory closed. The specific time marker makes this trigger easy to spot. When stressful events occur, we can stay alert to our increased vulnerability over a period of time."[3]

Sadness and depression know no marital, economic, career, or denominational boundaries. It is no respecter of persons. Great individuals in history were known to fight depression (John Quincy Adams, Abraham Lincoln).

perform. Then when they don't complete everything on the list, a feeling of failure results and the individuals become depressed.

- *Am I isolating myself?* Many people are most depressed and lonely in crowds. Though people are around them, they don't know how to connect because they risk being vulnerable. Search out individuals with whom you can be yourself and share your needs.

Can I get better on my own?

As long as your case is not severe, Poinsett recommends:

- Building your self-image. Goals. Managing your life. Accepting limitations.
- Transforming negative thoughts.
- Building spiritual resistance.[4]

I further recommend:

- Find a safe place to talk about how you are feeling.
- Do something you really enjoy once a week.
- Find new interests.
- Consider meeting with a Christian counselor.

Joy: What You Should Know

I found a reputable child-care facility to watch my children for me while I worked. For many months following the divorce, my oldest daughter would put a tape in the tape player of our car on the way to child care and play the song "I Choose to Be Happy" by Cheryl Pruett. Day after day, we would sing along: "I choose to be happy, happy, happy as I can be." That is except for the days when things were not so good and the tape never went in the player.

Happiness is a choice, but it varies with the circumstances. Happiness indicates a certain well-being or contentment. It occurs when things are going our way—the weather is sunny or we're having steak for dinner. But what happens when the rains fall and peanut butter is all that's left? Our happiness wanes. That's where joy can come in.

Joy is a "state of happiness or felicity." This state of happiness transcends circumstances. It's something down inside that is, well, happy. Happy anyway. And no rain or peanut butter or divorce or death can destroy it. The Bible talks about joy lots of places, such as Matthew 25:21 and John 15:11.

Ella Wheeler Wilcox writes:

*One ship sails east
One ship sails west
Regardless of how the
winds blow,
It is the set of the sail
And not the gale
That determines the way
we go.*[5]

I believe single parents can hold on to their joy even when

stormy winds blow. When a relationship into which we have sunk our hearts, souls, minds, and bodies breaks up, our world gets pulled from beneath us. The beautiful 1817 farmhouse my husband and I had laboriously refinished and stocked with antiques was gone. My name and position in the community and in my husband's family were redefined. Divorce took almost everything.

Yet my spirit remained. I chose to guard that spirit and not let anyone take it away or wield power over it. I turned to the faith my parents had instilled in me. I realized there was someone who was bigger than all my circumstances, and I could place utter and complete confidence in him. Eventually that gave me reason to smile again. But this time I smiled from the inside out. No one or no thing had the power to change that even when tears fell.

Questions You Ask

I thought I had met my Prince Charming. How can I ever be happy again—alone?

Many of us allow our total being and happiness to rest in the hands of other people. We confuse love with need. We spend our energy on fantasy and become dependent on love. We want another person to provide all emotional gratification. Cravings for love can never be fulfilled by other human beings.

Spend your efforts on your children and on building your own life back—personally, emotionally, and spiritually. Too many single parents go from one romantic relationship to another to fill those voids. Meanwhile, what do the children have? Where are they left?

Relationships with people are essential to help you and your children heal. Connect with extended family as much as possible. Get involved with community, school, and sports activities. Find a church where you and your family can become involved. You'll be surprised at the friends you will find. But the most important relationship you can find is with God. He can fill a void in you that no man can.

Once you become whole and happy again, perhaps you will find someone else with whom you can share a relationship. Be sure, however, that he is also whole and happy. You can discover this by observing him over time and through a variety of environments. Note his response to all kinds of individuals and the direction of his interests. These and other observations will tell you much about how he would handle other things.

I keep thinking that success at my job will make me happy.

Only you can define your success. You determine how successful you will be and what success means. Success brings more responsibility. Happiness does not necessarily follow success: Success just drives toward more achievement.

Sometimes things around me are going well, but I can't be happy for fear of what lies around the next bend. Am I being weird?

If you are weird, so are many others. Because our single-parenting circumstances are so intense, we often take ourselves far too seriously.

Sometimes when I walk to the car and stick in my key to unlock the door, a strange face stares back at me in the reflection—a sober, unhappy, serious, mad face. My face. I, like you, need to learn how to be happy and excited for the present and assured that no matter what comes, we will be okay in the future.

Does it help to laugh at ourselves?

It's a healthy thing to laugh when we goof—like the time I mashed my lips in the car door.

I was taking some classes. I walked to the car carrying my books, holding an umbrella, and keeping my skirt down in the wind. I unlocked the car, which was parked on a busy street, and I managed to throw in my umbrella, toss in my books, and get myself into the car, still keeping my skirt down, before the wind blew the door shut—on my lips, left angled in the door. After the swelling went down and the tears had stopped falling, I was able to laugh at myself.

God's gift of humor can be ours, even in the midst of turmoil. Although our situations may be quite serious, laughter can be a valuable escape. Humor can allow us to step briefly outside our sorrows.

Joy and Your Child

How important is play to a joyful child?

Fathers are particularly important for playing with children. Author David Popenoe tells us that from a child's birth through adolescence, fathers tend to emphasize play more than caretaking. A father's play is both physically stimulating and exciting. With older children it involves more physical games and teamwork requiring competitive testing of physical and mental skills. Popenoe says it often resembles an apprenticeship or teaching relationship.

Mothers spend more time playing with their children, but theirs is a different kind of play. A mother's play takes place more at a child's level. Mothers provide a child with an opportunity to be in charge, to proceed at the child's own pace. Kids, at least in the early years, seem to prefer to play with Daddy.[6]

Is a child learning anything else except for play itself?

Popenoe tells us that the way fathers play has effects on the management of the children's emotions, self-control, intelligence, and academic achievement. The more fathers play roughly with their children, the more the children learn the appropriateness of emotions and physical aggression such as biting and kicking. Fathers stress competition, challenge, initiative, risk-taking, and independence.

Mothers, as caretakers, stress emotional security and personal safety. On the playground, fathers will try to get the child to swing higher than the person on the next swing, while mothers will be cautious about accidents. Fathers' concern seems to be more for long-term development; mothers focus on children's immediate well-being. Input in play from both Mom and Dad is preferred for a child's normal development.[7]

How important is it for me to have fun each day? How can I fit it in?

Fun adds to happiness. Try to have fun every day with at least one item:

- *Recreation.* Pursue a new hobby or activate an old one, establish or maintain a regular exercise program, learn a new sport or hobby.
- *Family time.* Spend lots of time in family interaction free from distractions. Limit time on the phone and watching TV. I find weeknights best for this as kids, after their sports activities, are usually home getting ready for school the next day. We eat together, have Bible study, work on homework, and so on.
- *Time alone.* Read a book. Be creative through cooking. Study a topic to develop new knowledge. Repair something.
- *Communicating.* Go shopping with a friend, join a community group, enroll in a class, call someone you haven't talked with for a long time.
- *Building relationships.* Assist with a volunteer group, invite a new friend or coworker to dinner, visit with a neighbor, spend time alone with your significant other.

Does it hurt my daughter to see me emotionally distraught?

A child can learn many valuable life lessons by watching you work through hardships. Just don't let her see them too often or allow them to last too long.

One spring I had to deal with a problem concerning my older

daughter. I drove to where I needed to be and did what I needed to do. I cried—a lot—on my way back home. I didn't notice the beautiful purple Rocky Mountains I normally enjoyed. I couldn't look past the crisis of the moment.

I drove down our street and prepared to pull into our driveway. My son was playing basketball with a neighbor in our driveway. He stepped aside to let me drive into the garage. His eyes locked onto my own tear-stained, swollen eyes. The lump in my throat and weakness in my body caused me to shiver. I rested my forehead against the steering wheel. *How could I go on?*

I opened the door and swung my feet to the ground. I paused to gather my strength, then walked back out to the driveway. Clint was still watching me. I opened my mouth to speak as I spread my hands and said, "How about a game of H-O-R-S-E?"

A smile spread across Clint's face, and he said to his friend, "Wait till you see how my mom shoots."

I knew at that moment that my joy would soon return.

4

Who's Riding Along?

The Children

My children and I had just experienced our first Christmas in Colorado. A few days afterward, we drove a couple of hours to Copper Mountain for our first ski trip in the Rockies. It was a huge mountain, much different from the small Ohio hills where it took us thirty minutes to stand in line and thirty seconds to ski down.

The day was crisp and brilliant. I sat on the chairlift between twelve-year-old Ashley and eight-year-old Clint. We soon arrived at the top. Ashley, impatient to show her ability and independence, announced that she was going to go down and would meet us at the bottom. I watched with some concern as she confidently pushed forward and skied out of sight.

Clint, meanwhile, was staring wide-eyed at the slope before him. "I haven't skied for a long time, Mom," he reminded me in a low voice.

"Just follow me," I said.

Moving several feet down the mountain, I turned to watch him do the same. His ski tips were close and his legs were spread as he tried to follow in my tracks. But he soon fell, and fresh snow covered his face as he started to cry. "I'm scared," he said. "I can't do this. I don't want to go the rest of the way down."

I helped him up, dusted the snow from his pants legs and wiped the last tear from his cold cheek. I couldn't help but realize how much he had grown since the time I picked him up when he was learning to ride his bike. And I couldn't help but wonder how often he would need me after falls in the years to come.

We continued down the trail. Small clumps of snow dropped with a thud from a big tree and landed in the powder at our feet. Clint moved mechanically down the slope, his face quietly saying, *Are we having fun yet?*

I looked back to where we had come from and forward to where we were going. At that moment, I realized I had discovered a big truth. My role as a mom was being summed up in this simple trip down a mountainside:

- *I guided.* I showed Clint the path to take him to the bottom most quickly and with the least harm. The choices were many, but we needed to stay on the easy paths marked for us. I knew which trails were appropriate for our abilities. I modeled discretion by choosing the right paths, and Clint followed.
- *I protected.* Trees lined both sides of the trail, and skilled skiers and snowboarders flew by us: Both posed danger. I kept Clint far enough to the side so he would not obstruct others but not so close that he would crash into the trees.
- *I encouraged.* No one knew the little boy on that slope like I did, and no one had a greater opportunity to support and uplift him. "You can do it!" "Good job!" "That was great!" were some of the expressions he heard. I couldn't help but wonder how far he would have come if he had heard, "You clumsy ox!" "How stupid!" "Can't you do anything right?"
- *I taught independence.* Clint was careful at first to follow only in my tracks. But the farther down the mountain we moved, the more he gained confidence and made tracks of his own. He did fall again near the bottom, but when I skied up to him and asked if he needed help, he said, "I'm okay, Mom. I can get up."

Down at the chairlift, Ashley stood waiting for us. She told me she was going to ride back up with a girl she had met coming down and would catch up with us later. I squinted into the sun as I watched Clint finish the rest of the way down. "Come on, Mom," he said when he reached the bottom. "I want to go back up. Can't we go any faster?"

I smiled and moved toward the lift. This time Clint was in the lead. I realized that in the years to come, his tracks would become larger than mine, and he would choose paths far different from those I walk. But I also sensed he would always have a place in his heart for someone who would be there with him in his challenges to guide, protect, and encourage him, and to teach him independence.

14

Infants to Preschoolers

I have experienced both the hardships and the rewards of being a single mom to kids of all ages. Two-year-old Courtney and four-year-old Ashley kept me hopping while I cared for their newborn brother and managed a divorce. Warm memories are tucked in our hearts of the more than a decade since that time. I chuckle when I read a story from single mom Diane Guy of Kansas, who shared some of her own memories:

> After a day of baby-sitting, I sat down with my friend as we watched our children play. We were amazed at how quickly the kids were growing, and soon the conversation turned to birthdays and ages.
>
> "How old is Remme?" my friend said to my three-year-old daughter, Alison, referring to her six-month-old sister.

> Alison thought for a minute and smartly commented, "Remme doesn't have a number yet."

If you are the mom or dad of one of those little ones who doesn't have a number yet, you are probably already seeing what a challenge he or she can be. How does the absence of a parent through death, divorce, or abandonment affect a baby now and in the future? How do we know what to do to help?

What You Should Know

It is hard to go alone through something as difficult and emotional as a pregnancy. I took my best friend with me for my ultrasound when I first found out I would finally have my boy. My sister came to the birthing room when the time for delivery arrived. Though my ex-husband came, it was reassuring to know someone was present with my best interests at heart and who cared deeply about me.

Clint and the girls grew, and I watched other families growing around me as well. I quickly realized how important good parenting is in those early years. Our children depend on us to care for them, make the right decisions, and teach them what they need to know. Trust, security, and confidence become necessary traits to develop. They also need a safe environment in which to explore and grow and learn. Predictability and familiarity become important. Children of this age fear the loss of their primary caregiver and are threatened if they are taken out of their comfortable and predictable surroundings. When the loss of one parent has already been realized, this uncertainty can become especially serious when the child fears losing the other parent as well.

One Sunday morning when my children were two, four, and six and we were settled in our new apartment in Ohio, we went for the first time to the church I had chosen. I deposited each of the children into new rooms with new teachers, new surroundings, and kids they had never seen before. All three of them cried. I found an empty hallway, leaned my head against the wall, and shed a few tears of my own. When I finally found a class that

might work for me, I sat down beside a woman named Tammy. She introduced herself and asked me how I was, and I told her. In three minutes or less, I told her our life story.

Tammy became a lifelong friend and support as the children and I made these new surroundings and people into familiar ones. Meanwhile, during the preschool years, I paid special attention to skills such as:

- *Making careful decisions.* I prayed about them, asked others to help, weighed all the alternatives, and then acted. My kids were counting on me.
- *Finding support groups.* We connected as quickly as possible. I gave out as well as took in from others. We became part of larger groups at church, school, and through sports activities, and found individual relationships we could count on.
- *Establishing routines.* As we got settled, my kids could count on the schedules—when I picked them up, dropped them off, spent time with them, and when we ate. We made these routines standard and changed them only in emergencies.
- *Encouraging a relationship between my children and their dad.* In addition to their routine visit, I helped the kids remember to call their dad

and share important events that were going on.

- *Starting new traditions.* Making things special in our home. Creating a place that represents security, love, respect, and safety for my kids.

One day, I dropped my children off at day care. Then I went home and prepared dinner, since it was my night to go to class. I decided to do something creative, so I spread a tablecloth on the kitchen floor and packed a special brown-bag dinner for each of them.

All day long I couldn't wait to talk with my children. Finally I did. Courtney, who was my big eater, seemed chagrined when she took the phone. "Where's somethin' hot for dinner?" she said.

Old routines had been established. New traditions were still taking hold.

Questions You Ask

Birth to Eighteen Months

I am going through a lot of emotional turmoil since my daughter's father left. It's hard for me to be patient when she cries. How can I be sure I don't lose my cool with her?

Losing your cool is one thing, but if you think the possibility exists that you could hurt her in your anger, seek help.

If, on the other hand, you sometimes just get irritated with her, you're just going to have to tough it out. You need to be especially sensitive to your child's issues such as the pain of teething, ear infections, and the struggle to take her first steps. She also is beginning to test different personality traits. Help and encourage her as she explores. Guide her past the things she shouldn't do.

Ideally, meeting the needs of your child requires commitment from both parents. While it's important to have one primary residence, the noncustodial parent should have short, frequent visits if possible. Do all you can to help that happen. It will nurture your daughter and give you some short breaks.

It sounds as though you may not have that. If you don't, find other individuals to pick up the slack. You will need mentors for your child and yourself. You also could use someone who can care for your little girl while you care for yourself. Get involved in activities where you can meet other moms. Compare stories. You'll be amazed at how similar they are, and you'll probably find some friends besides.

I'm afraid my infant son will learn to mistrust all adults when he

learns his father abandoned him. What can I do?

At this age of your son's life, you should concentrate on filling his basic needs. By doing this, you will teach your son that he can trust you to be there for him. If these needs are not met, he will learn to mistrust adults in general and perhaps later see his father's abandonment as the norm rather than the exception.

Spend your time loving your baby in tangible ways: feed him, change him, rock him. Infants learn about life through their senses and physical movements. By understanding your love for him through your actions, spiritual development will become easier as well. He can learn trust not only for significant adults in his life but for God as well.

My baby is six months old. Is it too early to start talking to her?

Definitely not. Your daughter will not be able to talk back, but the sound of your voice will soothe her, help her feel secure, and send her on her way to understanding the meanings of her first words. Talk mostly about whatever your daughter is attending to for the moment—the bird she sees, her grandpa, or the food she is eating. She only understands the here and now, so references to nonpresent objects is ineffective at this age. Diaper-changing and bath times lend themselves to this type of teaching. But the earlier you start, the earlier start she will have on her own communications.

Should I just let my baby cry, assuming she is not in danger, or could her irritability be related to the divorce I am going through?

Your child will sense the tension in your life and may need some extra attention. Be sure she feels loved and secure. Research by M. Ainsworth at Johns Hopkins University shows that regular, prompt response to an infant's cry leads to more attachment between the caretaker and the baby. Sometimes you may have to let your baby cry it out, but don't let it become routine.

My son is one year old. I just left his father after many months of physical abuse. Will my son remember some of the horrifying events he saw and heard?

Children usually don't develop short-term memories until about one year of age. You can do nothing about what your child witnessed in the past, but you can control his future. Try the following:

- Allow him always to feel safe talking things out with you. This will set good habits for communication later on. You will need to guard your responses, however. Be sure not to overreact at things he says.

- Find appropriate adult outlets to discuss details of the conflict with your husband.
- Be sure your son is free from physical harm himself if the relationship between him and his father continues.
- Start building good memories. You can fill his heart full with good things in his life. The bad will pale as he starts feeling more safe in his environment. Your decision to get away from a conflict-filled home will help him do that.

I'm only sixteen and my daughter is fifteen months. On top of all I am trying to manage, I feel guilty for not teaching my daughter to read or count early. Older mothers I know seem to be doing this better than I. What should I do?

Provide a loving, stable home for your duaghter. That will outlast all the reading levels in the world.

When I was married, my husband and I flashed reading and math cards to our oldest daughter. She had not only a two-parent home, but academic and financial advantages as well.

Her dad's departure, however, caused me to accept a lot of new roles. There was no time left for flash cards. Suddenly, keeping my sanity and stability from hour to hour became a major issue.

If I were you and if I had my babies to raise again, I would still teach my kids, but I would do it in a more natural context. I would take time to relax at the end of a long day with a good book we all could enjoy. I would smell flowers with them and count the train cars at railroad crossings. These types of activities are less deliberate, but I believe they help heal—us as well as our children.

Eighteen Months to Three Years

When I try to correct my four-year-old, my two-year-old defends him. I feel as though I am alone in my efforts. Am I doing something wrong?

Sounds to me like you are doing something right. You are teaching your children to be loyal to one another. I would reward them for those efforts, then work hard to channel their attempts. They need to know what is appropriate and what is not.

One Thursday night after my husband left and Clint had been born, the children and I were eating dinner. The phone rang, and my sister-in-law from California launched a conversation. The call lasted longer than I wanted, and our dinner lost its continuity. The girls both excused themselves from the table.

When the conversation ended and I was clearing the dishes, I found two-year-old Courtney's plate clean and four-year-old Ashley's largely untouched. The baby, who was upstairs, was crying by this time. When I started nursing him, I told Ashley to finish her food.

Well, no four-year-old wants to be downstairs by herself eating food she didn't want in the first place. I repeated my request, then told her she couldn't watch Bill Cosby if she didn't eat her food. She said okay and went to her room. I finished with the baby, but I was uncomfortable about what was happening since it was the phone call that had caused the disturbance.

Courtney had disappeared, but I soon heard her coming up the stairs. She brushed past me and walked into Ashley's room and said, "Ashwee, you tan doe watch Bill Tosby now. I just went down and ate your food."

What could I say? We gathered on my bed and watched our favorite show.

My sweet little daughter is starting to pull away from me. She jerks back her hand when I try to take it, and she has a mind of her own when she wants something. What should I do?

While keeping respect for adults always in focus, recognize that your child is entering another phase. She is beginning to separate from her parents and is developing an independent sense of herself. Allow her to discover—through touching, seeing, tasting—everything a-round her, while still teaching safety skills.

Your daughter will go to the limits with you, so you need to set clear boundaries. Let her know what the rules are and what the consequences are for breaking those rules. Be firm and consistent and always follow through. I regret not emphasizing earlier to my children that what I said counted the first time I said it, and not to wait until the fifth time. I have often suffered as my children have ignored instructions or requests because they did not learn consistent consequences when they were young.

I want to be firm with my child, but he's been through so much with the divorce and all. Shouldn't I lighten up?

Of all times not to lighten up, it's now. He needs boundaries and limits and consistency more than ever before. Be affectionate and encouraging and let him know you will love him always, no matter what. But also be firm. All the time. No questions asked. Your hunches will let you know when you need to bend the rules slightly or tend to a specific need.

How do boundaries help a child this young?

Children from divorced or never-married homes spend more time away from the primary caregiving mom or dad than they ever have before. Rules and routines may be quite different at the other parent's house. The children need to realize who they are. Things need to be predictable. Children need a schedule as they switch back and forth between these two worlds. Contact with both parents confirms their security and feeling of being loved. It should be maintained at all costs.

My two-year-old son is very strong-willed. How can I raise him best while understanding this personal quality?

Any two-year-old wants to explore the world around him. This natural inquisitiveness sets the stage for you to shame your child for his curiosity or to gently and safely guide him toward his explorations within it. Safe discovery produces autonomy. He will begin to see himself as an individual and no longer just part of the larger family. He will test more boundaries as he explores more about who this person is inside of him. What can you do?

- Allow him to pull and push things in safe ways. Teach him about danger.
- Provide a consistent schedule, as well as clear boundaries around which he can conduct these life explorations.
- Be careful what you tell him. He will believe everything you say, and he will be the first to notice inconsistencies.
- Be firm on discipline. Your son's sense of right and wrong will be largely defined by whether or not rewards or punishment follow.

If you are encouraging autonomy in your son, you will likely see evidence of his strong will emerge. That could mean you're doing lots of things right. Draw clear boundaries around which both of you can understand and operate, and then help your little boy discover who he is within them.

Three to Five Years

My three-year-old son started wetting the bed soon after his dad left. Should I just let it go?

Like you, your child is trying to assimilate all the changes happening around him. He is no doubt fearful that more bad will happen and that he may lose you as well. Crying for you obsessively when you leave him with a baby-sitter, hitting others, regressing in certain developmental areas such as bed-wetting, or lapsing into baby speech— these are all common ways of expressing the pain he is going through. Be patient, kind, loving. Offer him security, constancy, trust, and lots of love. If the behavior persists, ask your pediatrician about it or seek help from someone experienced in dealing with a three-year-old who just lost his dad.

My husband died, so he's not here to help me know if our four-year-old son is developing normally. What are some of the things he should be learning?

You might watch for several things:

- *Gender identification.* Help him by exposing him to as many "boy things" as you can. Assist him in feeling good about who he is.
- *Control.* He's discovering what it is like to be in charge. Work with him carefully as he grows and help him know he is totally in charge of himself. Also, let him know he often cannot control others or circumstances around him. Strengthen his skills in those things he can do something about.
- *Find friendships.* This is the beginning of a lot of years of peer influence. Teach him good friend-selection skills and recognize the need he has to be with other children his age. At this age, your son should be learning how to cooperate with

others when he plays. Help him set limits in doing that.

- *Develop values.* Up to this point, you have imposed what you believe upon him. Now he is exposed to others' opinions through friends he finds and places he attends, such as preschool. Keep your eyes on the kinds of people he is meeting. You can strengthen his own identity in this area by reminding him of what you stand for. One mom I know reminds her son of their Christian beliefs through these simple words as he leaves for school or leaves with a friend, "Remember Whose you are and what you stand for."
- *Allay his fears.* Because he is asking lots of questions and there is much he doesn't understand, much will cause him to be fearful. He needs understanding and comfort.

To reassure yourself of the normalcy of your son's growth in these areas, get involved in a support group at church, in the neighborhood, or with other individual moms who also have four-year-olds. Ask questions of the parents at preschool. Compare notes on how your son is progressing and how you are handling things.

My son is five. He's starting to say more negative things about his mother, who left when he was an

infant. Should I correct him for disrespect or let him say what he is feeling?

Your son is at an age that he is starting to separate reality from fantasy. He is probably realizing—perhaps for the first time—that his mother is never coming back.

Allow safe places to talk out his feelings, but always reinforce respect for others as he does so. He learns most in this area by seeing how his father handles these same issues. Be sure you show the same respect you expect him to learn.

Take this time to help your son feel secure. Be certain he understands that you will always be there for him. Surround him with people who help him feel good about himself. Encourage his inquisitiveness of life. Help him explore all kinds of things and discover areas that will become his special areas of strength and purpose. Use concrete experiences to get all your points across. I once compared the stable parts of our family to a compass. The point stayed put while the pencil drew circles of all sizes.

Because my daughter usually visits her mom every other weekend, how can I keep normalcy in the situation at home?

The challenge is due to the fact that homes were never designed to be divided. At times, normalcy will be hard to achieve. Keep working hard to establish her home with you. Build your own memories and traditions that will always represent home to her.

In order to connect her two worlds, try keeping photos of your daughter's mom in her room. Allow her to talk to her mom by phone as often as possible and watch your reactions at the relationship they develop. You want your daughter to be able to say anything to you without fear of overreaction.

You might purchase a tape recorder for your daughter and allow her and her mother to send messages back and forth. If your daughter has a favorite stuffed animal or blanket, let her take it when she visits her mom. Encourage sharing important parts of her life with the other parent. Assure your daughter that the divorce was between you and her mother, not between her and either parent.

Consistency is hard to achieve with so many things going on. How can we get on a schedule?

Discipline yourself to restrict activities for both you and your child. If you don't, things will get much worse. You and your child need to learn the importance of both quiet time and moments spent with others. If not, you will raise a young adult who is unable to relax, unskilled at being with himself, or uncomfortable with developing intimate relationships within the family.

Try working with your ex-spouse in keeping a regular routine for playing, sleeping, eating, and socializing. Similar discipline habits should be practiced in both homes—such as what your son watches on TV and when he watches it. Consistency is once again the key.

My daughter is in preschool. She doesn't know what occurred between her dad and me. When I talk about it with others, I whisper and spell the things I don't want her to hear. Lately, I've been wondering if she deserves to know more.

If anyone needs to understand what is going on, it is your daughter. Explain things commensurate with her ability to understand. At the same time, don't go into unnecessary details. She lost her other parent because of some turn of events. What you don't tell her, she will fill in with her own information, such as, *It's all my fault*, or *Dad left because he didn't love me anymore.*

Your daughter already understands much more than you are giving her credit for. She notices not only what you say, but how you say it—especially when it concerns her dad. You have a wonderful opportunity to model for her how to resolve differ-

ences in constructive ways. It is best for children of this age to be able to see the other parent about twice a week.

How will I know if I need to get outside help for my son?

Observe him closely. You know his patterns. If those change and remain changed over an extended period of time, get help. Such alterations in his behavior may include:

- Not eating or sleeping.
- Withdrawing or being unusually needy.
- Becoming depressed or irritable.
- Digressing to babyish behavior or language.
- Losing interest in things he got excited about before.

Your son has lost a lot with the breakup of his home. In addition, you are undergoing much emotional and physical stress. Make things constant for him and supply things to fill in those losses—love, traditions, love, laughter, love, understanding, and love. Surround him with new relationships and places to become involved. If problems persist, get help.

Can I do the job of raising my son being only a mom with no dad involved?

You surely can. There's a job that needs to be done, and you get the privilege. Be confident in your abilities. Relate to your kids emotionally as well as physically and spiritually. Keep your priorities straight at all times. Create a parenting plan that reflects your goals and desires, then pursue it with determination regardless of what advice others give you. I'm amazed every day at great men I meet who have grown up in a single-parent home.

How do I help my son work through his fears?

Because I don't know your son or what his fears are, it's hard to make concrete suggestions. You probably will have to seek professional help if his fears are extensive. But in the meantime, there are things you as his parent can do that can help.

Control his environment. As much as possible, remove the reason for his fear. Assure him, for example, that you will not leave him. Keep as many things the same as you can, but try to alter difficult situations, such as the school or church he is attending. Keep the lines of communication open. Get him to talk as much as possible about everything he is feeling. Keep things calm and don't overextend your schedules. Do fun things together and take time to laugh. Also, don't hesitate to take him to see a doctor.

My husband was killed before our daughter was born. She is four now and has been screaming out at night. What can I do to help?

Toddlers fear being abandoned both physically and emotionally by losing your love and approval. She probably became extremely attached to you as a result of your husband's death. She could still be afraid that you will leave her like her daddy did. Assure her in every way that she is not alone—nor will she ever be.

Bad dreams are fairly normal for children, but if the problem persists, you might need to get her some help.

My son is now five. His father and I never married, and we signed a contract that he wouldn't have to pay child support if he had nothing to do with our child. Lately, as my son has met kids' parents at preschool, he has asked lots of questions about his dad. What should I do? Dad lives only about nine miles from us.

Be honest. Except for cases of abuse, kids need their parents—both of them. You should make that happen any way you can.

Imagine how you would feel if you had longed for your dad ever since you could remember, but you never got to meet him. One day you find out he's been living just down the road and that it was only a piece of paper that your mother and father had signed that kept him from seeing you. Who do you think you'd blame?

I would tell my son everything he needs to know for his age level. Then I would stop until he's ready for more. Listen carefully to him. I think you'll know when you need to introduce your son to his dad. I would also keep some kind of contact with the dad to assess his character and availability and interest in his son when the time is right.

Only you know the circumstances surrounding your son's father. If he is not a terrible influence or abusive, you owe it to your own future relationship with your son to introduce them.

I have to break the news to my five-year-old that her dad and I are getting a divorce. How can I bring such horrible information to such an innocent mind?

I handled this information much as I did the rest of the real world my children were beginning to experience.

- *I kept them close.* The divorce was an emotional time for me, so that had to be balanced while I also was trying to stabilize my children. I heard a man speak once on radio about sending his daughter to school for the first time. He was overwhelmed about all the things that would now bombard this heretofore innocent child. That night the dad

walked outside and looked up in the sky. A giant 747 could be seen way up in the sky. The mechanical genius that had put that monster with its flashing lights in the sky overwhelmed him and made him feel helpless. Suddenly a tiny firefly flew close to his face. The light from the firefly was so bright, it obliterated the lights of the giant 747 above. At once the man knew that his biggest defense for protecting his daughter from the monsters around her was to keep her close.

Divorce was the first real monster my kids encountered. But I have kept them close, and their experience through that hardship prepared them for the monsters they would later encounter.

- *I used common sense.* Many times my children would ask questions, such as why did "Daddy leave?" and I would explain just what they needed to know at that time. Sometimes we parents just need to know when to say things to our children.
- *I taught truths.* I got our family involved in a church with an active youth group immediately after we moved. We lived in that city for almost seven years. During that time I had many others who helped me raise my children. They

became extended family who confirmed the things my family believed in.

- *I modeled values.* My hands needed to hold six little hands, and my actions were constantly under scrutiny of three pairs of eyes. Even the smallest of things was noticed by the children—a lost temper, a "white lie," a lack.

One Sunday morning Courtney's Sunday school teacher told me how my daughter had asked the class to pray so her mom wouldn't say bad words. Embarrassed, I searched my mind to figure out what Courtney meant—as that was an area of my life totally under control. Then I found out: In the hubbub of the morning baths and getting them ready to go, I had said, "Stop that *crap* right now." It was a word I didn't allow them to say, and though I could have spoken much worse, Courtney made me accountable that day. She was right—it was only fair. If it was wrong for them, it was wrong for me. It was my opportunity to model what I wanted them to do.

15

Elementary Schoolers

One night my children and I returned from a visit with a friend at the university where I taught. The friend had a Picasso painting on her wall and a Ming vase on her mantle. Exquisite taste was evident everywhere. We enjoyed dessert while overlooking the city from her view high atop a hill.

When we returned home that night, my older daughter came into my bedroom and said, "Mom, Karen has a beautiful *house*, but we have a beautiful *home*."

I believe those words are the challenge of all single parents. Ken Canfield says: "They [the children] cross over from the four walls of home into a vast world, one that seems to be without boundaries. It is a time of great transition, which produces even greater questions. Our children need our help as they wrestle with such critical issues

as social status, spirituality, and sex."[1]

During the time that we raise our kids alone, we face many difficulties and stages and transitions. So how do we handle the challenges amid our many responsibilities while also trying to make our houses into homes?

What You Should Know

Raising children is a difficult job in the best of circumstances. This job for single parents is particularly challenging. Author Gary Sprague says elementary-age kids worry about things such as:

Survival issues:

- Who will take care of me?
- Will we have enough money now?
- Will I have to move to a new neighborhood?
- Will I have to change schools?
- Will I have to meet new friends?

138

Emotional issues:

- Is there anybody I can count on?
- Will my parents stop loving me, too?
- Is my parents' divorce my fault?
- Are there other kids who have divorced parents?
- Can I get my parents back together again?

Security issues:

- Will my parents get sick or die?
- Are my parents going to get married again?
- Will my parents fight over me?

Gary recommends:

- Tell your child the real reasons for the separation, even if it involves abuse, addiction, adultery, or abandonment.
- Describe the facts when telling about the reasons for the separation.
- Avoid blaming one parent or the other.
- Share what each parent did right or wrong.
- Allow the child to love both parents.
- Encourage and model forgiveness for what has been done.[2]

Questions You Ask

Six Years Old

My six-year-old son has witnessed his father being physically and emotionally abusive toward me.

He often doesn't want to leave me. What can I do to reassure him?

Your son does not need to be burdened with family concerns. Instead, he should be encouraged by you to constructively handle his new challenges at school. He needs tools to develop good work and play skills.

Resolve conflicts privately with your ex-husband if there is any way possible. This will teach your son how to manage his own personality clashes in positive ways. If you cannot find such solutions yourself or with the help of professionals, you don't need to see your husband alone. Drop off your son in a neutral location with another adult present.

I trust your son is safe from the same abusive treatment. If he is, you must also protect him from perpetuation of this abuse:

- Teach him this is not how a man treats a woman. Expose him constantly to gentle men who demonstrate respect toward women.
- Show him ways of managing his own anger.

My ex-husband has a history of losing his temper in destructive ways. My children have seen many of those incidents. One day my son, Clint, lost his temper. Then he said, "I get that from my dad."

I quickly nipped that rationalization in the bud. I snuggled with

Clint on the couch and we talked. A famous trial was going on where a man was accused of murdering his ex-wife. Angry temper flare-ups were brought to light during the much-televised trial. I reminded Clint of that information and asked how he thought such horrible anger came to be.

We decided together that this man's uncontrollable anger had possibly led to murder. His anger began when he was a toddler who got mad and didn't release it properly, and continued in a little boy on a football field who lost his cool, and then in a teen who expressed his anger without restraint.

Clint and I talked about constructive ways of taking care of his anger now and about how he was in total control of every one of his reactions. I hope I convinced him that while circumstances and actions of others around him were out of his control, his responses were totally his to choose.

Should I get my daughter involved in sports while she is so young?

Around six years of age, children begin to understand fairness. It is a perfect time to promote the development of friendships and participation in sports activities. Your daughter's logical thinking is beginning to develop. She no doubt feels good about high grades in school. Do all you can to promote the same feelings of high self-esteem in the friends she is developing and the outside activities in which she is becoming involved.

So much of what has happened in your child's life is beyond her control. She has witnessed the departure of one of her parents through some means she could do nothing about. Single-parent homes have become a commonplace thing. But to each child involved, it is a brand-new tragedy that leaves hurt and devastation in its wake.

Working hard to give your daughter strengths in these other areas hands her back some sense of control and better feelings about herself and life. Guard against overinvolvement and be sure she is not using activities to avoid handling emotions she needs to work through.

My ex-wife often changes the visitation schedule. I am afraid this will hurt my daughter's ability to adjust to all the changes. Will it?

Your daughter needs the freedom to feel love and to give love with both parents. That's the most important thing, though a regular schedule is important, too. Do all you can to resolve difficulties between you and your ex-wife. Try to reach an agreement with her for a more standardized visitation. But don't create a battle zone out of this issue. It's not worth it.

How do I know if my six-year-old daughter needs outside help?

Watch for problems from your child in social situations or with her work at school. If she frequently loses her temper, sulks, becomes depressed, or withdraws, get help—especially if she blames the family breakup for all the bad things going on in her life. You should also seek outside intervention if she denies the pain she is going through.

Watch for hatred developing toward one parent. Some single parents feel satisfaction and even encourage a child's negative reaction against the other parent. To continue in this frame of mind is to invite disaster. And the situation can quickly turn on the parent.

Seven to Eight Years Old

My eight-year-old son doesn't like for me to hug him like he once did. Is this normal or a product of the divorce?

Your son is growing up. His friends and outside interests are more important than ever before. Be there for him. Assure him of your love. Show signs of affection in discreet ways. Be creative about how you show your love. Though he doesn't express it, he needs your love more than he ever has. And demonstrating it to him in appropriate ways lets him know you understand him as well.

I am getting remarried. My son is seven. How should I explain the difference between the siblings involved in that union?

Explain the physical differences between birth siblings (both parents the same), half siblings (one parent the same) and stepsiblings (no parents the same). This seems to be a simple way your son can see the natural reasons why each is different.

But with the emotional variations, you are on your own. You will discover marked differences between the children living in your house and those living someplace else. There will be times when you will want to favor your own child and your husband will want to favor his. But you and your husband must make a pact with each other as to how you will administer fairness. This is an important agreement you should reach before you get married.

This is a stressful time of transition for all of you. If it is to go smoothly, you will need to have your ducks in a row as to how you will handle these changes. I suggest you read a good book on the subject, such as *Winning the Heart of Your Stepchild* by Bob Barnes, to help you with in-depth issues.

I'm a single mom of a seven-year-old daughter and six-year-old son. Right now we are surviving in a small one-bedroom apartment where I sleep on the living-room sofa. Please tell me at what ages my children should move into separate beds, rooms, and bath times?

The time is now. Take this opportunity to teach the importance of privacy, modesty, and occasional time alone. During family time, generate creative ways to do this.

What about partitioning your living room and making a "bedroom" in one corner? You'd be surprised how cool sleeping on a mattress on the floor can be to kids. The child who sleeps there would have certain benefits you can capitalize on, such as easy access to the kitchen, TV, or phone.

Go to yard sales together and get enthusiastic about helping your children decorate their areas. You might find used futons or daybeds that could contribute to your solutions as well. Make a fun sign saying "occupied" to hang on the bathroom door. Train each other to knock at closed doors and to honor the private spaces of others.

Don't forget your own need for time to yourself. Switch off with another single parent in taking the kids for a day. Your family will remain only as strong as you are.

I started dating someone recently for the first time since the divorce. My seven-year-old son is acting out like crazy. Why?

It's hard to say why. I don't know the circumstances involved in the person you are dating. I also don't know what you mean by "acting out." Some behavior requires outside help. But much can be very normal responses.

Remember that you and your son are working through stages of grieving, and he may still be experiencing denial or bargaining emotions where he hopes to get his mom and dad back together. Your son has seen a lot of changes take place recently. He may fear you will abandon him, too.

Assure him every way you can that you will always be there for him. Show him daily the priority that he is. Demonstrate affection constantly. Proceed with caution and much wisdom in your relationship.

One last caution: Remarriage is a serious step to take. Your son's reactions may be indicating something you are too close to see. Step back or involve an impartial party. See if there might be some red flags that you hadn't noticed before. It's much better to find them now than later.

How do I help my son split his affections between two homes?

When I was married, we had a Doberman pinscher. Every time before she would lie down—outside in the sun, on her cushion, or at our feet—she would circle her spot. Around and around she would walk and do something funky with her paws, and then she would plop down.

I've often seen the same nesting instinct in my children. In their rooms, they pull their possessions close around them, hang things on the walls, and my son even conducts makeshift experiments there. I've learned to let them circle. Within reason, they are allowed to hang whatever they want if they do it in ways that do not destroy.

I, better than anyone else, know what my kids like best. I know what foods to have in the fridge and what posters they prefer. My kids have moved between two homes now for more than a decade, but a home base, where they are secure and are an integral part, has never been more important.

I learned long ago that I am not responsible for the relationship my kids develop with their dad, but I have worked hard on their lives with me. On weekends when they are with their dad, I find time to be alone, be with friends, read a good book, study, or catch up on my work.

No matter what has happened during their weekends away, on those Sunday nights when they have returned, my kids have built more than ten years of memories walking into a clean home with a full refrigerator, a schedule they could count on, and a mom who was rested and thrilled to see them return.

Nine to Ten Years Old

When my daughter turned ten, she seemed to accept the divorce better. Why?

One of several things could be happening. You may have just done a remarkable job in helping her adjust and move on with life. She could be getting through more stages of handling her losses. Her age is also a factor. She is starting to be a more independent thinker. Kids her age often don't try anymore to put the parents back together. She probably doesn't take a black-and-white position on issues between the parents. Chances are, your daughter feels love and empathy for both of you, but she also recognizes the faults of Dad *and* Mom.

Your daughter's friends are becoming more and more important to her. Yet at this age, her parents are still the primary influence in her life. She still wants participation from both of you in the things and people that are a priority in her life. Stay in that place, even if it doesn't seem to work at times.

My husband made me get an abortion when we were first married. I was not strong enough to refuse, and I agreed to have it done. During the divorce many years later, he told my daughter and refused to take any responsibility at that point. She didn't ask me about it until she was almost eleven. Why did she wait?

She probably was not able to handle that one yet. A concept such as abortion is so tragic that children cannot comprehend its reality. Also, her emotions may not have been stable enough to deal with it. One mom I know had a similar situation. She waited and watched and listened to her daughter. When her daughter asked, she told her the truth. They cried together as the mom told the story of the most terrible, far-reaching decision she had ever made.

Your daughter probably is ready to have more questions answered. "Why did you and dad divorce?" "Were you happy while you were married?" She probably will ask a lot of questions about your life as a child as well: "Mom, what was it like when . . . ?" Your daughter is searching for security, and she is trying to put the pieces of her life together

in ways she can understand. Be careful how you help her do that.

My son has never seen his father. But he has seen tough talk on the streets about being a man. How can we raise our boys to be awesome men?

When I first became the editor of *Single-Parent Family* magazine, I was amazed at how many great men—even famous ones—were raised in single-parent homes. God's original design, of course, included both a mom and a dad. When this doesn't happen, however, you can still bring up some great men, but not without a lot of work and planning.

- *Give them masculine jobs around the house.* While my daughters do chores such as folding laundry, dusting, and sweeping, I try to expose my son to masculine types of activities so he will know how to do them. Then I look around for jobs that can belong just to him. He changes furnace filters, takes out the garbage, shovels the driveway, and tightens screws. I also give him jobs to figure out around the house. Last week he fixed the garbage disposal.
- *Expose him to heroes*—great men in history and the Bible as well as current ones. Media heroes are hard to find, but there are some sports and

Christian music heroes that have made moral stands.

- *Give him heart.* One Saturday last winter, my son had a friend over who comes from an affluent two-parent home. I asked what he got for Christmas, and he proceeded to list electronic games, sports equipment, and so on. I looked at Clint, who was shooting a crooked bullet from his Nerf gun and was settling down to play the dinosaur Nintendo someone gave my children several years ago.

"I thought your Nintendo didn't work," I said.

"It didn't," Clint answered. "But I followed the wires and found the problem and fixed it."

My first reaction was to feel sorry for my son who had far fewer things than his friend. Then I realized Clint was learning to navigate his way through life by fixing or creating the things he needed. He was realizing that life doesn't always work out right and is sometimes unfair. He was learning to keep on going and not give up no matter what obstacles he faced.

Clint has become a really good basketball player by playing in the driveway, hour after hour. Whether his six-foot, thirteen-year-old sister was playing mercilessly against him, his dear ole mom was giving him a run for the money in H-O-R-S-E, or he was shooting alone, my son was developing heart and perseverance and tenacity and balance. And one day, too soon, all these qualities will have grown up into a man I will be proud to have as my son. If you have a boy, you know the feeling.

My son isn't motivated to keep up his grades in school. I have tried everything, but nothing seems to help. What do you suggest?

Negative approaches don't work well for long. Grounding, for example, often doesn't reflect the real-world consequences of neglected work.

The best thing parents can do is to motivate their kids toward goals of their choice. If your son would like to work with computers someday, help him start working in the direction of that goal. You can do that in creative ways that not only promote his enthusiasm but also teach him needed skills in planning and in working alongside the people who care for him the most:

- Obtain a college description of a computer science degree. Outline prerequisite classes and grade-point averages required to enter the program.
- Reward him with software you can pick up at used computer stores when he pulls high marks in school. Also, lots of affirmation and greater

responsibilities around the house will go a long way.

Assistance, enthusiasm, and encouragement are better motivators than coercion and control—and a whole lot more fun for you.

Eleven to Twelve Years Old

My son is ready to go to junior high. He seems to like his friends more than me. I've raised him on my own since he was five. Have I done something wrong?

For eleven- and twelve-year-olds, peers become more and more important. They share their secrets with each other instead of Mom or Dad. You still have a lot of influence on your son's adjustment, feelings about himself, and values. Work hard on those things. Equip him to make good decisions. Teach him right from wrong through the clear boundaries you draw. Give him positive strokes often. Encourage his discernment skills when it comes to finding friends.

If you are filling his pockets full of life skills while he is with you, he will be equipped to use them when he is not. Remain loving, kind, safe, and trustworthy. He'll come to you when the time is right. And in a little while, you'll probably be his best friend again.

My daughter is eleven, and she is starting to ask more questions about the divorce. Why? Should I answer all of them?

At this age, your daughter has more of her own sense of right and wrong and is making more moral judgments. You can use this knowledge and interest to reinforce her own personal values. Find ways to reinforce them with the church you attend and the activities in which your daughter is involved. She is also connected more on an emotional level. Because she is learning from every front, she is understanding issues on a larger scale than ever before. She is probably much more informed than you think. Yes, I would answer her questions. Give her language that is appropriate for her development, and don't demean the other parent.

My son is having trouble finding friends in our new neighborhood. He has started yelling and blaming his absent father for the changes.

Remember how important your son's peers are. When he is rejected by them, he assumes that he is rejected, unloved, and unworthy to all. He probably will draw closer to you during this time, but don't draw too much strength or reinforcement from your son. He still needs to deal with his feelings about his father as well as his friends.

So while you are there for him in his time of need, encourage him to talk and spend time with your ex-husband. Do all you can to promote that relationship. Then build up your son's self-esteem and help him attract appropriate friends. You might allow him to ask two or three other boys to a local arcade. A basketball court in your driveway will attract guys from all over.

I know one single mom who relocated when her daughter was twelve. For months, the daughter struggled with the issue of finding friends. Mom was consumed with responsibilities at her new job and did not help enough with the skills her daughter needed. So the daughter got in with the wrong crowd and compromised their values in order to fit in. Months of misery followed for both child and parent.

It's an important time to help your son make some really important decisions. Be sure you are helping to make that happen.

My twelve-year-old son has become depressed. I have leaned on him a lot the last two years. Now he's mean to me and his younger brother, and he never talks about his dad. How can I draw him out?

Be careful how much responsibility you are giving your son. Don't give your son so much to do in the home that you don't allow him to be the boy he needs to be. This can be very unhealthy for a preadolescent boy. Find other adults to become your confidants.

Your son's withdrawal is but one signal that something needs to change. Excessive anger or misbehavior may also be a sign that something is not right. Get help for him through counseling. Assist him in getting involved with wholesome activities, youth groups, and even volunteer organizations. Then ease up emotionally on him and don't give him more responsibilities than he needs. Above all, reinforce for him absolute boundaries for personal values. Give him a framework in which he can organize his life. The outside people and activities you find to involve him with can reinforce these.

Though my son sometimes resists his father's interference, I notice his grades are up and he remains more balanced when his dad is there for him. Should I just let the two of them work that out?

Researcher David Popenoe says that a father's involvement seems to be linked to children's improved quantitative and verbal skills, problem-solving abilities, and academic achievement. The amount of time fathers spend reading to their children is a strong predictor of their daughters' verbal ability. Fathers' involvement produces strong quantitative and mathematical abilities in their sons. Those dads who spend time alone with their children more than twice a week—with meals, baths, and other basic care—rear the most compassionate adults.[3]

As you can see, the more a father stays in touch, the better off a child will be—unless a father is abusive.

How can I really get to know my child?

Many times the simplest attempt helps the most. A good place to start is to talk less and listen more. How about:

- Asking your child questions such as what he wants to be or why he admires his favorite ball player. Then just listen without judgment.
- Spending time on your child's turf. Go to his games. Walk through the mall and understand his peers. Listen to his music.
- Providing your child with plenty of opportunities to discover personal interests and talents—musically, athletically, spiritually.
- Giving your child feedback and praise. We all master the art of selective listening. They know when you aren't listening, and eventually they stop talking.
- Listening to your child's friends, his teachers, his coaches. They can provide insights you might be too close to see.

If I should be honest with my son on why the marriage broke up, how do I define adultery?

Gary Sprague defines it as "pretending to be married to someone else."[4] Explain to your son that this is wrong and hurts a lot of people.

Since I became a single mom, my son has been the man of the house, providing a lot of strength and companionship. He is mature for his years and has grown protective of me. Is this okay?

Single-parent kids will naturally have a tendency to be more independent and responsible. It's okay to expect some things from your son commensurate with his maturity. But always remember to let your "little man" be a little boy.

Author Doug Easterday tells you to ask yourself these questions to see if this might be a problem for you:

- Do you feel guilty after disciplining your child and back down from imposing consequences? When too much emotional support is drawn from the child, it controls the parent's actions, words, and feelings.
- Do your child's opinions control you? While it is helpful to give a child options, giving him responsibility beyond his years is harmful.
- Do you have to get angry before you require your child

to do something against his will? When a parent has to work himself up to insist on obedience, the child has ceased being a son or daughter and has become a companion.[5]

Both you and your child need to develop lives of your own. Pursue separate hobbies, interests, and goals as well as solid relationships that fill both your needs. This will keep the two of you separate people and make the relationship one of mutual love instead of desperate emotional need.

My son seems so angry since the divorce. What can I do?

First, look at the ways your child is acting out his anger. Does he tear himself down (self-criticism)? Have you ever found him fighting with another child (aggression)? Does he yell and scream at the one he is angry at (ventilation)? Do you find him going off somewhere by himself (withdrawing)? Or does he defy all authority with his actions (passive aggression)?

Start learning how to deal with your child's anger by creating a loving environment. Don't be afraid to discipline your child when needed, but encourage him to express his anger appropriately, not stifle it. If you don't allow him to say what he feels, he is more likely to act it out—cheating, lying, fighting.

Talk often with your son. Be careful not to judge what he says. Be sure your unconditional love comes through, no matter what he says or does. Help your son generate positive solutions to problems he faces.

Finally, learn to defuse your son's anger by controlling your own. It takes two to fight. If you meet your son's angry outbursts with kindness, control, and self discipline, you can often redirect him toward a constructive solution.

Can you give me ways to move my child toward more independence?

During the elementary school years, children become more independent: walking to a neighbor's house, riding a bike, making a snowman. They also become more involved outside the home with lessons and activities. Hold yourself accountable for the growing responsibilities you are releasing to your child each month. In addition, don't forget these:

- Spend all the time you can with your child.
- Don't try to shelter your child from all outside influences. Teach him alternatives.
- Don't condemn your child's friends and their families.
- Let your child start deciding how he wants to get his hair cut and what he will wear to help him prepare him for the bigger choices.

- Don't overreact by trashing TV or punishing a child for repeating a bad word.
- Talk and listen to your child often, without overreacting.
- Watch for teachable moments.
- Pray for God's protection for your child.

- Expose your child to wholesome friends.
- Model strong values in your home.
- Don't panic about how fast your child is growing up. Just get more involved.

16

Adolescents

My children were twelve, ten, and eight when we moved from Ohio to Colorado. I had accepted a position as editor of *Single-Parent Family* magazine. School was almost out for the summer, and we were all excited about the move and the new friends it would bring.

I hit the deck running. With a brand-new magazine to get off the ground, I worked hard while also settling the children into their new home. My parenting felt secure as things had gone well so far. My children were really neat people. When one colleague at work mentioned that her child had an "attitude," she had to explain to me what that meant.

Then my oldest daughter turned thirteen, and life changed. For all the stability I had achieved, my daughter inserted instability. I pulled in tighter and forgot that my job as her mom was more than three-fourths over. She pulled harder for her independence.

Then I knew what having an attitude really meant. Every parenting skill I had relied on to that point seemed ineffective. I read all the books I could find on adolescents and talked to others who understood. For the first time, I wondered if we would make it.

I had heard a man on radio humorously define adolescence as:

The years of fears, jeers, sneers, tears.

The dynamic time that comes in with a pimple and out with a beard.

Flirtatious time when girls begin to powder and boys begin to puff.

But there was nothing funny about what I was going through. I began to wonder, *Is it possible for single parents to make it through difficult years of adolescence?*

What You Should Know

When I taught junior high school, I also coached girls' track. I worked on the relay races, and one of my jobs was to teach my runners how to pass the baton. In the 440 race, we have only a certain period of space and time at every 110 yards for one runner to give the baton to the next runner. The new runner takes over from there. We worked tediously both with the passing and the receiving. If the baton was dropped, the runner had to stop, pick it up, get back in the proper lane, and resume running. Valuable time and effort were wasted when that happened. The whole race could be won or lost with the passing of the baton.

Adolescence covers the last five years (ages thirteen to eighteen) that our children are still under our parent/child nurturing influence. It is the most difficult time of all because it involves the passing of the baton, and we have only a certain amount of space and time in which to do it. We are handing them what they need to continue with their leg of the race.

While the challenges of this age often stump me, I am awed by the process that involves the infants we gave birth to just a short time ago who are now accepting the challenge to take into adulthood.

Puberty takes place for the average male in the U.S. between ages thirteen and fourteen and for the average female between twelve and thirteen. Once puberty begins, the physiological changes by themselves are not usually as traumatic to the kids as the changes in the way others view them. As their adolescent bodies begin to look more like adult bodies, others begin to expect them to think and act mature as well.

Questions You Ask

I heard someone say that a thirteen-year-old is like a two-year-old. Is this correct?

Some psychologists agree that there is a similarity. Infants think they are part of their mothers—one and the same—and they panic when Mom is not around. At about ten months and continuing through about eighteen months, the baby starts to need more independence, and he begins separating from his mother and exploring the outside world. He takes risks for the first time, tries everything, and begins to use the words "me," "my," and "mine" for the first time. At about eighteen months to three years, the child realizes he can get hurt, the world can be dangerous, and he still needs his parents.

In a similar way, the adolescent emerges from a time when she felt as if she were an extension of her parents. She hasn't tried a lot on her own. Between the ages of thirteen and fifteen, she starts to need more independence and begins to separate herself from her parents and explore the outside world. She can take some pretty nasty falls during this time, and this process can be most difficult for parent and child alike. Usually, however, the child realizes she still needs her parents, and she reunites with them, but this time as a distinct individual.

What is my adolescent daughter really searching for?

All adolescent girls are searching for their identities apart from their parents. Most single-parent kids have suffered disappointment through death, divorce, or abandonment. Depending on how this was dealt with and how much continued conflict the child observed, she comes to adolescence searching for new ways to make sense of the world. She is looking for:

- *Security.* Whatever safe places she found during earlier challenges have become suspect. She discovers the human weaknesses and limitations in her parents. The black-and-white way she viewed things following the family breakup is no longer reliable. She finds out her parents have less control over the world than she thought they did.
- *Effect.* By the time they reach preadolescence, most children have discovered how to get their world to take notice of them. Often this means acting out.
- *Intimacy.* The adolescent needs to bond with others emotionally, spiritually, and physically. That is why she places such importance on her peer relationships. Sometimes, intimacy gets lost during the earlier years in single-parent homes. This can be due to the overwhelming responsibilities and difficulties faced by those who parent alone, leaving little physical or emotional energy for bonding. Whatever the cause, if a hunger for intimacy exists, the adolescent will go to search for it.
- *Love.* An adolescent sees the actions and motives of others more clearly. She begins to recognize selfishness and lack of love beneath people's actions in ways she never thought she could as a child. This can make her feel unloved in spite of verbal assurances to the contrary.

My son is fifteen and doesn't talk to me anymore. What has happened?

Psychologist and author Dr. James Dobson talks openly about teens. He says the first and most important change is hormonal, which causes the teen to misinterpret his world and impairs his social judgment. Dr. Dobson says a teen's "greatest anxiety is the possibility of rejection or humiliation in the eyes of his peers.... It is impossible to comprehend the adolescent mind without understanding this terror of the peer group." Dr. Dobson says that physical beauty drives the girl, and power motivates the teen boy. To work best with your son or daughter through these turbulent times, he suggests:

- *Keep them busy* with outside interests and youth groups.
- *Don't rock the boat.* "Idealistic and perfectionistic parents who are determined to make their adolescents measure up to their highest standard can rock a boat that is already threatened by the rapids."
- *Maintain a reserve army.* Parents must reserve the energy to cope with these new challenges. Keep the schedule simple, get plenty of rest, eat nutritious meals, and stay on your knees.
- *Reestablish the boundaries.*[1]

My fourteen-year-old son doesn't seem to want me involved with his schoolwork. How can I stay in touch and still make him feel comfortable?

No matter what they say, our kids want us involved in their lives. Troubled kids will often read uninvolvement as lack of love.

High-school counselor Jeenie Gordon suggests the following for staying involved:

- Keep on top of grades. Know when report cards are due.
- Always attend school events.
- Talk by phone with teachers, counselors, and attendance office when necessary.
- Encourage any and all signs of improvement.
- Nip skipping classes in the bud. Fast!
- Volunteer once in a while.
- Choose classes with your child. Include a little fun in the schedule.
- Allow your failing senior to be in total control of his graduation—whether he makes it or not.
- Be kind and considerate to school personnel. It pays off.[3]

I can't seem to do anything right when it comes to my fourteen-year-old daughter. What does she want?

Your daughter is trying to define herself apart from you— her values, tastes, interests, desires. My daughter Ashley would say, "Mom, I don't do this because I don't want to, not because you tell me not to."

Your daughter probably is demanding freedom you feel she has not earned. What her friends think and do seems more important than what Mom or Dad thinks and does, and priorities shift to how she looks compared to the models she knows by name in the magazines.

When I drive my daughter and a friend to soccer practice, I listen to their conversation. Their priorities are on things that don't matter. What can I do?

I call this a mall mentality—when our adolescents' minds are consumed by shallow things. Discovering what things are really important in life and what things are really unimportant is part of maturing.

Many of these changes are products of our times and society. Some of us grew up when we had more chores to do, and the survival of the family depended more on the joint efforts of all. As only one in a family of eight, our needs were added to the needs of everyone else. Having my family build their schedules around my soccer games was unheard of. As a matter of fact, I didn't get an opportunity to play soccer. Once a week, I had to help my mother do the laundry for eight to ten people with our old wringer washer. When I was

in the sixth grade, we got an inside bathroom. Things were, indeed, much different than they are today.

As I have mentioned before, we should not take anything away from our children without putting something better in its place. We need to help them discover their purpose—the reason they are here, different from anyone else on the face of the earth. We need to encourage them to express that difference, and we need to help them know the meaning of giving out—not just taking in.

None of these are small tasks. But you and I can help our children discover and then pursue their gifts and passions—art, sports, computers. At the same time, we can get them involved in regular activities where they are giving to others. Recently, we called a Christian radio station in our city to start sponsorship of a fatherless boy in Honduras. For $12 a month—the cost of one pizza—my children are able to provide a better life for another single-parent child. They learned the value of tithing their money regularly when they were very young. We also have volunteered at soup kitchens.

What shouldn't parents be to their adolescents?

Parenting adolescents is hard work. I have found that many of the ways I feel like responding are ineffective. At all costs, I have to guard against being:

- Controlling.
- Dictatorial without room for opinions.
- All talk.
- A bad listener.
- A comparer of my adolescence with my children's adolescence.
- Inflexible with rules, curfews, friends, and privileges.
- Intolerant.
- Impatient.

What qualities are especially important in responding to my adolescent?

When I found myself faced with the challenges that adolescence brings, I held my ground firmly. At first. It was easy to see that I was the one with more life experience. I knew what was best, and I would make my daughter see that, too. Wrong.

The more stubbornly I insisted on my way, the harder my daughter resisted and the bigger the gulf grew between us. I realized how little control I really had over the situation or my daughter's choices. I decided to go to work on me instead. And I discovered it wasn't only my daughter who had a ways to go in the learning department. I did as well. I found I needed to:

- *Understand.* Kids live in a different world than we did. I needed to combine what I did remember about being a teen with the changes our teens face today. We need to understand.
- *Communicate.* Choose positive attitudes. Listen nonjudgmentally. Use words our children understand. Take advantage of the teachable moments.
- *Love.* Stay close. Clear the schedule. Affirm.
- *Discipline.* No matter how much our children push against limits, they want and need them.
- *Teach.* Just because your child is older doesn't mean he or she ceases to need instruction from you. Keep an eye out for ways to teach values and life skills.
- *Stay involved.* This is not a time to withdraw, no matter how much you misunderstand motives or actions.
- *Remain open.* Your child may not be seeking your guidance today, but keep the door open to conversation.
- *Promote self-discipline.* Feed into your child's desire for independence any way you can. She wants to be independent? Leave the laundry for her to do. He wants his independence? Let him earn the money he will need. Help your adolescent become self-disciplined.

In addition:

- Don't argue and fight over every little thing.
- Don't overreact and lose your cool.
- Don't take what they say as literal truth. One friend of mine says, "Don't take it personally."

My son mistrusts people and feels they do not keep their word. He withdraws when people try to get too close to him. What can I do?

It sounds as though your son has had one or more important people let him down. He probably has coped by numbing his desire to be close to people. If he continues to think he doesn't need connections with others, he may never pursue a deep relationship with God or others. Instead, he will continue to deny he needs anyone.

Adolescents from single-parent homes often become aware that they are missing this relationship component. When they try to tell someone about it, they often get shot down. The listener attributes it to adolescent acting out, and the teen feels unsafe and withdraws, hides, or denies his needs to a greater degree even though he needs to be in relationships more than ever.

The more help adolescents get in clarifying what their desires really are, the less likely they are to find immorality attractive. It is when kids are left entirely to their own devices to cope with the disappointment and confusion of adolescence that they are likely to direct their desires toward that which is bad.

But does my fourteen-year-old really know what she wants from me? I certainly don't know.

Your daughter's relational styles with you are probably deceptive. She disguises what she wants in relationships. Instead of directly asking you to meet an unmet desire in her, she feels compelled to win it from you one way or another. Maybe she doesn't feel you understand or care for her deeply enough to give her what she desires. So she finds ways to get it from you through acting out. Adolescents learn early in childhood to be deceptive about what they want.

Since my divorce, I've leaned pretty heavily on my son for emotional support. Should I try to eliminate this now that he is an adolescent?

During divorce, one or more parents often look to their children for sympathy, understanding, or support. Parents cannot avoid draining their adolescent when they involve him in their own marital or emotional problems. This can lead to serious damage to the adolescent's developing identity, especially when he inevitably experiences failure at keeping Mom or Dad pumped up.

Many parents are tempted to use their relationship with their kids to quiet the desires in themselves. Up until adolescence, children are often the least threatening source of relationships for parents because kids' behavior is usually far more predictable and controllable than that of adults. When their kids become less predictable in adolescence, parents can experience a crisis that is just as great as the ones their kids go through.

Let your son be a normal adolescent—if there is such a thing. It's his turn now. He's the one who needs you for sympathy, understanding, and support. Put everything you can into giving that to him.

17

Older Teens

When my oldest daughter started school, I would watch from our bay window as she made her way down the driveway to board the school bus. She sometimes stopped to kick the snow or smell a flower, but she would always scuttle toward that bus and a new adventure with enviable childlike enthusiasm.

I would watch, wrapping my robe more tightly around me, not knowing what my family would face tomorrow but knowing that today was okay. Her tummy was full of warm oatmeal, her curls were still damp from her morning shampoo, and lots of love said good-bye at the door and would greet her when she returned.

Recently I was talking to Ashley, now a teenager, about a struggle she was experiencing. Her little curls have turned to long brown strands. She still scuttles toward new adventures with the enthusiasm only a child can know. But the challenges have grown more intense with the years. Oatmeal and warm baths are no longer enough to protect her from the dangers that seek to destroy her very soul. How do we adjust our parenting to combat that?

What You Should Know

Though it may seem your child doesn't want your love, the truth is that she really does, but in a new way. Parenting skills you used on your daughter as a child need to be altered. Raising a teen requires a smarter, more subtle, and sophisticated style of parenting. It demands compassion, good communication, and diplomacy, and provides many opportunities to solve problems productively. This means a more deliberate effort on your part and lots of practice. Don't get discouraged and give up in the process. It will be worth the effort. Keep reading good books on the subject and remember these ten nuggets:

- Laugh with your child at situations and at funny things she has to say.
- Choose your battles carefully and cool down before you respond.
- Keep your own interests so hers stay in perspective.
- Say "I'm sorry" when necessary. It will set a good example.
- Involve her in important decisions.
- Give her greater responsibility as she earns it.
- Never take away anything without putting something better in its place.
- Expose her to other adults (at church, for example) who share your values and echo your beliefs.
- Talk a lot about things she enjoys. Listen to her input without condemnation.
- Pray for her every day.

Questions You Ask

My son will graduate from high school next year. How much should I interfere in his life at this age?

Your son is almost an adult. He is busy with such things as deciding what he wants to be when he grows up, determining who he is as a person and what he wants, learning how to accept responsibility for himself, and asserting his independence.

Your son still needs guidance from you that is flexible and appropriate for his age. He needs to continue meaningful contact with both you and his father, if possible, and he needs schedules flexible enough to accommodate his friends and outside activities. Learn to consult with him and listen to him while still being his mom.

Some parents are so preoccupied with their own needs that they don't respond to their teenagers in times of crisis. Also, it's easy to project hostile feelings toward an ex-spouse onto a teen—especially mothers onto sons. Resist doing either of these and be there for him. He's going to need you for quite a while yet.

My daughter will graduate soon. She seems depressed and scared. What can I do?

When I was ready to graduate from high school, I reconsidered all my efforts to push away from my parents. I discovered for the first time what a scary world it was out there. I needed my mom's and dad's love and support— but in a different way. Just think about all the changes your daughter will face soon:

- *Leaving home.* When I got my first apartment and all the responsibility that came with it, I was scared I couldn't do it. I remember my mom saying, "If you can't do it, you can just move back home." It was the consolation and extra boost of courage I needed to make the plunge.
- *Going from school to work or college.* These are decisions that need major input and guidance.
- *Becoming self-reliant.* Mom is not going to be around to do everything anymore. I hope you've taught your daughter how to sort laundry, balance her checkbook, and change a lightbulb.
- *Getting different friends.* As she moves from high school to work or college, her friends are likely to become scattered.

You need to remain available to your daughter for this last juncture. Help her, guide her, instruct her only as she asks. Otherwise, your input could be perceived as intrusion. Just be there for her.

I have two daughters. Since my divorce seven years ago, they visit their dad every other weekend. But within the last year, my teenage daughter doesn't want to spend a lot of time with her dad because he still treats her like the child she was when he left. They both need to realize that growing up in a divorced family makes changes more difficult. Can you recommend reading material for them?

Many good books on the market teach parents about teens. It's a hard time at best for all parents, but you're right, divorce further complicates everything. I recommend:

Parenting Isn't for Cowards by James Dobson,[1] *Parenting Adolescents* by Kevin Higgins,[2] and *Parenting Passages* by David Veerman,[3] just to name a few. Read every quality book you can find and pray every day for your child.

Not as much material exists to inform kids about parents. In addition, reading may not be the best method of getting across the information to a child. You might try talking through some sample scenarios with your teen and model ways she could respond appropriately to her father. You also might help her draft a letter addressing everything that bothers her. Another suggestion is to read together a section from one of the books mentioned earlier. This lets her see that the parent isn't weird, and neither is she. Both should understand the other and work together.

One thing that you must keep in mind is that your ex-husband may be offended or threatened by your interference with his father-daughter relationship. If he is, you need to honor his wishes and not get involved. But both parents should cooperate and be flexible about the visitation schedule. It often needs to change as children become older and have more activities.

You are only one parent. The relationship your daughter forges with her dad is not your responsibility. A single mom once said to me, "Leah likes grape juice, and her dad never has it in his house. What should I do?"

My response? "Show Leah how to communicate her needs to her dad. Then *you* have grape juice in *your* house all the time. That's what you're responsible for."

My sophomore daughter is always forgetting her lunch, gym bag, homework, and I'm always running to school to bail her out. How can I teach her more responsibility?

Leave her to flounder.

Yours is a classic case of rescuing. Your daughter has been conditioned to think that Mom will always cover for her. She experiences no consequences for forgetting her lunch, gym bag, or homework. How many days of going hungry or getting zeros on assignments or for not participating in sports do you think it would take before she remembered to be responsible for herself?

I suggest the two of you draw up a contract. Let her know

everything she is to be responsible for. Make sure she understands that it is no one's responsibility but hers to make these things happen.

At first you may appear as the heavy. But as your daughter learns that she is in control of what occurs and the consequences she faces, she will knuckle down and probably learn one of the most valuable lessons of her life.

Until you stop rescuing, your daughter will never learn independence. It looks like it's up to you.

My son asks a lot of questions about his dad and why we divorced. I have dodged the truth thus far about his dad's adulterous affair. Does my son deserve more?

Tell him the truth, but do it lovingly. When you describe what the ex-spouse did, focus more on his behavior than his value as a person. Your child still needs a good relationship with his dad. Leave out the emotional charge the affair has for you. Do your venting among understanding adults.

Be sure you accomplish two goals in speaking with your son: Convince him the divorce was not his fault, and assure him that the cycle of divorce does not have to follow him into adulthood. When and how you tell your son the truth will make all the difference. But if you avoid the truth, it will come back to haunt both of you when he learns it from someone else. Be the first to the punch with the truth, spoken by someone with his best interests at heart.

What's going on with my teen daughter?

Think of yourself on your most bombarded day—balls flying at you from all directions: the washer breaks, the insurance comes due, you get an overdraft notice from the bank, and the child-support check doesn't come. That might be comparable to what your adolescent feels like every day.

Her body changes almost daily. Socially she is leaving behind old friends and selecting new ones. She is beginning to notice the opposite sex. The most important thing in her life usually has something to do with relationships. Spiritually, your daughter stands alone among her peers. She learns to keep her beliefs quiet. Mentally she is still thinking in black-and-white terms and finding it hard to figure things out. So what can you do?

- Talk, talk, talk. Try to make it her language.
- Listen, listen, listen—with your eyes, heart, time, and nonjudgmental responses.
- Reserve your battles for the big things.
- Stay calm. This confidence can steer you through some rough waters and often defuse tense moments.
- Walk in her shoes. Understand what she is going through.
- Teach. Use object lessons to bring home important points whenever you can find places to insert them. The opportunity might come from a news item or experience one of your children has gone through. Clarify what happened and let them, for example, suggest ways it could have been handled better.
- Draw clear boundaries.
- Be firm but loving in your discipline.
- Affirm her.
- Love her unconditionally.

How does the absence of a father for my daughter affect her now that she is sixteen?

David Popenoe says that teenage boys without fathers are more prone to trouble because they don't learn what it means to be a man. Girls learn about trust and intimacy and how to relate to men. They learn to appreciate their own femininity from the one male who is most special in their lives (assuming they love and respect their father). Most important, through loving and being loved by their father, they learn that they are worthy of love.[4]

Be sure that your daughter has been assured of your love for her.

What do I do about my daughter's rebellion?

The truth is that we cannot run our children: They run themselves. What we as parents do is build a safe, secure, affirming home around our children in which they make the transition into adulthood in good health. If our kids want to bang their heads against the walls, that is their choice, but we can build soft, resilient walls. We still have the same function as parents of teens, but we need new approaches from what we have been using. We should remain involved and find new ways to spend time with our teen. We need to close our mouths and listen more.

About subjects such as sex, imposing your views on your children is outside your control. Having a view, however, and living consistently according to it is within your control. About vocation, don't dictate, but rather help her discover and develop her own unique gifts and passions.

How do I know which stage my teen is in dealing with her dad's death?

Look for tell-tale signs and statements:

- *Denial.* "I'm okay. It doesn't bother me."

- *Anger.* "How could God let this happen?" Gary Sprague[5] describes four ways of handling anger: rage (throw tantrum, yell, punch), repression (keep it all inside), resolution (tell the person you are angry), and redirection (throw angry energy into another activity).
- *Bargaining.* "God, if you will bring my dad back, I will ..."
- *Depression.* "Life stinks."
- *Acceptance.* "It may be difficult to put life back together, but I can't change the past."

How often does divorce occur when teenagers are in the home? What problems does this pose?

Approximately 20 percent of the divorces that occur today happen in families in which the parents have been married for more than fifteen years. Thus the importance of the impact of divorce on older children cannot be overstated.

All children go through developmental tasks, and these tasks are more successfully completed when there is consistency and continuity in children's lives—particularly with their parents. Family stability is a crucial element during these developmental stages. Adolescents and young adults are trying to negotiate the states of intimacy versus isolation. Therefore, in divorce

Don't Forget These No-Failers to Use with Teens:

- *Communicate.* To encourage trust and independence, tell your children that you assume the best of them.
- *Enforce.* Enforce the rules you set.
- *Compromise.* Allow your high schooler to mature and move toward independence. I wrote a letter to my teenager during a hard time telling her I would say yes on as many things as I could, but the answer would always be no to other things that had been around long before I was a mom.
- *Affirm.* This encourages mature and responsible actions. Offer them rewards for positive behavior.
- *Get help.* Start with church or counseling.
- *Be sensitive.* Give your child the privacy she needs. Release more and more decisions to her as she earns them—clothes, classes, and use of leisure time. Understand that she won't be as eager to have you around.
- *Don't panic, overreact, give up, or despair.* Independence is a natural next step.
- *Build a relationship.* You and your child are working toward being friends and relating as adults.
- *Prepare.* Your child needs to be ready for the adult world. Teach her how to manage money, drive defensively, fulfill responsibilities, and act responsibly.
- *Connect.* Put your high schooler in touch with positive Christian role models and youth ministries that can help her grow in her faith.
- *Remember, this, too, shall pass.*

situations, the mom and dad should work together to bring as much stability to the teen's life as they can.

A comparison is made in chapter 39 of the book of Job. It talks about a couple of different kinds of parents. One is represented by the ostrich. She lays her eggs in the sand, then leaves them for predators to eat or step on. She is a polygamous bird who feels her job is finished after she gives birth.

The eagle, on the other hand, is a monogamous bird who builds her nest up on high and returns to it year after year, making improvements. One nest discovered in Ohio weighed almost a ton.

It is safe up in the eagle's nest. From there, she can nurture and teach her babies as they grow. She shows them where the good food is, where the dangers lie, and what awaits them up above. They remain in the nest with this clear perspective for about a year. Then the mother pushes them out to fly on their own.

May we learn from the words of Job today. Wherever you are in this pushing-out thing, love your child, nurture him, and teach him. Build your nest on high where you can show him how to eat the good and stay away from the bad. Give him a clear perspective. Then as you watch him soar on his own, you can smile, knowing you have finished your job and done it well.

18

Boy or Girl?

I drove into the driveway, stopping for my son to move his things. Courtney waved from the yard where she stood with a friend and a soccer ball. They'd kick, then talk; kick, then talk. Ashley smiled from the front porch step where she sat chatting to a friend on the phone.

Clint stayed busy moving a small pile of stones that lay on the concrete, and close by was a tattered paper sign secured from the wind with a rock. The sign read:

> FOR SALE
> ROCKS $~~1.00~~
> $~~.50~~
> $~~.25~~
> $~~.10~~
> ~~2 FOR $.05~~
> FREE

I smiled and felt a warmth deep inside as I realized all over again how uniquely God had made each of my children.

What You Should Know

All of our kids are distinct creations—even down to their fingerprints. While recognizing this uniqueness, there are also some principles governing the sexes that can help equip us to raise our sons and daughters.

Boys tend to be physical and competitive. Their conversations and play involve who's the biggest and the best. They even tend to integrate how they feel about themselves based on how they rank in the biggest and best categories. As they grow older, their competitions change. It becomes who knows more or who's the best at sports. Meanwhile, girls are more emotional and like to collaborate, work together, blend in, be accepted.

Boys need room to discover. I can't count the number of times I have walked into my son's room only to trip over a new experiment or to pick one up off the floor. He has always tinkered and fixed things that didn't work or needed to be made better. Boys can also be big dreamers. Clint's passion is to one day play for the NBA. He talks about it, plans the house he's going to build for his dear ol' mom, and discusses the positions he's going to play.

My girls, on the other hand, are often more interested in making their discoveries and doing their tinkering on the social scene. What they look like and how they are perceived have become paramount in this journey toward womanhood. In return, they expect appropriate relational responses from me. They want to be listened to and talked to and have time spent with them, while also recognizing their blossoming maturity.

Questions You Ask

Snails and Wails and Puppy Dog Tails? Boys

I constantly feel like there's no way I can raise my son without a man around. Am I tackling an impossible feat?

Many great men have been raised by their moms. Author William Beausay II says, "No matter what your circumstance—single, married, divorced, or widowed—you can raise a healthy young man if you know what to do. Your contribution as a mother involves demonstrating your maternal love for your boy, realizing that what your son sees of you is what he will see of women in general, developing his 'softer' side, and pushing him toward masculinity."[1]

Just because your son doesn't have a father around doesn't mean he can't be exposed to men. Connect him in places where that can happen. No one expects you to be a dad to your son. You are the mom. Do your best at that job and keep your eyes open to opportunities for others to fill in the voids. You're sure to find them.

Ever since my son was a little boy, he has liked to roughhouse. It doesn't take much to get his engine revved up. Does this mean he is violent?

It means he's a boy. Boys like action. They express themselves more physically, while girls express themselves verbally and emotionally. When my son gets particularly antsy, I force him into some kind of physical expression. More than once we've been in the car, and he's bouncing all over the place. I have let him out at the entrance of the subdivision where we live and let him run home while I followed in the car. We all laughed, he ran hard, and he emptied some of that pent-up energy that we girls have a hard time understanding.

For your son, I would continue to find constructive outlets for this kind of expression. Involve him in a sport of his choosing. Walk or run with him; it will give you time to connect. I would also closely guard against destructive outlets for physical expression. Monitor the TV programs he sees. Watch the friends he chooses to hang out with. You don't want your son growing up thinking that real men are physically violent.

How can I find healthy male role models for my son?

You can help him see positive qualities in men. These may be men at church, the grocery store, or the soccer field. Help him to see the benefit of a man holding the door for a woman. Draw attention to a man who saved another human life. Read to him about great men of the Bible and in history and in today's newspaper, men who stood for what they believed in no matter what those around them did.

My son has been the man of the house for three years and now, at fourteen, he seems to resent that role. He has gotten rebellious and disrespectful toward me.

Many factors could be contributing to your son's rebellion. Perhaps one of them is your belief that he is "the man of the house." It sounds as though he was eleven when you became a single mom. What has being the man of the house required him to do or be? Has he been able to be a little boy? Have you relied on him emotionally?

I know a man who says the best time to plant a tree is years ago. The second best time is now. No matter what else is contributing to your son's negative reactions, you need to change your expectations for him around the house, and do it now. Try:

- *Apologizing.* Tell him you were wrong to depend on him for the things you needed emotionally.
- *Involving him.* If he's always wanted to play football, let him play. Help him become a part of an active youth group at a church in your area that teaches solid biblical principles. There are some wonderful things going on in groups such as these.
- *Giving him responsibilities of different kinds.* Allow him to volunteer with some worthwhile endeavor: helping younger boys at a boys home, coaching a sports team, and so on.

- *Letting him see you connect.* If you've relied on him too long emotionally, it probably means you need more adult friends in your life. Model for him how to develop solid friendships and reciprocal accountability.
- *Being there for him.* If you're working that second job away from home, try finding work instead that can keep you home and available for your son.
- *Talking, talking, talking.* He has a lot to say at this age. Listen to what he has to say. Let him know he is important enough to be heard. Make responses that help him know you are tracking with him.

My son challenges my parenting a lot lately. I have to stand my ground often. Is this normal for a nine-year-old boy?

Yes, it is normal. He is testing the boundaries. He is examining just how firm—or negotiable—they are. You should stand your ground. Don't let what he says rock what you say. He needs to see something solid, unchangeable, and confident when around him things are changing and unreliable. He is also testing the waters to see where his own values lie apart from yours.

Your role for your son is changing. You must be confident in what you represent to him, and then do it with confidence no matter what changes around you. Your confidence will give him confidence in something solid and always there.

How can I ensure my son will develop manly qualities?

Nothing is ensured in this parenting thing, but a lot of principles have stood up through the test of time and situations. Expose him to men who represent the qualities you espouse. Teach and model your values consistently, then allow him to demonstrate them in his own way. Respond as he talks about feeling sorry for the bencher on the basketball team. Let him cry when he needs to, and let him know that's okay. Don't forget to pray for your son every day as well as for yourself and for the wisdom you need to raise an awesome man.

What do I look for in a good male mentor for my son? Where do I go to find one?

This is a question many single moms are asking. In searching for a mentor, I would consider the following issues:

- *Values.* Be sure he stands for what you do. A good place to start your search would be in church. Big Brothers/Big Sisters clubs, the YMCA, athletic clubs, and community centers are also places to look. Don't assume, however, that every man from these seemingly safe locations would be either suitable or safe. Also, don't make your search obvious. Just keep your eyes open to qualities you need.

- *Interests.* A mentor can broaden your son's interests as well as affirm existing ones. Be sure that what the man does is of interest to your child.
- *Commitment.* Find someone who wants to be involved with your son for the long haul.
- *Safety.* Know the person well who mentors your son. This is a big issue. I know of a mom who relied on her next-door neighbor for friendship and mentoring, only to find out sexual molestation was taking place over a long period of time.
- *Motives.* One man asked me if he could be a mentor for my son. I wasn't acquainted with him, but I made a few phone calls. He came from the church we were attending, and many knew him well. This all seemed to check out okay. So I agreed to a first meeting—in our basement—where this man had a couple of hours to help Clint build a table to mount his train set. That way, I could go about my own day while keeping an eye on the situation.

When I felt this man had proven himself, I allowed him to take my son skiing. They returned later that day, how-ever, and his motives became clear. He was looking for a wife and a ready-made family. That was the end of that.

Mentors are essential, but also very, very chancy. You can actually do more harm than good to your son if you put people in and out of his life. He needs someone solid and committed to him who says to your son in all kinds of ways, "You matter to me."

I want to raise my son into a wonderful man. What are some things I should always keep in mind?

I have been amazed at the famous men who grew up in single-parent homes: neurosurgeon Benjamin Carson, and football player and motivational speaker Mike Singletary, to name a couple. In all cases, I would keep the following in mind:

- Pray much. I talk to God each morning for my children. His plan in the Bible is to pass godly principles from generation to generation. It is more important to God than it is even to me. I ask for wisdom to do that.
- Expose your son to appropriate role models.
- Monitor TV viewing and the company your son keeps.
- Let him respond in his own way, though it may be different from yours.

- Give him "guy" experiences in addition to the regular chores he is assigned, such as running the sweeper or cooking something. I assign chores to my son around the house that encourage manly development—tightening screws, taking out garbage, mowing the lawn, changing furnace filters.
- Refrain from negative statements about men in general or your ex in particular. Vent to other people. Allow your son to be proud of being both a male and the son of his dad.
- Be confident. Your high self-esteem and sense of direction is a great source of comfort for your son in such a changing world.
- Don't worry. You and I can fret and fume so much, we don't enjoy what is happening around us. You are a single parent. Put everything you have into raising that son. He's going to be okay, and you can enjoy the trip along the way.

Sugar and Spice and Everything Nice? Girls

My fourteen-year-old daughter seems unhappy and uncaring about her appearance. I wonder, if her dad were around, would things be different?

You will never know, but you do need to get at the root of what's going on in her now. What makes her happy? Unhappy? Is this a recent thing? If so, what prompted it?

One of the ways I have found to correct an undesirable behavior in my children is to focus them on a better one. You know her and what she likes. Encourage her to explore new interests. Help her achieve success in something that belongs to just her. Girls, especially, want to express themselves apart from their mom or dad. They want their own opinions, interests, and activities. Not only encourage this, but help your daughter find her way. Release more and more responsibilities as she earns them. Ask her opinions on more things. Build her up and bite your tongue when you feel the tendency to criticize. She needs you, of all people, to affirm her.

Finally, be careful about how you look at her appearance. Too many of us see our daughter's looks as extensions of our own. We want them to make better choices than we did. If I could raise my oldest daughter all over again, I would celebrate her adolescence more, rather than dread it. I would sit down with a catalog and let her talk about styles, as distasteful as they might be to me. I would go window shopping with her more and express my opinions less. I would allow her to make her own decisions without my comments. I would be more of a friend and less of a critic. I would be her greatest fan through all her phases.

I have been a single mom for a long time and done so successfully. This experience has made me strong in many areas, but I don't want my daughter to be a ramrodder just because she has watched me survive. How can I nurture her gentle and feminine side?

This is an issue with which I struggle every day. The qualities in me that have helped me survive this single-parenting thing have, in other ways, created a monster in me. I like things done quickly and efficiently, and I get impatient when they are not. To help my children find more balance, I try to:

- Let them participate in decisions. "Do I or don't I?" This helps them to be informed decision makers.
- Think long, talk short.
- Be tall on patience and short on criticism.
- Be compassionate by helping others we see in need.
- Show my vulnerability. I tell my children when I am scared. But they all know a Bible verse that says, "When I am weak, then I am strong."[2] They've heard their mom quote it many times.
- Let my children see their mom praying about the issues we face.

Through it all, I want my girls to see a woman who can make it through anything, but not by herself. I want them to know me as a woman who lives by godly principles and, as a result, relies on God's strength. That's why I am able to go on successfully, not because I am a superwoman.

Twila Paris has a song called "Warrior Is a Child." Some of the words go:

> *People say that I'm
> amazing, never face
> retreat.
> But they don't see the
> enemies that lay me
> at His feet.
> They don't know that I go
> running home when
> I fall down.
> They don't know who picks
> me up when no one is
> around.
> I drop my sword and cry
> for just a while
> Cause deep inside this
> armor, the warrior
> is a child.*[3]

I have decided that part of helping my girls develop their soft sides is to make sure they do know the struggles I face and the One I depend on to help me navigate my way through them.

Will my daughter be promiscuous?

Many things contribute to a person's experimentation with sex, but being from a single-parent family doesn't have to be one of them. You should be teaching your daughter what to choose and what to avoid. Model all kinds of good behavior all the time. Put good things in the place of things that might do her harm, such as:

- Follow some of the neat suggestions for "moral dating" found in *258 Dates While You Wait*[4]:
  - Create your own pizza.
  - Visit an animal shelter.
  - Design your own holiday.
  - Host a "bubble mania."
  - Engage in a fast-food progressive dinner.
- Buy a True-Love-Waits ring and present it to her in a special way.
- Expose her to Christian personalities and musical artists who uphold abstinence.
- Model purity in you own life and in those you expose her to.

How can I help my daughter identify her boundaries?

Hopefully, you've been doing this since she was very young. We can help our daughters fix things that are less than perfect. We can help them find the answers when the questions stump them at first. We can help them be strong in their beliefs when those around grow weak. We can help them learn how to appropriate their time and money and to spend both wisely.

One day I sat with my children and gave them each a piece of blank paper and a crayon. They laid a hand down on the paper and traced around it. When they lifted their hands, a profile remained. Then we talked. I asked them to write words inside their hands that represented what they believed in, what they liked and disliked, where they wanted to go, and things they wanted to avoid. Before long, each of their profiles was filled with things they chose to include. And surrounding these things on paper was the profile, the boundary that each child had drawn.

We must teach our daughters to draw clear boundaries around who they are. And we must let them know that they alone are the ones who choose what goes inside.

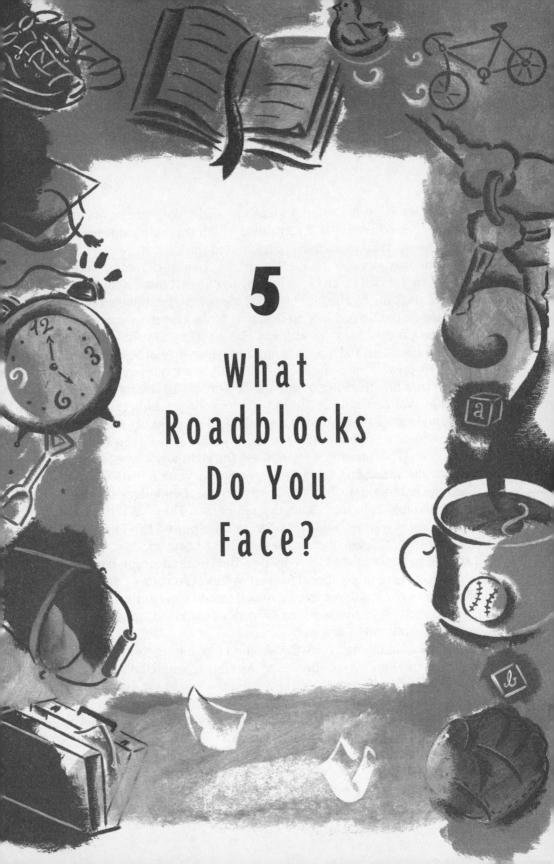

5

What Roadblocks Do You Face?

Parenting Needs

It was late Saturday afternoon. I was about eight. We were on our way to the church where my dad pastored, which was thirty-three miles from our home. While walking into a five-and-ten-cent store in a small town on the way, my dad noticed the grand opening of a bank across the street. He told my mom he was going to check it out. I ran to catch up, and he took me by the hand to lead me across the busy street.

Once inside the bank, I saw an ocean of faces. One man was talking over a microphone. "Step this way and choose a key. If your key opens this treasure chest, all the money from inside that you can hold is yours."

My dad followed the crowd to the man. We took our places in line. I stood in that line thinking of the man's words, "All the money from inside that you can hold is yours." For one of six kids (two more would come later), that sounded appealing. I looked at my dad's giant hand, confident he could hold a hundred dollars at least. So I started praying, "Oh, God, please let my dad get the right key."

Our turn drew near. I repeated my prayer. Soon it was my dad's moment.

The man extended the box full of keys. Sweat beaded my forehead as I watched my dad's hand span the selections. Then his thumb and a finger came together, and from the box he pulled the key to our financial future. "Please, please, please, God," I prayed.

I started to step forward with my dad, but the man stopped me and held the box close to my face. I looked at him. "Your turn," he said.

Me? But that's my dad's job. I glanced uncertainly at my dad, who was standing behind another man in front of the chest. I reached out my sweaty hand and took a key.

I stood behind my dad for what seemed like a long time. The man in front of us didn't have any luck. At last, it was Dad's turn. He stepped forward. His arm lifted. I pressed the key in my sweaty right palm with my left thumb.

Dad's key was in. He turned it. I fixed my eyes on his face as he looked at me. He shook his head. Nothing.

Disappointment overwhelmed me until a gentle hand from behind nudged me forward. It was now my turn to stand in front of the treasure chest. I lifted my key, convinced there was no way I would have what it took. Soon the key was in the lock.

I turned it to the right. CLICK. The lock opened!

The man standing behind the table smiled and lifted the lid. All kinds of coins! And my eyes were as big as the biggest of them. I put my hand into the treasure, sunk it deep, and closed my fingers around all I could handle. I lifted the money, pulled it quickly to my chest, and scurried across the room to my dad, where I sat down to count the money.

I got to $2.98, $2.99, $3.00, $3.01. I don't remember exactly how much over three dollars I had, but I do remember treating my family that afternoon to ice cream at a shop down the street.

Needing the Key Again

Many years went by without my giving much thought to my lucky key. I grew up, went to college, got married, and had children of my own. I had the same fears all new mothers face, and I called my mother often for advice: "How do I know when her temperature is high enough to take her to the doctor?" "Why isn't he sleeping through the night?"

I didn't feel very confident in my own abilities or decisions. Someone else could always do it better.

But then Mom and Dad moved far away, and Dad became very ill. My husband was gone. All those who I thought held the key to opening what we needed had stepped out of my life. Yet the treasure chest— my children—remained squarely in front of me. It was my turn at the lock. My thumb pressed the cold key into my palm once again.

I stepped forward. I put everything I had into opening that one. I realized nothing would ever be more important. I dipped my hand deep into the riches. Sometimes I had a handful. Sometimes the things I held fell through. Other times I gathered just what I needed.

Many years have passed. My treasure chest has grown—my three children are nearly as big as I am. Every day the lock changes. Every day the key feels more inadequate. Every day I stand alone facing the day's new challenge—sometimes gigantic, other times minute, but never boring.

My turn's not over yet. I still sweat a few bullets, and I wonder what challenges tomorrow will offer. I am still the one who needs to make everything work. But I have found God faithful. And I am confident that when tomorrow comes, my key will somehow fit the lock one more time.

19

Discipline

Shortly after we arrived in Colorado, the children convinced me to buy a ten-week-old Labrador retriever pup we named Colorado Rockie. He was the cutest thing that could melt even the coldest of hearts—including mine, though I didn't need one more thing to handle.

At first, everything Rockie did was sweet as he romped and played and found his way in his new world. But then he started chewing—anything from shoes and balls to fences and the siding on our house.

I hired a man to come and train Rockie. He showed us how to take hold of the lower parts of his legs with our hands and "flip" Rockie. Supposedly, this would allow us to regain the upper hand. The trainer explained that if Rockie looked us in the eyes while on his back, he was still in charge. If, however, he looked away instead of staring at us head-on, we had won, and the dog had become submissive to us.

This trainer made several trips to our home. Courtney took on the tasks of not only flipping him as we sought to regain control, but she worked with the trainer in teaching Rockie how to be led.

I decided to bite the bullet instead of shooting it at the dog. I waited for our new discipline to make a difference. The poplar tree in the backyard that Rockie had stripped of its bark was now dead. The ponderosa pine with its broken branches barely made it. One day I hired a cleaning lady to do our house. I looked forward to coming home to spotless surroundings. When I arrived, however, more disaster awaited me. She had left the back door open, and Rockie had done his thing in our home for hours. Beheaded and destuffed teddy bears lay on the carpet amid the remains of other toys, shoes, a CD player, and clothes.

The trainer found a new home for Rockie following an irate call from me. We haven't seen Rockie since he left, but I remember him often (not fondly, I might add) when I think of discipline. I realize how he needed time, consistency, guidance, and an opportunity from me to learn and then enough space to run and practice acceptable behavior. I failed with Rockie, but I trust my children will be okay and I'll not have to call someone to find them another home.

But how do we as single parents find the time and the energy to provide consistency, guidance, and opportunity to discipline our children correctly?

What You Should Know

Discipline involves teaching our kids how to do something, giving them the space and opportunity to do it, then rewarding or correcting them, depending on how they did the job.

Let's say you want to teach your son how to make his bed. You show him how this is done, and you explain the expectations you have of him—to make his bed every morning. You will also need to describe the consequences if he does not follow

through, such as not going out to play after school. Next, you give him the opportunity to practice this new skill. You might have to remind him until he gets self-motivated. You are helping your son develop good habits and a certain level of proficiency in this area. Finally, you must apply consistent consequences. These consequences should be chosen to fit both the task and the child.

You might be surprised that as far back as the Bible times, disciplining our children was addressed. Listen to these words as if they were penned today:

- "He who spares his rod hates his son, but he who loves him disciplines him diligently."[1]
- "Foolishness is bound up in the heart of a child; the rod of correction will drive it far from him."[2]
- "Do not withhold discipline from a child; if you punish him with the rod, he will not die."[3]
- "Discipline your son in his early years while there is hope. If you don't you will ruin his life."[4]
- "Those whom I love I rebuke and discipline."[5]

Questions You Ask

Because my children have been through so much since their mother died, I sometimes hesitate to discipline them. Is this wrong?

Probably every single parent has wrestled with this same

issue. But they need consistency and something sure and always the same—now more than ever. They are redefining themselves under new rules. Just as you helped when they were younger with outlining the pictures in their coloring books with crayons, help them now draw the right boundaries. This will help them get a true "picture" of the real world. Then teach them how to stay within those lines.

My husband left while I was pregnant. My daughter is now one. I love her so much, and my whole world has come to revolve around her. She has helped me through so much grief. It's hard to imagine ever having to punish anyone so sweet. Am I wrong to feel this way?

I hear several statements from you that cause concern. You say, "My daughter is":

- "My whole world." This is not a good thing to do. You need to draw around you a circle of support consisting of adults who can hold you accountable, mentor you, become a sounding board, and teach you from their own experiences. If you keep your daughter in a role in which she doesn't belong, both of you will develop unhealthy tendencies and some unhappy days are ahead.
- "She has helped me through so much grief." You need to experience a normal grief cycle.

You should work through these stages in an adultlike manner that has nothing to do with a one-year-old. She will go through her own stages of grief as she gets older. The severity and direction depend on how much continued positive involvement your ex-husband has in her life.

- "It's hard to imagine ever having to punish anyone so sweet." Your own attitude toward discipline seems more like punishment. Discipline should be positive, loving, and encouraging. As with our puppy, if you don't show her who's in charge and define clear boundaries early on, no amount of cuteness will compensate for the consequences later on.

Methods of Discipline

I suppose the question is not so much "if I discipline," but "how will I discipline?" Right?

The idea is to keep your love, support, and guidance high as you nurture your child while also maintaining appropriate control. In chapter 20 on self-esteem, we talk about different kinds of parenting styles based on the research of D. Baumrind.[6] Take a look at how single parents with these various styles might tend to handle control and discipline:

- *Authoritarian.* Bill is not interested in what his daughter thinks about issues when they arise. He demands respect and compliance with the rules. Bill puts his daughter's obedience before his relationship with her. He responds with, "Don't argue with your father." Bill is rejecting and restrictive. This makes him a low nurturer and high controller.

- *Permissive.* Tammy is a single mother who struggles with saying no and setting limits with her daughter. She amply shares love with her daughter but does not try to control her behavior. This comes out in letting her daughter do as she pleases, giving little guidance on decisions, and refusing to correct bad behavior. Tammy is high in love but low on control in her parenting and disciplining.

- *Authoritative.* Audrey asks for and gets response from her son because he knows that it is best for him. She sets limits, but she allows her son to have freedom within those limits. Audrey is loving and supportive and available to her son. She has found a balance between caring and disciplining him.

When I talk to my daughter and correct her, what should I remember to do?

Look directly into her eyes and lean toward her. Talk firmly (though not harshly) to your daughter and let her know you mean what you say. Tell her exactly what you want her to do. Never make requesting or begging statements such as, "Don't you think you should get your homework done?" Say simply, "Please do your homework now."

Don't make empty threats. Don't count. Your children will learn not to listen to you until you get exasperated with them.

My children's father undermines me every way he can, including discipline. He sways the kids by being extra nice to them when they're with him, leaving me to clean up the mess when they return. What can I do?

Organize yourself and see that what you are doing is what you want to do. Then do. And keep on doing.

- Write out a one-sentence mission statement. What do you stand for? What do you believe in?
- Designate a goal. Where are you heading? What are you trying to accomplish?
- Decide what steps will be necessary to reach your goal.
- List rules that must be upheld in order to get to your goal.
- Determine what consequences there will be if those rules are not upheld.

- Allow your children to participate in developing these guidelines.
- Enforce these rules consistently, gently and lovingly, while interspersing enjoyable rewards. Model for your children how to be firm yet kind and self-controlled. They'll be learning far more than you could ever imagine, and you'll be investing in the lives that matter the most to you—in spite of any opposition you may get.

Your children need to be aware that you are heading somewhere, and everything you do should be getting you to that destination. Sooner or later, your children will see the lack of plan and organization your husband shows. In contrast, they need to see you with your act together, not vengeful, and actually enjoying the direction in which you are heading.

My kids try to play me and their stepdad against each other. What do I do?

Stick together. At all times and in all matters. When you are confident, and when you're shaky. When you're positive, and when you're unsure. If you determine that from this day on the two of you will always present a united front, no one should be able to pry you apart or play one of you against the other.

I have always admired the spunk in my daughter, though it has proved exasperating at times. How do I discipline appropriately while still keeping that sparkle in her eyes?

What you call your daughter's "spunk," I will call her "spirit." Distinguish between what is your daughter's will and her spirit:

- *Will* involves your daughter's ability to decide her own actions. These may be the same or quite different from yours. A child's will can vary from being compliant to being strong-willed and determined to become her own boss. You need to take charge as your daughter begins to go her own way in spite of the rules you have imposed. The younger she is when you do this consistently, the better off both of you will be.
- *Spirit* includes those abstract character qualities that distinguish your daughter from others and make her a unique individual. This part of her is fragile and sensitive and can be easily injured. My mother calls it a tender rose inside of each of us that can only withstand so many bruises. To protect your daughter's spirit—or spunk as you call it—provide her with the deepest respect you can muster for her person.

Be aware of the methods you use in handling your anger when your daughter disobeys. Make a list of the ways you respond to her actions. Then target your inappropriate responses—yelling, overreacting, disciplining in front of others—and decide better ways of dealing with them. Your goal is to guide your daughter's will without breaking her spirit.

Should I spank my child?

I believe spanking has its place up to a certain age (between eight and eleven) if we take a few precautions. Spanking should be used, however, only for deliberate acts of disobedience or defiance of authority (refusing to come home when told). Do not spank for things the child does that simply represent a mistake or misjudgment (spilling his milk). Always keep these rules in mind:

- If you have a tendency to abuse your child, do not spank.
- Cool down before you spank—always.
- Spank in private, then assure your child of your love.
- Help your child verbalize the rule he broke so he understands why he is being disciplined.
- Make the spanking swift with painful hits only on the bottom.
- After you spank the child, hold him close.
- Spank with something other than your hand. Reserve your touches for acts of tenderness.

If I am supposed to be teaching my son new skills, providing opportunities to practice those skills, then giving correction after he does them, how do I discipline effectively at all those levels?

It is possible to discipline at all levels of the training process. Try these suggestions:

- *Discipline while you teach.* At this level, you impart information to your son. Show him, for example, how to make good decisions about the friends he selects and then stand for what you preach. Teach him at both formal times (when you get together for the purpose of talking about certain matters) and informal times (when, after reading a newspaper article, you are able to review what you have discussed).
- *Discipline while he practices what he has learned.* What better way to discipline than to help your son develop expertise in areas that will affect his future? Stick close after you have instructed him. Keep an eye on how he is pulling off what you showed him. Teach him a more complex task step by step. While you are together, you can go into further depth and answer his questions. Reward him when he makes good decisions.
- *Correct.* This becomes necessary if the child makes a

wrong choice. Adjust your child's behavior by helping him remember his instructions and do the job right. Depending on the age of your son and the type of misbehavior, you may need to spank him, talk directly with him, or allow consequences to do their job.

I want to rescue my son instead of allowing him to face the consequences of his actions. Will I regret this?

No doubt you *and* your son will. By allowing him to suffer consequences, you permit him to experience real-world results of decisions he makes. You can use *natural consequences*—those things that occur naturally.

Once when Ashley got a new video game, she asked me if she could take it to school. I said no. But Ashley sneaked it anyway, and another kid at school broke it. When she returned home, she explained what had happened. Ashley had faced a natural consequence. I didn't have to do any more.

Logical consequences are built in by the parent. They involve a negative consequence that is logically related to the thing the child has done. If a child scribbles on the wall with crayons, he might get to scrub all the marks off the whole downstairs. Logical consequences can be used with any age child and are effective because they put the responsibility for upholding the rules back with the child. It follows a pattern: *If . . . then . . . . If* your son decides to break the rules, *then* he makes a choice to face the music. Remember that the goal of discipline is to help your son develop self-discipline and self-control. As he grows older, his control should increase while your control decreases.

I once heard a story of how Michelangelo was criticized for wasting so much marble when he sculpted the "David" statue. His response? "As the chips fall away, the image emerges."

Let's use discipline as our own tool for helping our children's images emerge.

Examine Your Own Discipline

Do:

- Vary your disciplinary techniques. Sometimes a time-out may be appropriate, but at other times, no TV might work better.
- Focus attention on the specific misbehavior that upsets you without bringing up things done wrong earlier.
- Recognize and reinforce correct behavior.
- Be consistent and firm in carrying out correction. Empty threats are worse than ignoring the behavior in the first place.
- Keep the correction specific.
- Let your children experience the consequences of their misbehavior.
- Make correction last for only a limited period of time.
- Practice both patience and understanding when you are confronted by misbehavior. Remember, the kids are just kids, and there are some pretty tough things going on in their lives.
- Adjust your discipline and punishment strategies to reflect the ages and maturity levels of your children. Being sent to bed at eight may be appropriate for an eight-year-old, but not for a teenager.
- Put the punishment into effect as soon as possible after the inappropriate behavior. Immediate consequences emphasize the relationship of cause and effect that you want your children to understand.

Don't:

- Get into a no-win power struggle with your children. ("You will sit in this chair until you eat your dinner.")
- React to everything your children do that displeases you. Some things are best ignored. Choose your battles.
- Fail to recognize that each child is different. Each has different strengths and weaknesses and reacts to things in different ways. Personalities are neither good nor bad. Each has positive and negative characteristics.

20

Self-Esteem

When my daughter Courtney was twelve, she came home from school one day with her report card. It listed a few more average grades than I prefer. But Courtney looked at me with a smile and said, "Mom, I know my grades aren't the best in my class. I'll work harder next quarter, but I'm really good at soccer, basketball, and track. The kids and teachers all like me. I'm kinda happy about all that."

How could I question a couple of C grades on her report card after an attitude like that?

Unfortunately, such solid self-esteem has not always been the case for Courtney or for my other children. All kids, but especially those from single-parent homes, wrestle with low self-esteem at times as they ask questions such as: *Did Dad leave because of me? Why do I have to come from a single-parent home?*

What You Should Know

Self-esteem is a confidence and satisfaction in oneself. Building solid self-esteem in children helps them adjust better to life's challenges without both parents, take control of their lives, have better temperaments, and not blame others. They are also comfortable with people, they don't tear others down, they make better decisions, and are confident, optimistic, and willing to try new things. When single-parent kids have high self-esteem, it takes a lot to get them down.

Questions You Ask

How much does a child's talent affect his self-esteem?

Much of your child's self-confidence is based on his opinions about his abilities. Children need an opportunity to succeed. They also need to learn what it means to deal with failure, achieve challenging goals, and handle themselves in a variety of situations. By watching, listening, and following your lead, your child can learn essential life skills.

Give him confidence. Give him a view of his potential and capacity to grow and adapt. Give him independence. Give him hope. Give him the chance to have a high self-esteem.

Why is unconditional love so important to self-esteem?

Love from a parent assures a child that his acceptance will never change. It's a given. A done deal. A nonnegotiable truth.

Unconditional love provides a child with a solid foundation on which to build everything else. That child should know, *Mom will always be in my corner. I can always count on my dad.* If the child fails to find it at home, he will seek it someplace else. You can help by sharing your own emotions, such as fear and anger, and apologizing when necessary. Kids know and demonstrate unconditional love automatically. A child can better understand the perfect love of God by seeing unconditional love modeled through his parents.

Can we control all the things that contribute to our feelings about ourselves?

From before our birth, everything that happens to us affects how we feel toward ourselves, either positively or negatively. Characteristics such as race, sex, birth order, and socioeconomic status are not controllable, but what we do with those factors is. Our children are watching. Let them see us navigate our way through the rough circumstances of a relationship breakup and come out okay. Let them learn from us how to forgive and never give up.

My daughter thinks if she doesn't look like the models in the magazines, she is not acceptable. How do I combat that?

"Beautiful people" stare at all of us from the media. Models walk across the runways and spread across the magazine pages in perfect proportions. Our daughters cannot see the pain or drastic alterations or sacrifices that made those positions possible. Instead, our developing teens often come up short when they stand in front of the mirror and compare their own appearance with what they see. This can create a desperate sense of inadequacy and low self-esteem.

Stay emotionally and physically close to your daughter every day. Be sure she understands what is real and what is not. Help her see the plastic, hype, and makeover involved in a model's line of work. Reward her for efforts that reflect strong character qualities. Expose her to more meaningful things in life by allowing her to get involved with others through volunteer work, youth groups, or benevolent activities. By doing all these things, what you model will speak louder than all the other models in the world.

My daughter's grandmother always told her not to think too much of herself and often cautioned her against bragging. How do I now teach her that having a high self-esteem is okay?

Your daughter must understand positive self-esteem is not the same as self-centeredness. Bragging about oneself is actually an attempt to hide low self-esteem. Many think they are important as long as they are producing or measuring up to standards someone else has imposed.

Help your daughter create her own standards of performance and her own value system. Teach and model the values your family stands for. Discipline consistently while listening, praising, having fun, and showing parental self-control. The younger your daughter is when she gets the message that she is worthwhile through positive reactions from you, the deeper and more lasting the impact on her self-image. Children act like the persons they think they are. It will be up to you to help your daughter see what a special person she really is.

Does teasing hurt a child's self-esteem?

Don't tease. Teach your children not to tease. Show them instead how to build up one another.

For the most part, teasing is never good. Many times, the things we are teased about when we arc young are the very things that distinguish us from all the others. But because our feelings about ourselves are not yet in place, we internalize the teasing and convince ourselves the trait is a terrible flaw.

I took a lot of teasing about my height when I was young. I towered over everyone during all my elementary school days. Sports were not big for girls at that time, so I couldn't capitalize on that strength. Therefore, I compensated by slumping over and wearing clothes and shoes that diminished this "flaw." It wasn't until I gained some maturity—and some weight—that I realized what a gift my height actually was.

Parenting and Self-Esteem

Why does the family have such an important role in building self-esteem?

The family is the first place where children begin to discover who they are. Reactions and encouragement received while making these discoveries will largely determine self-image. Whether parents are living together or apart, they teach their children values (or a lack of them) and a sense of who they are. Whoever (parents, grandparents, day-care workers, teachers) or whatever (TV, radio) spends the most time with your children will have the greatest influence on their self-image. Both parents should be aware of who and what those primary influences are.

I parent differently than my sister does. How might our different parenting styles affect our children's self-esteem?

Psychologist D. Baumrind discusses three different types of parenting styles. These styles of parenting are especially evident in single parents I know:

- *Authoritarian.* This style of parenting is heavy on discipline. Single moms and dads have lost control over so many other areas of their lives, it is not uncommon for some custodial parents to clamp down hard on what they feel is still controllable — the children. They can get uptight when their children disobey or show disrespect toward them. They also expect a lot from their kids and make them think that their love is dependent on how the children behave. The kids, in turn, can develop low self-esteem.
- *Permissive.* Overly loving and supportive but lacking in disciplinary strengths are marks of the permissive parent. Some single parents feel their children have suffered so much through the loss of one parent due to the home breakup or death of a parent that they relax their discipline. Their boundaries are vague and not consistently enforced. They look past bad behavior so they won't have to deal with it. The children from permissive homes often have unrealistic self-esteem and feel victimized by bad things that happen to them.
- *Authoritative.* When a parent is balanced in his or her discipline and self-esteem, Baumrind says the parent is authoritative. Children in these homes clearly know their boundaries and eventually learn to define themselves based on these outlines, regardless of the difficulties they face. Disobedience brings consistent consequences. Parents maintain a sense of self-control, even in moments of aggravation toward the child. Authoritative parents encourage independent and creative thinking in their children. As a result, the kids grow up to be confident, competent, and better adjusted, with healthy self-esteem. And plenty of them come from single-parent homes.[1]

But I'm so busy with work and housework. Do I have time to work on my son's self-esteem?

If you don't, someone else will—either to his good or to his detriment. What does an "I-don't-have-time for you" attitude tell your son? Many parents are workaholics. An obsession with work inside or outside the home devalues the worth of a child. It says, "You are worth less than the stuff I have to do." Ignored children find creative ways to get attention.

The first step for any nurturing parent in building a child's self-esteem is to spend quality time with the child. Half of all fathers (not just single fathers) spend less than fifteen minutes each day with their adolescents. The old saying is never more true: "A child spells love T-I-M-E." When a child sees he is important enough for you to carve out time to spend with him, he is much more equipped to face the rest of his world.

If we as parents knock our own abilities, "I've always been lousy at math," is this same discontent passed on to our children?

It certainly is. Continuous criticism or abuse—even directed at oneself—with little or no positive affirmation is almost certain to affect self-esteem.

The greatest gift you can give your child is to convey your own healthy sense of self-worth. Find ways to work on this in yourself through reading, support groups, or counseling. You will also need to examine your goals and determine where you want to go and how you will get there. Be sure that what you do every day is helping you to accomplish that.

Once you as a parent feel good about yourself, it's easier to work on your child's self-esteem. Comment on her good qualities: "I really admire the way you handled that" or "You look beautiful today" or "Of all the kids there today, you made me most proud." Demonstrate how to accept a compliment and then lavish them on your child.

Sometimes when I punish my little boy, I'm afraid I will hurt his self-esteem. Is that possible?

Parents sometimes do not distinguish between the misbehavior and the child himself. Then when the child is reprimanded, he thinks the love from that parent is in question. This makes that parent's love conditional upon the child's behavior and can be devastating to his self-esteem.

Is my child really affected that much by the things I say?

I once heard motivational speaker Zig Ziglar tell about a class that everyone considered incorrigible. Two teachers had resigned through the course of the year. The administration brought in a retired teacher to take over. The kids straightened up and grades soared. At the end of the year, when the teacher was honored by the principal, the teacher responded, "Well, when you gave me the kids' names and their IQs—Mary, 150; Anthony, 163—I knew they had potential."

The principal responded, "Those weren't their IQs. Those were their locker numbers."

When we demonstrate solid belief in our children, they have a way of producing. Our kids are often products of the comments they hear or fail to hear from their parents. Be careful that what you communicate to your child is what you want your child to become. Future artists and teachers and even good dads and moms are created the minute they hear that kind of affirmation. We just need to stop and think about what we are really saying.

When my son makes his bed, it's still a mess. I can't resist redoing it. Do his sloppy methods say anything regarding his feelings about himself?

His actions might not, but your actions definitely do. When your son does something and receives continuous criticism for doing it, he can begin to feel like he doesn't measure up. You can avoid doing this by:

- Being sure your child understands, both verbally and non-verbally, your unconditional love for him, no matter what he does.
- Giving your child jobs to do that he can handle in incre-

ments. Maybe the job you have given him is too hard.
- Not being such a nag about less-than-perfect performance. Praise him for jobs well done. Watch for improvement. Then move on.
- Resisting comparisons between children.
- Being sure you teach him the skills before each task is begun. I used my son's bed-making once as an object lesson. I showed him how when the bed is lumpy on the inside, no amount of work on the outside can hide it. Then we talked about how important it is to work on things on the inside of us (our character) before anything else. Clint sometimes still does a messy job, but he knows how to do it right—both the bed and his own character.

How do I find something good to praise my son about? He's been doing everything wrong lately.

Praise is hard to come up with sometimes, but it must be given regularly and correctly if you are going to foster a good attitude.

Make a list of every good thing about each of your children. Use this information to praise them. Be specific. Build details into your comments. You can even put it in writing to each child. Catch them being good at something—such as putting the bread away without being told or saying a kind word to someone. There's good in everyone. Sometimes we just need to step back to see it. All the time, we need to acknowledge it.

Do I just ignore the things my son does wrong?

If done the correct way, criticism can be a motivator. Just be sure that your criticism to your child has a positive purpose.

- We need to help them rethink wrong actions into something better.
- When we start with the positives, it's easier to challenge the negatives. Such a statement might be: "John, you have the marks of a really strong and effective leader. That gives you a lot of responsibility to recognize when to use those strengths. In cases like today when you yelled at your brother, how could you have dealt with him differently?" This helps us concentrate on the behavior and not the person.
- We should provide clear instructions for performance. If we say, "You put the dishes in the dishwasher pretty quickly. Tomorrow if you get it done by 6:30, you can go out and play before it gets dark."
- We need to forgive and forget. If you throw old mistakes up in your son's face, he'll do the same in his relationships.

- We need to correct our children in private. Don't humiliate them in front of others. Humiliation shreds self-esteem.
- We should verbalize confidence in our children. "I know you can do it." Once when I went to speak at a camp and had to stay overnight, the babysitter didn't show up. The camp was inaccessible, so I couldn't be reached by phone. My children alerted the neighbors and made some really good decisions. While I was visibly shaken at the mistake, I rewarded my children for their maturity and good planning.

Does teamwork in the home help self-esteem?

When kids are consulted over something as simple as "How do I look?" it raises their self-esteem. We have family meetings in which everyone contributes equally to the issue at hand. Sometimes we choose something fun to do. Other times we dissect a problem that must be worked through. All members of the family contribute suggestions, information, and opinions. One single dad I know had his children brainstorm with him and then draw up a family mission statement. The words were broad yet specific enough that they described what the family stood for. Once that was done, goals—as well as boundaries—were easier for them to set as a family.

When teamwork is used in the home, everyone is more likely to buy in to the rules. Each member feels like an important part of the process and better, more thought-out decisions, result. Everyone learns to respect everyone else's opinions. Rules are kept and goals are reached more quickly as the members feel good about themselves and the product.

How important is it that I touch my child?

Very important.

When I was married, I helped my father-in-law deliver twin foals one morning. Immediately the mare was beside her babies licking, nudging, nursing, and rubbing them. My father-in-law explained that bodily functions of the horse, such as the excretory system, do not start working until the baby experiences touches from the mother.

Touching is important and should be as natural as breathing. Kids and adults who get eight to ten meaningful touches a day are known to maintain better emotional and physical health. Think of how much you and I need hugs sometimes. Your kids need them every day. Do it with your eyes, arms, and words.

But shouldn't my child be self-motivated?

When I was trained to be a teacher, I was instructed to reward children outwardly a great deal in the beginning of an activity. As progress continues, reward less frequently, and finally replace reward with the satisfaction of a job well done.

Intrinsic motivation is the goal for all of us, but you might need to help the process along. It doesn't come naturally for everyone, but it can be learned and developed. Instilling internal motivation in your child will keep him moving forward in spite of discouragement, mistakes, and setbacks. How can single parents build in this inner desire?

- *Believe in yourself.* Do all you can to correct things, then concentrate on the many good things in your life. Allow positive thoughts to dominate your thinking such as: "I am worthy." "I can handle what comes my way." A verse in the Bible reminds us to dwell on the good things: "Whatever is true, . . . noble, . . . right, . . . pure, . . . lovely, . . . admirable—if anything is excellent or praiseworthy—think about such things."[2]
- *Develop necessary qualities.* Welcome challenges. Adapt to change. Develop pride in your achievements—from baking a cake to getting a raise. Set goals that are stimulating and challenging. And in all these things, let the kids observe the process.

- *Overcome fear.* Use the things you are afraid of to motivate you to action. Starbuck, mate of a ship in Herman Melville's book *Moby Dick*, said, "I'll have no man in my boat who is not afraid of the whale." Fear creates stress, panic, and anxiety and immobilizes your achievement of plans and goals. But if used constructively to motivate you toward change, fear can be a constructive force.
- *Model motivation.* We delay diets, exercise programs, and letter writing to long-lost friends. Get in motion, today. As your momentum builds, so will your motivation. Your kids will catch the vision—guaranteed!
- *Focus on the rewards.* Help your children visualize the positive consequences you will enjoy. Make it such a good picture that you will do almost anything to be part of it.
- *Assign chores.* Having duties assigned in the home is one of the most effective ways to teach responsibility.

Thirty-Two Ways to Build Self-Esteem in Children

Only you know your child, what motivates him, and how to help him feel good about himself. Read through the following suggestions and see if they spark some ideas of your own:

- Let your child be "special" for a day. We have a red plate that says "You are special." On birthdays or special-event days, the honored person finds the red plate at his place at the table.
- Allow each child to help make decisions and give opinions. When I moved Courtney to another school in March one year, she found the adjustment difficult. Rather than hand all the decisions down to her without input, she and I discussed the matters and their options, such as the other schools she could attend. Even when our conclusions were not her preferences, she enjoyed being brought along.
- Keep promises. We have an understanding in our family that promises will always be kept, though sometimes they are delayed. This makes me careful about what I promise, and it makes the children aware of just how important their word is.
- Laugh at your child's jokes. You'll be surprised at how funny she really is.

Thirty-Two Ways to Build Self-Esteem in Children

- Compliment him often. Too often we zero in on the negatives and fail to recognize the positives in our children's lives.
- Display your child's school and activity pictures, work, and awards.
- Let your child teach you something.
- Stop and answer your child's questions without judgment or condemnation as they are asked. Keep those lines of communication open.
- Do all you can to help your child pursue dreams and interests. Let him try out things he chooses. Teach her how to reach beyond the ordinary to excellence.
- Be involved in school and extracurricular activities with your child.
- Allow for your child's individuality. Encourage exploration of things that interest him.
- Teach your son or daughter rejection-coping skills and instill the courage to follow through on issues.
- Draw clear boundaries and allow your child to experience consequences. Be consistent. Kids will complain and test the limits to see if you really care what they do, but inwardly they appreciate adults who are consistent, respectful, and firm.
- Allow your child to fail at some things and teach him how to respond to failure.
- Instill in your children accountability for their actions. Model how you have people in your life who hold you accountable. Never blame others for your mistakes.
- Say "I'm sorry" when necessary. Be plentiful with the "I love yous."
- Get your child a pet. The companionship of pets can boost a child's emotional health and self-esteem. Pets are loyal, ask no questions, pass no judgments. We have had dogs, cats, gerbils, guinea pigs, a bird named Dixie, and a one-armed frog named Captain Hook.
- Keep reminding your children how much God loves them. God accepts each one as a beloved child, never forgets any

Thirty-Two Ways to Build Self-Esteem in Children

child, and is always with each child. Ask God for the ability to accept each of your children with a love patterned after the generous, unconditional, dependable divine love.

- Treat children as if they already are what you want them to become. Youngsters react to such trust by striving to live up to parental expectations.

- Work every day on being a better parent. The longer I go and the better I get at some things, the more areas I see that I need to work on. There is always room for improvement, and it's good to let your kids see you making those improvements.

- Drop your concerns and problems when you come home, and focus on your children. When you arrive home from work, you may still be under the stress of job-related problems. Identify a receptacle near the door where you can mentally stuff the cares of the day before meeting your family.

- At bedtime, affirm your love and comment on some strength in each child. These words will go to sleep with the child that night.

- Express confidence in the child's decision-making ability.

- Regardless of your individual interests, support the group activities in which your child participates.

- Make your child's friends feel welcome in your home.

- Create opportunities for your children to bond with their grandparents and other relatives as often as possible.

- Show your children how to defuse the negative elements in their lives that destroy high self-esteem.

- Help your child establish goals.

- Allow your children's own self-confidence to motivate others.

- Don't overprotect your child. Let him know you believe in him and his ability to do the job. My daughters complained to me that I was "always" (it seems to be "always" or "never" with kids) defending their younger brother. Just as I was about to defend him once again, Clint spoke up. "Mom, you do. Let me get myself out of the situation." It took a little waking up, but I was reminded to step aside and let my "baby" work his own way through conflicts.

Thirty-Two Ways to Build Self-Esteem in Children

- Don't humiliate your child—ever. Once when I was a child, I was playing with a man in the back of our church. I loved the attention, and I got carried away and stepped on his toe. I made the decision to do this just as my dad walked up to us. My dad promptly pulled back his hand and slapped me across the face in front of everyone standing around. I don't remember the pain, but I do remember the total humiliation that I felt long after the event. I cowered after that when I saw people who had witnessed the slap. Our efforts and those of our children should build each other up. Constructive criticism should be delivered in private.

- Resist perfectionism. Today, I walked into the house at the end of the day and before I said hello to my children, I listed which of their chores weren't done—the garbage can was still at the curb, breakfast dishes were still on the counter, and beds were unmade. As I stirred the macaroni that night, my heart ached as I thought about my unretractable words. I wanted to walk in the door all over again and shower love on them and listen to them first. Then I wanted to affirm them for what they did do right—got an A on an exam, made the basketball team, and so on. Though the undone chores needed to be dealt with, my perfectionism came through in lots of nasty ways—including the unspoken words, "You're never quite good enough."

I'll try to do better tomorrow.

21

Preparing the Kids

Though I went to college years ago to become a teacher, my real teaching has taken place at home, with my children. I can impart to them what they need to know to move out on their own—if I remain available, observant, and wise. They need to be adept at things such as choosing good friends, managing money, and making the right value choices.

"Train a child in the way he should go, and when he is old he will not turn from it."[1]

The list is endless of all the last-minute things we think about as we pack our kids for the inevitable venture into adulthood.

What else does your child need?

What You Should Know

The saying goes, "Give a man a fish, and he'll eat for a day. Teach a man how to fish, and he'll eat for a lifetime."

As busy single parents, we often don't think we have enough time to sit down and teach skills to our children. Instead of being bothered with the way my daughter folds the laundry, I find one more way of doing it myself.

When my husband and I were building our house, we began by having a foundation dug. Then we brought others along to contribute to that construction process: builders built, plumbers plumbed, brickers bricked, and drywallers drywalled. Each worker used their skill to build upon the work of the one before, and each took pride in the ultimate product. Think of what it would have been like if the drywallers had come to do their work before the walls had gone up.

Our goal is to make our children independent thinkers and doers. They should not have to start from scratch when they leave us to go out on their own. Instead, they should have been involved in the building process and gained from the skills of both parents along the way. This can be done by:

- *Teaching.* Once I asked my six-year-old daughter to load the dishwasher. When I opened the door, things fell on the floor, and I was irritated. But then I realized I had never instructed her how to do the job—no matter how simple it appeared to me. As your child takes on new responsibilities, be sure she knows how to do them.
- *Being specific.* I can't usually say "Go clean your room" to my son. Rather, I make lists that describe specific areas for him to work on—his closet, bathroom, and drawers.
- *Allowing for creativity.* Give them creative license. My son likes to wash the dishes, put them in the sink, then drown all of them with the spray rinser. This object intrigues him greatly. Though this isn't the way I do things, I have found it best to let him do some things his way. It may not be as quick or as thorough as mine, but it gets the job done and he has fun in the process.
- *Praising them.* When a job is done well, let your children know. Release them from some small task because of the

thoroughness with which they did another. Watch them beam when you tell them these things.
- *Sticking around.* Don't leave them on their own too long before they are ready. In order to teach your kids, you must be available. Carve special time to spend with your children. Include them in the things you have to do. Leave them as infrequently as you can.
- *Giving the opportunity to make decisions.* Your children need experience in making sound decisions. Allow these while they are still under your watchful eye.

Questions You Ask

Character Traits

My 8-year-old son lies a lot. How can I reinforce how important it is to tell the truth?

I have often had to deal with misbehavior from one or the other of my children. But every time, I have tried to reward them for their honesty. Ashley was about four when I discovered crayon marks on the wall of the guest bedroom. "Who did this?" I asked as I stared at Ashley and two-year-old Courtney. "I did," Ashley responded.

I handed her the cleanser and a clean rag. She had to scrub the mess instead of watching her favorite show, but I praised her for her honesty. I would have opportunities to do this over and over again as the years went by. What came of it? A child whose word I could count on no matter what she had to lose.

Be sure to model the importance of telling the truth in your own life. Set specific consequences your son can count on if he lies again, such as losing TV privileges for a week.

I experienced a lot of physical abuse from my husband while we were married. Since the divorce, our daughter has watched and listened as my ex-husband has berated and showed disrespect toward me. Now that she's older, she is beginning to show the same disrespect for me and a disregard for adult authority in general. What can I do?

Begin by respecting your daughter. When Ashley was three, she poured fish food on the bathroom floor. I sent her to her bedroom, cleaned up the mess, then went to have a stern talk with her. I decided the best punishment would be to take away a short trip we were planning for the next day. I informed her we would not be taking the trip.

Ashley looked at me and said, "But you already gave me that."

That's the moment I learned respect for my child. I had already rewarded her with something because of good behavior she had exhibited. That deal was done.

It was a nonnegotiable item. I responded, "You're right. If you were the mom and I were the little girl, what would you do?" I think Ashley learned much about respect that day herself.

After you have modeled respect for your daughter, demand it from her. Do not respond to requests that are not polite. Design consequences for acts of disrespect, then carry them out: "If you speak disrespectfully to me one time this week, you will not spend the night with Julie on Friday." You are teaching your daughter there are consequences for our actions, and you are demonstrating a code for right and wrong behavior.

How can I make my son more thankful for what he has?

I like to sing hymns to God for his gifts. Many of the psalms demonstrate thanksgiving, such as Psalm 95:2.

Most of us struggle with teaching our children gratitude. Expose your son through volunteer work to those less fortunate. Sponsor a hungry child overseas with money you save from not eating out one meal. Help your son be happy with what he has. Here are two areas where you might start:

- *Budgeting.* Let your son see how much money comes in and then how much goes back out. This will teach him that money does not flow from an endless stream. Columnist Mary Hunt advises that we stop giving allowances as soon as our children are ready and start giving "salaries." Agree upon those things for which your child is responsible and have him set priorities in making his own purchases. It sounds as though your son may be ready for this valuable lesson.

One parent from Indiana allowed her children to choose only three gifts for Christmas to simulate the three gifts Jesus was brought—gold, frankincense, and myrrh.

Also, limit your son's extra-curricular activities. If you don't, you will become a slave to his schedule and will reinforce his need to be in charge.

- *Giving.* Model for your son the concept of giving back part of what you have. This includes giving to the offering at church. You can also help him find ways to share—outgrown toys and Christmas presents for the needy. On Thanksgiving morning, start your day by volunteering at a local soup kitchen. Let your son experience the joy of giving to others. Chances are he will enjoy that turkey leg a lot more when he returns home.

How do I help my daughter be content? When she was young, she wanted everything she saw advertised on TV. Now she wants what everyone else is wearing. What should I do?

I hope you asked this question and did something about it when your daughter was much younger.

I recently took Courtney and a friend to the mall. Her friend went from store to store picking out the things she wanted. She even called her mom to see if I could buy something for her and her mother would pay me back when we returned. Courtney looked on and, while she admired many of the things she saw, acquiring any of them did not become her passion. My children know the Bible verse "Godliness with contentment is great gain."[2]

Let her see contentment in you through your conversation ("I can wear the dress I wore last year. It still looks good."). Let her also see those who have much but are not happy. Let her know what it is to go without and then be happy with what she has. Let her hear you give thanks to God regularly for all things.

Single parents have an advantage when it comes to contentment. Because most of us can't afford to lavish gifts on our children, what we can give has more value.

Because of my working schedule, my son comes home to an empty house. By the time I get home, he has done nothing but sit in front of

the TV for hours. He has become more aggressive towards kids in the neighborhood and toward me. What can I do?

Television can have a terrible effect on our children. One study involved a Canadian community where TV was introduced in 1973. Inappropriate aggression was monitored before TV's introduction and two years afterward. The rate of aggression in the community increased 160 percent after the introduction of TV.[1]

The Center for Media and Public Affairs in Washington D.C. tallied the violence that appeared on on April 7, 1994 across 10 TV channels from 6 a.m. till midnight. They recorded 2,605 violent scenes, an average of 15 acts of violence per channel per hour. This number represented a 41 percent increase over a similar study two years earlier.[2]

By the time the average child leaves elementary school, he will have witnessed 8,000 murders and 100,000 other acts of violence on TV. Saturday morning TV viewing hosts 20–25 violent acts per hour.

You should not take anything away from your son without putting back something better in its place. See if one of thse suggestions works for you.

- Make arrangements with a friend and business owner you know, and see if he or she has odd jobs that can occupy your son after school.
- Put your son on a salary and hold him accountable to completing certain jobs in a given period of time.
- Get your son involved in sports or other extra curricular activities. This commitment involves many after-school practices and might be costly in time and money. But it will be far less expensive than leaving your son to flounder on his own.
- Become a mother/son team and work with some volunteer organization—reading to occupants of nursing homes, feeding the homeless, etc. Allow your son to become a giver and see you doing this as well.
- Do things with your son he likes to do—camping, riding bikes, taking pictures, building, or traveling. This will give him other things to do besides sitting in front of the tube.
- Set specific rules for monitored TV viewing. If these are not abided by, get rid of your TV. I know one single dad in Boulder, Colo. who raised his son and daughter alone for about 13 years. For 11 of those years, they have been without a TV altogether. Both teens are involved in sports, and the daughter even sews her own clothes. They are two of the

most well-rounded and gracious kids I know.

Whatever you do, do it now. Take charge before it's too late for your son.

How can I teach my son to stick with something?

Our kids come from homes where only one parent has been around most of the time. They often see the weak commitment to marriage so prevalent in today's society mirrored in other areas of life. I have worked hard to stress to my children the importance of commitment through:

- Having them finish out the season of a sport they tried but didn't like.
- Finishing a task in a timely fashion—cleaning their rooms, washing the dishes.
- Doing what they promised.
- Sticking with a job when the benefits are not observable.

What are the best ways to instill responsibility in our children?

As you know, schedules and routines have been important since your children's youngest years. Work around the house should be no different. Your children need to learn that furniture still gets dusty and laundry is soiled even during vacations and on days when they can sleep late.

Create a chart or list of what chores need to be accomplished, with a deadline when each chore

needs to be done. If you and your ex can coordinate, work together on which chores are to be done at both houses. Then allow your children to develop good work habits by functioning within those limits and making some decisions about when chores get done. Be sure to administer appropriate consequences for incomplete or unacceptable work on chores— no TV or playtime or time spent with friends.

Because of what your children have been through, it is even more important that you provide routine and standards. Clearly communicate expectations, and consistently administer discipline.

Life Skills

Since my time is so limited, how will I know which life skills are the most important?

When our children were infants, it seemed they would be with us always. But we learned quickly that they are only on loan to us. That's why we must start giving them back from the beginning. To attempt to keep them to ourselves is a violation of God's plan and is why we often feel resistance from the kids.

Children start to separate themselves in their early years by doing things their way in their own time and by seeking their own identities.

We should prepare our children to leave instead of making them dependent on us. Everything we do with them should get them ready for their own adult lives. Most of the information we gather through on-the-job training or through books we read can be adapted to teach our children. Give your kids strong foundations in the following areas:

- *Money management.* Let your child choose a pretend profession that earns him a specific salary. Show him how to subtract his taxes and tithes, thus showing his net spendable income. Then cut him a pretend check. Together, generate a budget by helping him determine the categories and what percentage he should spend in each. Then hold him to it. Share as much as you can of your own pay stubs and your capital outlay each month.
- *Boundary development.* With young children, begin with a picture to color. With a crayon, outline the border of each item in the picture, noting that the elements of the picture would blend together without that clear definition. Start the child thinking from her earliest years how she can take control of her own life and dictate who she will become and what she will stand for in the areas of friendships, values, and communication.
- *Goal setting.* Help your child set small goals while he is young (e.g., to save twenty dollars by Christmas.) Then assist in establishing objectives for achieving those goals. As the child grows, help him decide what he wants to be when he is out of high school and what it will take to get there.
- *Time management.* This area is often overlooked, but it is never too early to start learning. Let your daughter know that she has only five hours from the time she gets home from school until she goes to bed. Dinner preparation, eating, and cleanup will involve one hour. One hour should go toward homework. Thirty minutes should be spent on bathing and getting ready for bed. That leaves a little over two hours for play, talking on the phone, doing chores, and so on. Help her budget that time appropriately.
- *Decision making.* Teach your children to recognize different propaganda devices found on TV and in advertisements: "Everyone is doing it" or "To be cool and fit in, you simply must . . ." Then start showing your children refusal skills and ways to make informed decisions based on God's value system, which you have made clear to them over the years

by reading the Bible with them. Give your children opportunities to make their own choices as they grow. This way they get practice with not only making the decisions, but in living with the consequences. Resist rescuing your children.

- *Communication.* Impress on your child the importance of conveying her feelings and beliefs. Teach your child non-threatening, assertive communication skills—from the importance of eye contact, a firm handshake, and dialogue when introducing your child to a stranger to long-term interchange between friends.

- *Self-help strategies.* Anything you must do around the house can be taught to your child, including laundry, housekeeping, and minor maintenance.

Seize the moments that you have with your child now. Love, spend time, listen, and share everything you learn—all while you are helping him pack for his own trip into adulthood.

Relationships

My children seem to fuss at each other all the time. Are there things I can do to promote friendship among them?

At one time I could relate each and every sordid detail that broke up our home. It took a long time for me to begin turning loose

those things. But I soon discovered how true the old saying is: "If mama ain't happy, ain't nobody happy." Holding on to those yucky things was like being in control of the light switches in a dark room. No lights came on, and few advances were made as long as the one in charge was remaining a prisoner to the past.

I finally realized that we were still a family, and families needed people and rules and a whole lot of love. Since the children had no grandparents or aunts and uncles around, our church filled those roles. My children became comfortable around strangers, adults as well as children. We were a team joining many other teams. Our home operated according to specific rules—things we always or never did. My children learned a sense of encouragement and responsibility for each other. Though they had minor tiffs, more often than not they were huddled in a corner whispering or playing in the backyard. We have learned through the hardships to band together and defend each other. When one of the members is weakened, our team cannot play the game.

Two keys become necessary: Focus on the good things. And laugh. Life wasn't always drudgery. Learning to see the fun in the day, the humor in situations, and the funny things my kids do and say brought back the laughter and unified the team. And we have become good friends along the way.

I have never talked to my son about sex. How do I know when it's time? What do I tell him?

One day Clint and I were riding home from the doctor's office. He was seven, and though I had broached the subject before, I felt it was time to do it again. We were having one of our rare moments alone, so I made a stab at it.

"Clint," I began, "we have talked before about where babies come from? Remember when you helped your dad breed horses? . . ."

My white knuckles squeezed the steering wheel as I asked, "Do you have any questions?"

"Yes," he said.

Oh rats! I thought. *I don't have time for this today.*

"What do mountain lions eat?" he asked.

We talked about mountain lions for a second. Then I ruffled his hair and said, "About this baby thing. You are going to hear other kids talk about a lot of different things. Come to me with any questions you have. If I don't know the answers, I'll find them out and get back to you."

I learned a lot about talking about sex that afternoon.

- Don't make it harder than it is.

- Be aware of what your child is being exposed to. Be the first to explain things—the right way.
- Use things existing naturally around you to help in that explanation.
- Tell your son what he needs to know now. He will let you know when you've said enough.
- Keep the lines of communication open. Never treat sex or the questions about it as a dirty thing.
- Replace fiction with fact. Tell him the way things really are so he can be informed.

How can I teach my children to do a better job of selecting a mate than I did?

To be most efficient at the grocery store, you take a shopping list to avoid forgetting the essentials. When your child is young, generate a family shopping list for selecting friends. This begins the habit of judging character and selecting relationships based on specific criteria. Once your children begin looking for a possible mate, it will be natural to choose qualities that will outlast the fireworks of first love. Your list might resemble the following:

- *Character.* What values do I see displayed in this person's life? Integrity? Honesty? Responsibility?
- *Parenting skills.* How does he respond to others—children, the less fortunate? Does he

More Ways to Prepare Your Kids

- Talk often about how to treat others and how one should expect to be treated.

- Give your daughter mock situations when she will need to make a quick decision, resolve conflict, or manage her anger.

- Communicate effectively about everything—even the touchy issues. One single mom wrote to tell about her young daughter asking once how to make *babies*. The mom frantically was thinking about the answer she would share when the child interrupted her thoughts: "Is it 'ies' or 'ys'?" Don't let the delicacy of the topic affect your explanations. If your child can't get the answer from you, she'll go someplace else.

- Watch for moments to bring home certain points—then bring them on home. When my children were little, we lived on a horse farm where we bred our horses. They saw the act of procreation in a natural way. So when it came time to talk about sex, we talked about the "birds and the horses."

- Teach your child to be inquisitive, discerning, and attentive. This will often allow him to distinguish between the truth and a lie.

- Allow for some creativity. Let your child know about alternatives to getting into compromising situations. Be candid about sexual temptations before dating is even an issue. Share the dangers of premature sex and the benefits of waiting for sex until after marriage.

show compassion and patience? How self-centered is he?

- *Appearance.* Is a large measure of what he loves about me something that could change, such as my looks?

- *Ambition.* Does she strive for her best and want to learn more? Is she helping me reach my goals?

- *Chemistry.* Will the physical attraction I feel stand the test of time and difficulties?

- *Spirituality.* What does he truly believe in? Do his priorities square with mine?

- *Flexibility.* Is he willing to adapt to suit others' needs or wants?

- *Life skills.* How well has she mastered important life skills such as communicating, resolving conflict, handling anger? Have I noticed ways her values, habits, use of money, or interests differ from mine?

6

What Are You Learning?

Skills

Two and a half years after my husband left, our divorce became final. Those years were a busy time when I felt every emotion one could feel. I cried constantly, prayed daily, and sought help and direction from others. Besides giving birth and raising three children on my own during that time, I, like most others, had to find a way to make a living. I had taught school before I married and had no desire to continue with that profession.

For eighteen months the children and I remained on my husband's family farm, so moving became necessary. I began to look around for both a job and a new home. Eventually I found an opportunity to go back to school to earn my doctorate. We moved to a city about eighty miles away in a neighboring state before the final divorce was issued. It was far enough to start a new life, but close enough to keep my children in contact with their dad. I taught courses for the university while I earned my degree. This paid for all my schooling and gave me a small salary each month. We moved into an apartment and our new life began.

Who's the Leader of the Band?

My program involved work in several areas. Among them were classes in corporate training and administration. As my course work progressed, I began to learn much about leadership skills. Some definitions in particular got my attention, such as the following:

- Individuals in leadership influence, inspire, rally, direct, encourage, motivate, induce, mobilize, and activate others to pursue a common goal and purpose while maintaining commitment, momentum, confidence, and courage.
- The price of leadership is personal sacrifice, rejection, criticism, loneliness, pressure, perplexity, and mental and physical fatigue.
- Qualities of leadership include purpose, passion, integrity, trust, curiosity, and daring. Leaders clarify the vision, provide the quality, create the future leaders, and keep the momentum going.

Why did this information interest me so?

Because every morning and every night, I worked at a job that was much more demanding and important than the one I called my vocation. I was an administrator who influenced, inspired, rallied, directed, encouraged, motivated, induced, mobilized, and activated three little kids to pursue a common goal and purpose while maintaining commitment, momentum, confidence, and courage.

I was well acquainted with the personal sacrifice this job demanded. And some days, it took all the purpose, passion, integrity, trust, curiosity, and daring I could muster to keep the momentum going. I was involved in my own leadership training on the home front.

I began to look at my parenting responsibilities in a new light. No leader anywhere has more crucial tasks to perform than moms and dads have—especially those who are single. I discovered that sometimes we inherit this position simply because there's no one else to do the job. And just because we do does not mean we are automatically effective leaders. It takes attending a lot of courses, tons of homework, and extensive reading and teaching by others.

That's when I took a second look at my skills in areas such as setting goals, finding balance, dealing with conflict, combating stress, coping with change, enhancing communication, finding time, and managing money.

My children are now eleven, thirteen, and fifteen. I sometimes get more opportunities than I like to practice these skills. I'm not proficient at all of them yet, and sometimes I fail the tests. But my hard work pays high dividends in the end. After all, I, like you, am helping to clarify the vision, provide the quality, and create future leaders. That makes it worth the effort.

22

Setting Goals

During the most desperate times of my life, I have discovered I have no more dreams. I don't know whether the lack of dreams causes me to slip into down times or whether difficulties cause me to lose focus on my dreams. Whichever it is, I have begun my healing process more than one time by reexamining my dreams and goals.

When people go through times of great hurt and disappointment, they often discover that life no longer holds any purpose. Their dreams have been dashed. They live life from day to day.

When we as single parents work through the frenzy of the circumstances that brought us to parenting alone, we are forced to regroup. But with the fatigue, fear, and low self-esteem we feel, this becomes difficult to do. What we need is a clear grasp of purpose and a rebirth of our dreams.

"Purpose is the key to life," says Myles Munroe. "Without purpose, life has no meaning. . . . Purpose is the master of motivation and the mother of commitment. It is the source of enthusiasm and the womb of perseverance. Purpose gives birth to hope and instills the passion to act. . . . Until purpose is discovered, existence has no meaning, for purpose is the source of fulfillment."[1]

Everything in life has a purpose. Purpose is the why of our existence. If we lose sight of this, life can become haphazard and can lead to disappointment and dead ends.

What You Should Know

It's never too late to develop dreams. Poet Langston Hughes writes, "Hold fast to dreams, for when dreams die, life is a broken-winged bird that cannot fly. Hold fast to dreams, for when dreams go, life is a barren field covered with snow."

Author Carl Sandburg wrote, "Nothing happens unless first a dream."

The Bible says, "Record the vision and inscribe it on tablets, That the one who reads it may run. 'For the vision is yet for the appointed time; It hastens toward the goal, and it will not fail. Though it tarries, wait for it; For it will certainly come, it will not delay.'"[2]

Dreams help us discover talents and potential we might never have known we had. Dreams give us a direction and a purpose to work toward. Dreams allow us to see the possibilities that something good will happen when things around us really stink. Dreams revive hope. Dreams help us see reality through God's eyes.

Divorce can't destroy our dreams. Dreams look at life as God meant it to be—even when we have buried a spouse. Dreams add color to our black-and-white existence—even when the one we counted on has walked away. Most great steps taken by human beings have begun with and have been sustained by a dream. Don't let anything or anyone take that away from you.

If you breathe, you have a purpose and a destiny that grew out of your God-given passions.

What do you need to know about your passions?

- *You were born with passions.* What talents, interests, desires, and experiences have burned inside you through the years?
- *Passions evoke emotions.* What do you want more than anything?
- *Passions don't have to be forced.* What would you fight for?
- *Passion is accompanied by fear.* Pursuing your passions is sometimes scary.

Questions You Ask

Since my divorce, I have felt so victimized. How can I have dreams when I don't feel like I'm in control of my life?

A victim mentality will fatigue and frustrate you and cause you to depend on other people, relationships, and situations to provide your security. My husband had become the object of my affection and the center of my existence. I depended on him for my well-being, and when he let me down, I despised him. I felt as though things were happening to me over which I had no control.

Almost always, single parenting stops us dead in our tracks on the path we are walking. It often launches us in a whole different direction and forces us to regroup. If we continue to believe our lives are beyond our control, we just stumble along and take whatever life hands us and our kids.

But we have another choice—we can have a say in how things turn out. We can make plans, dream dreams, and decide on goals for what lies around the bend for our families. The choice is ours, and our children are watching while we make that choice.

I don't even know who I am anymore. My identity was wrapped up in my husband and in our ten years of marriage. I don't know where to begin to find my way.

You must come to grips with your own identity before you can move forward with your plans. Get acquainted with your strengths and weaknesses, skills and gifts, interests and ambitions. Defining your identity will keep you focused as you set your priorities, organize tasks, deal with emergencies, and meet challenges.

Be careful not to define yourself based on externals—your job or possessions. Rather, look at things that last—ethics, goals, integrity, and spiritual identity—qualities fundamental to how you behave.

Start by examining the following: self-esteem, personal relationships, time management, leisure moments, strengths, and weaknesses. Remember how life looked before you married. Look

at pictures, read diaries, talk to your family—rediscover the characteristics that made you who you are. Old interests may spark new enthusiasm to pursue unique challenges. Close examination of these areas will help you decide what you want to eliminate, change, or make better in the days ahead.

I was married for eight years. My husband made all the major decisions in our family. Now that I am alone, I am trying to sort out my own values. Is this unusual?

Unusual? Maybe, but it happens. When we moved to Ohio following the divorce, my oldest daughter was starting kindergarten. None of our children had had any vaccinations. My husband had read much about the adverse effects they could cause, and we did not subject our children to them. I had relinquished control in this area to my husband since he knew more about the topic. But when the schools were telling me I had to get her vaccinated or sign a paper saying that it was against my beliefs, I was confused.

Was it against my beliefs? What were my beliefs? I was fearful after all I had heard about the possible side effects of vaccinations. Yet I knew the value of them as well. In addition, I was conscious of the feelings I had against my ex-husband. I didn't want to act out of vengeance toward him in an area that had such a profound effect on the children.

The day arrived when I had to make a decision. I took my daughter to the doctor and had him vaccinate her. The same day, I prayed for protection for Ashley. I also prayed that God would keep my heart feeling and reacting the way he would want it to in all these situations involving my ex-husband.

It takes a while for most of us single parents to sort through these kinds of issues—especially when the former mate has betrayed us in some way. We try to decide which values we genuinely own and which we turn away from—independent from the person we were intimately connected to before. This is true for the divorced, the never-married, and the widowed.

By clarifying what you stand for, you will create a basis upon which to build your personal life and career. Here are some questions that will help you determine your personal values: What is my attitude toward other people? What moral issues are important to me? What are my responsibilities to my family and community? What values do I want to impart to my children?

Then take a look at other parts of your life and ask yourself: How important is having contact with people? What do I value most at work? Do I feel a need to make the world a better place? What are my priorities for personal fulfillment? Based on the information you discover, make your decision and don't look back.

I have been a single dad for two years. I am more stable than I was in the beginning and feel I know who I am. How do I go about establishing goals for myself?

If you don't keep your sight on a specific goal, you could wander off course, so you are wise to plan.

In your personal life, goals should be an extension of your values. They should be challenging, realistic, and stated specifically such as "I will read two books this month to help me grow spiritually," or "I will lose five pounds."

In your professional life, your values are also important. Set specific goals. Write them down and reward yourself when you achieve them. Share your vision with people at work. Your goals can be a powerful motivational tool such as "I will take a course this year to expand my knowledge in _____" or "I will work on my communication skills."

I think I know who I am and where I'm headed. How do I get there?

As soon as you determine your goal, create a plan toward

reaching that goal. List your goal, the activities you need to do to reach it, who or what can help you accomplish each step, and a target date for accomplishing each activity. Suppose you decide you want a better job, and to do that you want to fulfill your life-long dream of completing your college degree. How many credits do you need? Do you require counseling in your field? Where can you go to find financial help? Who can help you with the children while you work?

Brainstorm all the factors that will contribute to making this dream come true. Decide what people and resources you need to accomplish your dream. Then go for it. As challenging as it will be, accomplishing a goal such as this will do wonders for other areas of your life, such as self-esteem and parenting.

How can I be sure my motivation is not like last year's New Year's resolution—quickly forgotten?

Develop discipline. Stick to an action plan even when you'd rather do other things. Develop the necessary self-control to achieve your goals.

When I chose to go back to school and get my doctorate, I had to become more disciplined than I had ever been. While people I knew were out having fun, I had my nose in a book. When other lights in our apart-

ment complex remained out in the wee hours, mine came on and the books came open, sometimes as early as 3 A.M.

Once when I set my alarm, I accidentally advanced the time by two hours. I got up, studied, fed the children, and got us out the door. I wondered why it was so dark, but I assumed the weather had something to do with it. But in the car, the clock said 4 A.M. I turned and looked at my two-, four-, and six-year-old children in the back with their heads against the seat, sleeping. We gathered our things and went back inside for a little more rest.

Self-discipline involves doing what needs to be done rather than what you would like to do at that moment. Only you can make it happen. Don't wait! Practice good habits in small ways—exercise regularly, eat in moderation, spend quiet time, and make time for fun.

While I was involved in my course work at the university, I found an outlet in wallpapering my house. Over time, I finished five rooms. It was a creative, non-intellectual activity that I enjoyed when the kids were gone and showed immediate signs of progress. Developing control in your daily life is the first step toward learning that you can control your success and happiness.

How can I teach my kids that they can do things now toward reaching their goals?

You are already doing much by setting your own example. Show them how big tasks can be completed through small steps. If your daughter wants to be a graphic designer one day, expose her to shows and magazines that promote that interest. Get a description from a local college on what is required to earn that degree. Help her plan her high-school classes to be working toward that end.

Assist your children in identifying time wasters such as talking on the phone too long or failing to organize. Show your children how to focus on specific goals. The key to self-discipline is to defer your gratification from the present to the future. Guide them toward saving their money for that big purchase a month down the line.

How can I begin setting my goals?

Many successful individuals claim you can be anything you want to be, have anything you want, and do anything you choose—provided you set some goals and prioritize the necessary steps to achieve them. When you want something badly enough, it's usually worth your time and effort. List your goals, using the questions below, even if your goals seem unreachable.

My most important CAREER goal (e.g., a new job, more pay)

in one year _____ ,
in three years _____ ,
in five years _____ .

My most important HOME goal (e.g., family time together, organization)

in one year _____ ,
in three years _____ ,
in five years _____ .

My most important LEISURE goals (e.g., travel, learn tennis)

in one year _____ ,
in three years _____ ,
in five years _____ .

Then list your steps to achieve each goal. What people and resources will you need?

What do I do once I have reached the goal?

Reward yourself with something that matters to you. Then work toward new goals. Focus on the things you did right in the process and learn from the things you did wrong.

I can think of so many things I wish I had done with my life. How can I encourage my children to pursue their dreams?

Perhaps the greatest way to encourage your children is to let them see you fulfill a dream of your own. It's never too late. And yet, Oliver Wendell Holmes wrote,

"Most people go to the grave with their music still inside them."

Every day your children will share with you the seeds of their dreams—interests in sports, music, drama, or talents in writing, speaking, or dancing. What you do with those seeds will determine how they grow. You can destroy them with discouraging words or by ignoring their interests. You can nurture them by listening, encouraging, and providing opportunities to develop them.

What we do with the seeds of our children's dreams is up to us, the parents.

Florence Littauer writes:

Do you know someone
  who has a song waiting
  to be sung?
Some art waiting to be hung?
A piece waiting to be played?
A scene waiting to be staged?
A tale waiting to be told?
A book waiting to be sold?
A rhyme waiting to be read?
A speech waiting to be said?
If you do, don't let them die
  with the music still
  in them.[3]

That includes our kids.

23

Finding Balance

When I was in first grade, I was playing on the teeter-totter at recess one day with my friend Dottie. When the teacher blew the whistle to signal the need to return to class, I jumped off—though I was in midair. This threw Dottie up with a jerk and then back down with a thud. She hit her chin on the teeter-totter. She has me to thank for losing her first tooth.

I have struggled with balance many other times since first grade, especially as a single mom. I often can't relax or enjoy the quiet. Satisfaction eludes me, and I resort to overachievement.

Years ago on *The Ed Sullivan Show*, a man would juggle balls. He had no problem handling two, three, four, or maybe five of them, but more became a real challenge. He worked hard to keep all the balls in the air and not let any of them fall to the floor. How can single parents do the same? How can we distribute time, energy, and thoughts among the infinite needs of work, family, and personal interests and obligations?

What You Should Know

Setting priorities involves balancing family, career, and personal growth. It involves deciding what is important and distributing our efforts among the things that matter. A balance in this area requires that we ask ourselves, *What do I choose to do?*

One day after Clint had returned from morning kindergarten, he and I ate lunch in the backyard on our old blue picnic table. He soon finished eating and walked across the yard to new adventures. I reached inside the back door for my briefcase. Since it was too heavy to carry, I dragged it across the cement. When I opened it, a to-do list sat perched on top of the contents. I laid it on the table and prepared to accomplish as many of the twenty items as my day would allow. Soon my concentration and copious planning were interrupted by a little six-year-old. "Mom," Clint said, "show me how to make something with my sticks."

My eyes drifted to the bundle of small branches Clint held in his arms, then to the list on the table blowing in the breeze, then back to Clint's big brown eyes— wide with anticipation. I walked into the house to gather glue and scissors and made my way back outside where Clint and I built a little house. At bedtime that night, Clint came to my room and hugged me goodnight. He walked toward the door, then turned around and walked back to me and kissed me on the cheek. "That's for helping me to make something with my sticks."

I didn't accomplish one thing on my list that day. As a matter of fact, I don't even know what happened to the list. But what I chose to do that afternoon still matters over the long haul.

Deciding What's Worth Doing

Ask yourself, *What will it matter in five years? Do I need it? Can I simplify it?* This will help you prioritize, decide what not to do, and discern which things are worth the effort or not worth doing at all.

Reduce your wants! One way to get financial independence is having enough money to buy everything you want. The other is wanting less. Simplify, simplify, simplify. William and Nancie Carmichael say, "Contentment comes not from great wealth but from fewer wants."[1]

Most of the demands on our time come from work, home, and personal obligations. Others come from church, school, friends, and neighbors. Most experts agree that the mind can consistently concentrate on three things (for example, fixing dinner, talking on the phone, and answering the door). You simply have to choose what three they will be. If you decide to do something with a friend, you must slice that commitment from another area, such as rest or time with the kids.

The highest priorities of life fit somewhere within the three mentioned—home, work, and personal. Decide each day on the single most important thing you can do for your family, for your work, and for yourself. List these three under "I choose to do" before listing any "I have to do."

Questions You Ask

I have two children, aged two and four. How can I work and be the mom I should be?

For many of us, our identity is our job. But single parents can explore options such as: job-sharing, part-time, flextime, or working at home. There are many creative ways to raise our children and make a living, too.

Whatever you do, don't trade freedom and time for money and things. Do you really need the better and newer gadget enough to give up the more important things—freedom and time? I recently had a visitor to my home who looked at our old TV (fifteen years old) and an even older VCR and stereo set. "Your house is a burglar's nightmare," he said.

I hope the choice to keep those old products bought more time and freedom with my kids, even if we do have to pound the side of the TV to make it work.

How can I establish priorities?

Among the first things you should do is recognize that work is actually third on your list. Take care of yourself first so you can take care of your family. Then look at what you are doing in these two areas and put them in order of priority: interaction with family members, housekeeping, meal preparation, child care,

laundry, bill-paying, and so on. Do the same with your personal time: sports, hobbies, shopping, and movies. Once you think you have these in order, do the same for your work.

Picture your day as a pie. You slice eight hours for work, eight hours for sleep, and the other eight for the remaining important things in your life. Divide that last part very carefully.

Personal Time

I have trouble keeping a balance with all the things I have to do in a day. It seems I can cover only one or two areas well at a time while excelling at none. How do you recommend I find balance?

We spend the most time on those areas of greatest importance to us. You may be focusing solely on home and career which are demanding a lot of energy from you. You may need to spend more time in leisure.

Private time stabilizes and pulls you away from your responsibilities and allows you to do something for yourself. Most counselors recommend at least three hours a week for personal relaxation and recreation. This time might be spent engaging in a hobby, additional education, or some form of exercise to help you to refill your reserves. However you choose to use it, leisure time is necessary in order to put home and career in true perspective.

Where do I find leisure time?

Start by listing ten of your most important responsibilities at home and at work. Number them from least to most important. Can you eliminate any of these items? Perhaps you will find you can do something over your lunch hour—read a book, take a walk, or write a letter.

Since you have more control on the home front, maybe you should start there to make changes. Ask yourself these questions:

- What responsibilities can I delegate to others?
- Which expectations can I eliminate?
- What new tasks can I teach someone else to do?
- How can I better communicate my expectations?
- Which of my attitudes can be more positive?
- Where do I need to be better organized?

On airplanes we are instructed that, in case of an emergency, the adult is to put an oxygen mask on her own face before helping those who are dependent on her. Time away from career and home responsibilities can refresh your

---

Author Kathy Peel offers "quick-me-ups" to help you save time, money, and stress. Her suggestions include:

- Don't put things down, put them away. Ten minutes a day spent searching for misplaced items adds up to nine lost days a year.

- Listen to your body's circadian rhythm, its daily up-and-down cycles, to discover which time of day is your best. Do your most important work at that time.

- When a bill arrives, open it, put the statement in the mailing envelope, stamp it, and write the due date on the outside. Pay bills twice a month.

- Buy clothing staples such as hosiery and underwear in bulk twice a year.

- To many people, minutes are like pennies—not worth picking up. But add them together and they become valuable. Instead of managing the day, try managing the minutes and see if you have more time to do the things you really want to do.[2]

spirit and make you more efficient for those who are so dependent on you—both at work and at home. Leisure time is a necessity, not a luxury. Go ahead and put the mask on. You'll be glad you did.

I asked my daughter recently where she would like to go on a Saturday when we had nothing scheduled. Her response—"Let's just stay home"—got me thinking. Are our lives too jumbled?

We live in a time that demands overexertion in every way. Compare your life to decorating a room. No matter how much attractive, coordinated furniture you have, too much furniture will diminish the beauty of the whole. All the pieces may be valuable and important to you, but they probably are not all essential.

Your life is much the same. Look around and see what you need to keep and what you need to get rid of. To do this, record your activities for a week and the time it takes you to accomplish each. Next, allow your daughter to help sort the activities into "essential," "nonessential," and "maybe." This will allow you to set some priorities and boundaries that will help both of you guide future decisions.

Does my imbalance reflect bad habits I have developed?

Imbalance often results from bad habits—habits that stress work at the expense of family, structure at the expense of spontaneity, or accomplishments at the expense of relationships.

How many times have you come home from work with no energy left to invest in your family and personal needs? We get so caught up on routines, schedules, and structure that we forget how to be spontaneous, flexible, and fun.

At one point in my single parenting, I was without a job. When people asked me about myself, I realized just how much I measured myself by my achievements and how little by the relationships I had forged—more by my vocation and less by the values I lived by. "Well, I make pretty good meat loaf," I would respond. But because I didn't take enough pride in the meat loaf, both the recipe and the presentation suffered. It was time for me to reassess my priorities.

Everyone I know has time for exercise. I don't. This makes me look and feel bad as well as guilty. Can I change that?

Those you know who are exercising do so simply because it has become their priority. It *is* possible to fit exercise into your day.

Begin by thinking about the kind of exercise you want. Consider your enjoyment, health guidelines, time, and money resources. You may want to join a class or purchase equipment for your home.

Through the years, I have bought at yard sales a small trampoline, stationary bicycle, stepper, slant board, and rowing machine. Do they all get used? No way. But my favorite two—the trampoline and slant board—are accessible to me in my bedroom to use early in the morning, in the evenings while my children do their homework, or while we watch TV.

Commit yourself to one or more activities. Sign up, buy what you need, and tell your friends and family what you plan to do and when. Accomplishing the activity will become more of an issue of accountability and you will get involved.

Finally, follow through. Keep track of the time you have committed to physical exercise. Consider doing your activity with a friend to help ensure commitment. Make it a priority to always show up if you join a group.

I feel guilty doing things for myself.

I had a particularly enlightening airline flight recently. As we were taking off, the stewardess said, "In case of an emergency, leave all your belongings behind."

I stared out the window as we made our ascent and remembered one more time how important it was for me to stay healthy so I could be the best for my kids.

This reminder told me to work the hardest on the things I could take with me—my relationships.

When I still feel guilty about doing this, I read the Bible: "And Jesus grew in wisdom [intellectually] and stature [physically], and in favor with God [spiritually] and men [socially]."[3] He managed to take care of himself, and he had a lot more kids to juggle than I do—since we are his children.

The remarkable thing about doing the right things in the right proportion for yourself is that it is the most unselfish thing you can do.

It seems that on the soccer field and at the parenting meetings at school, all the parents have great accomplishments. I am a dad who is raising my son alone, and it's all I can do to put a roof over our heads, food in our stomachs, and help coach his soccer team.

Moms and dads who live balanced lives with their kids may be less likely to have a bridge or a park or a fountain or a monument named after them. Markers in cemeteries don't tell what books the people they honor wrote, the companies they were president of, or how many times they were on TV. Instead, their monuments explain that they were someone's wife or someone's mother or beloved father or brother. Relationships are what matter in the end.

Kudos to you, Dad. Keep on doing what you're doing. And do it with your head held high.

The Skill of Balance

I have a list of things to do. How do I build balance into them?

Balancing needs to occur daily. If we think about it only once a month or even once a week, we get away from balance on a daily basis. Try setting one priority daily for each important area of your life—family, personal, and work. Then plan everything else around those priorities.

You can also do weekly planning in much the same way every Sunday. Let these choices guide you as you make daily calls. You are controlling your priorities; they are not controlling you.

I structure everything. I am not spontaneous anymore. How can I help my kids discipline themselves and at the same time enjoy life?

Balance involves both structure and spontaneity, both firmness and flexibility, discipline and dreaminess. Balance in attitude allows for planned-for needs and unplanned-for opportunities. This is sometimes hard for the single parent.

I went bike riding last summer with a new friend. It was a rarity for me to get out and do some-

thing I love so much. We talked while I puffed a little up and down Colorado paths. We only had four hours to stay out, so we planned how far we would go. My friend was really intent on the ten-mile-and-back trail we would follow. He stared straight ahead and pumped hard as he talked. I, on the other hand, did not care if we went ten miles or two. I was more interested in the little ants darting from their sandy homes along the trail, the coyote we saw from a distance, the owl that swooped down to a low branch of a tree, and the trickling brook along the way that would not let me pass without my toes dipping in.

In trying to balance our lives, we have two goals: One is to get there, the other is to enjoy the journey. The most balanced person would find an achievable distance that may not be ten miles and ways to enjoy the journey.

One single dad I know, Jerry, realized this just in time. His wife of twenty-something years had just divorced him. All he had left of that relationship were his grown children and a few belongings in his car. He took off on a trip and realized he had gone hundreds of miles and wasn't able to recount anything he had seen along the way. Jerry began to reshuffle his life at that point and search for ways to enjoy his journey in spite of the unplanned-for destination.

Let's also teach this skill to our kids.

But why doesn't filling in my calendar help me get where I want to go?

Getting more done is not the goal. We should want more quality, not more quantity. Most planners we use do not help us achieve the balance we seek. Almost all of what is written in planners has to do with work or money and does not consider the other two areas, family and personal needs. If we are not careful, our lists start to control us. If we do something not on our list, we feel compelled to write it down. We view things that are not on the list as distractions. Planners focus our attention on getting and doing, not on people and giving.

A balanced life is more prone to move individuals toward family, spontaneity, and relationships. It helps us spend time on things that are most important whether they are planned or not. Tight schedules blind us to the opportunities, people, and beauty around us.

But I'm afraid that if I set my mind in a play mode, I won't accomplish what I need to get done.

Once again, balance is the key. When I lived in Ohio, I tried to write a children's story. The desire and motivation were there, but the time and creativity were not. Writer's block resulted. Nothing happened until I was on my way to teach a class at the university one night. I drove by a grove of maple trees along the highway and started thinking about the maple syrup festivals I had taken my kids to when they were young. On the back of a deposit slip on the car seat that evening, I jotted down my story. After more thought and research, the "masterpiece" was done.

Often our most creative thoughts and solutions to problems do not come when we are hurrying around and worrying. Rather, they occur during the down times in bed before we go to sleep or in the shower or while driving the car.

Before going back to work after Thanksgiving one year, I woke to find myself worried about some problems I didn't know how to solve. So I made a list of everything that was bothering me. Beside the things I could do something about, I wrote down my plans for the week. All the other things were beyond my control. I prayed about them, then tucked the list in my Bible. It was both relieving and fun to revisit the list a couple weeks later when two of the items had already worked out and others were on their way.

And it happened without my shouldering the worry.

Sometimes I think I have it worse than anyone else; then I'm forced to see I don't. I'm glad when that happens.

It's good for kids as well as their parents to come to this realization. My children and I were able to go to Venezuela on a mission trip one summer. We visited an orphanage where the children lived on dirt floors and ate food that we couldn't imagine. The atrocities they had suffered were dimmed by their thankfulness for each new meal and the helping hand that was extended to them. My children and I walked away with new thoughts about what it meant to be rich. We were suddenly more thankful for each other and for the things we possessed. But the things we possessed tended to take a more balanced place of importance.

I walk fast, talk fast, eat fast, and even think fast. Is this keeping me from achieving balance?

When we slow down and center ourselves, we begin to see more. Part of what we see may be a shortcut or a better way or even a more desirable thing to do. We become aware of what is really important.

Once I was in a department store accomplishing one of the many things on my to-do list. I stood at the counter writing my check. I was deep in thought about where I needed to go from there and what I needed to accomplish. A little girl who sat on the counter beside me interrupted my thoughts: "Are you mad?" she asked.

In her words, I heard the message, "Chill out. Slow down. Look around you. If you are happy, why don't you tell your face about it!"

What about fun? What part does it play in achieving balance?

My children were two, four, and six. My oldest daughter was in kindergarten. I was in my first year of a doctoral program, working as a teaching assistant, finishing a divorce, and handling my father's failing health. Life was pretty full, to say the least.

In the spring, I set aside a day to go to the zoo with my daughter's class. I blocked out everything else on my calendar. Three times that day my daughter made a comment, but it was not until the third that I really heard: "Mom, laugh and tell jokes today."

That little girl hadn't seen her mom laugh for a very long time. She had watched me become so consumed with the serious side of life that I had forgotten to smile. We are told by doctors that laughter is the best cure for ulcers and aids in digestion. And

I know it makes me a better mom for my children.

I have trouble taking risks. Does that keep me from balance?

Never trying anything new and always taking the easy route won't bring happiness or even safety. The real joy in life lies not in accumulated security but in moments when we take risks and allow ourselves to feel. Risking does not mean foolishness or disregard for danger.

Risk means valuing progress and uniqueness more than you fear failure or ridicule. When we follow our hunches, we risk. But when we ignore our promptings and nudges, they come to us less frequently. When we stop trusting our feelings, we also stop valuing them. People who stop feeling, stop living.

It's hard for me to give up the things I had when we were married.

Giving up things is a challenge in two ways, physically and mentally. Sometimes we are forced to give up things physically. Choosing not to hold on to them mentally is another hurdle.

Connie lived with her husband and twin daughters, fourteen months old, in an old Indiana farmhouse filled with antiques. On Christmas Eve, the temperature was thirteen degrees below zero. Connie prepared food for the dinner, which was to be at her in-laws' house, and finished wrapping the gifts so she and the girls could meet her husband, who was already there. When it was time to leave, she warmed the car and buckled the girls in seat belts. When she went back in to get the gifts and food, she smelled smoke. As she moved to the rear of the house, she saw flames. She called the fire department and her husband, then moved quickly through the house. What should she save? Her attempts were futile, and she went outside and watched the men battle the flames in the frigid temperatures. The last thing she saw was the porch swing blowing in the wind. Connie thought that all she could lose was lost that night.

Two years later, however, her home was destroyed once again, this time when her husband left. She was left once more with only a few possessions and was forced to rebuild again. But she still had her children and her family and friends who came out of the woodwork to help her in that process.

The Bible tells us not to treasure the things that a thief can steal or a moth or rust can destroy.[4] Single parents are in an excellent position to do this. They are often forced to turn loose things and to grasp hold of the eternal things that no one can take away—people and love and friendships.

The first Christmas I was a single mom, I put up a very scant tree. Everything had been divided in the divorce settlement, including the few Christmas decorations we had gathered in our short years of marriage.

During a recent holiday, I couldn't help but notice the multitude of ornaments that now hang on the tree. Many Christmases have come and gone. New people in our lives shared mementos for our tree. Other ornaments represented events. Still others, the most valuable of all, were the ones the children made. There they were for me to see: a stately tree proudly displaying the things no one can take away—love and friendship and new adventures.

I've been a single dad for some time. I do enjoy being with other people, but I enjoy my times alone. Am I becoming a hermit?

Once again, balance is the key. Get comfortable being with yourself. Like yourself. Stand tall for what you believe in and represent. Then you will be able to share most fully with others.

In finding time to be with others and with yourself, however, don't neglect these rituals in your home. Make some things special and don't let other events or people preempt them. Bible study time in my bedroom at night has been special through the years. The dinner hour is a time when the TV is off and the phone goes off the hook so nothing interferes with those few minutes together. Fresh pastries have been shared for breakfast on the first day of school every year. The most simple of rituals and ceremonies have become traditions my children can count on. It makes for stable nonnegotiables—the givens. The things that will remain. We can count on that.

I can't do it all, but I can stop trying to do it. Can you help me?

That is one place where a faith in God helps. A major premise behind the Christian faith is that we will never be able to hack it, but if we trust in God, he will do it for us. That takes a major weight off our shoulders.

Steps To Finding Balance

- Give daily attention to the three areas of life—work, family, and self.

- Decide what you choose to do in each of these three areas.

- Spend part of each day for relationships and away from accomplishments.

- Leave time for spontaneity.

- On Sunday, determine what is important for the seven days ahead in the areas of family, self, and work.

- Do the same on the first of the month for the month that lies ahead.

- Keep track of unexpected thoughts and opportunities that come your way.

- Detach yourself slightly from your work environment in order to become more objective.

- Compliment your boss for contributions to your balance.

- Buy birthday, anniversary, and special-event cards in advance. Pre-address and sign them. Mark them in a calendar so you will remember to send them.

- Buy gift items ahead of time. Make the most of sales and one-time shopping.

- Arrange direct deposit of your paycheck.

- Declare the first ten minutes after you arrive from work as time-out.

- Teach your kids to sort and do laundry.

- Assign one night a week for your teen to plan and prepare the evening meal.

- Take each child to breakfast or lunch once a month to allow one-on-one communication.

- Establish family events that teenagers control. Go camping or rent a cabin from which you can commute to work. Let them handle the plans and do the cooking.

24

Dealing with Conflict

Moms and dads encounter all kinds of conflicts in a day. Consider this: Single-dad Tom gets his kids up for school in the morning. They fight over who showers first and who gets the last bagel.

At work there's gossip around the coffee machine, and the boss announces a new rule that ruins Tom's day. On the way home, he gets behind a car in which the driver is honking and shaking his fist at a slow driver.

As he walks in the door at home, the phone is ringing. It's Tom's ex-wife. She can't take the kids this weekend, and she yells at Tom for not returning her call.

The mail informs Tom that the check to pay his electric bill has not been received, and the children fuss about who was supposed to have taken it to the mailbox. Dad sits down and props his head while he stares out the kitchen window at their two dogs fighting over a gnawing bone.

What You Should Know

Conflict is inevitable in every home, including those headed by one parent. It exists with former mates, children, and outside relationships. Because single moms and dads are so consumed with everyday tasks and are exhausted from fulfilling them, they often do not deal with conflicts at all.

Conflicts arise when disagreements threaten something of value to both parties. It will not occur between two or more people if they do not care passionately about something. The most simple way of reducing conflict is to terminate the relationship. But that is impossible between a parent and a child and between the single mom and dad who both need to continue being active in their child's life.

Though conflict is common in all families, causes vary in single-parent homes. The reasons for difficulties between individuals include:

- *Different role expectations.* Specific guidelines do not exist for single moms and noncustodial dads. Each has to forge his or her own way, with the children's best interests in mind.
- *Role pressures.* Single parenting is tough for both the mom and the dad. Resources and time are limited, and concerns about the adverse effects on their children of growing up without the benefit of a two-parent home plague each parent.
- *Competition for power.* Competition between custodial and noncustodial parents often keeps the issue of power in the forefront. Who gets what? Who pays what? Who makes the decisions? When time and money get tighter, conflicts intensify.
- *Status problems.* Nearly everybody involved in a single-parent situation takes a blow to his or her self-esteem at some time or another. We feel embarrassed in public for our failures. We feel hurt toward the former mate when old feelings of love are replaced by disgust. We feel guilty when our children suffer as a result of our life changes. When both parties are grappling with these feelings, the stage is set for many conflicts.
- *Value differences.* The parents often do not adhere to the same values once the separation is complete. The child is torn, and the parents become embroiled in conflicts about whose values should prevail. I wanted my children to be in church on Sunday mornings. Their dad wanted them to be at the barn with the horses. I had to let that go and strengthen their faith as much as I could while they were under my roof. And as important as I felt their spiritual lives were, I had to recognize they were getting things from their dad they weren't getting from me, such as experience on the farm.
- *Perceptual differences.* Both parents have different experiences with the same situation. Say the parents need to reach an agreement on the dates and length of summer stay with the noncustodial dad. Dad may look only at his pain of missing the children and want as much time as he can get. Mom may view the issue from her own knowledge of schedules, needs, and convenience. These differing viewpoints create platforms for many conflicts.

- *Differences in needs and wants.* You may, for example, want the children to stay home for the weekend because your sister's family is coming to your home. Your ex-husband needs to see them.
- *Incompatible goals.* Your goal may be to keep the children fulfilled at home, while your ex-husband is trying to be with them more. He will try to make that happen in all situations. You can recognize the need and try to fill that longing in him to see the kids more, or you can fight him every step of the way.
- *Inaccurate or incomplete information.* Be sure you are conveying important information to the children's other parent about schedules and special needs. Otherwise, much conflict can result.
- *Unacceptable methods, poor support.* Your former spouse may not like the way you dress the children or the activities in which you involve them. You both need to communicate and clarify your expectations.
- *Differences in emotional responses.* You respond out of your need to hold on to the children. Your ex-husband responds out of his need to take hold. Emotional needs and responses are different and will manifest themselves in varied ways. Become aware of these differences and try to understand.
- *Differences in behavior and thinking styles.* The two of you are different. You discovered this while you were married. Remember those differences and work on showing empathy toward your former mate.
- *Lack of awareness or sensitivity.* Once my ex-husband was scheduled to bring our children home. Not knowing what time he'd be there, I grabbed a rare opportunity to take a bike ride. I went farther on the trail than I had planned, and a very disgruntled ex-husband was waiting in the driveway when I returned. He threw the kids' stuff onto the lawn. My behavior lacked sensitivity to his needs, and conflict resulted.
- *Unwillingness to work on issues.* Many times, one or both parents refuse to get along or give up after only a few attempts. Accept personal responsibility, manage your attitude, and agree to win-win situations for the sake of your children.
- *Antagonistic feelings.* Some moms and dads can't or won't let go of the past. Instead, bad history and negative emotions control their responses.

- *Emotional problems.* These may be depression, excessive anger, or false guilt. It may be a case where only skilled professionals can help.
- *Selfishness.* Many conflicts are the result of one or both parents considering only themselves. Disregard is shown for the best interests of both the former spouse and the children. This will take a toll on your family. Your children need to see you compromise and work through conflict successfully.

Methods of Resolving Conflict

Every day, every conflict in every single-parent home is dealt with in some way—even if that means not dealing with it at all. The methods include:

- *Avoiding* (denial, withdrawal). Issues that cause the conflict are not addressed. Instead, withdrawing, ignoring, postponing, sidestepping, or substituting issues may be involved. The parents ignore their differences by failing to communicate. They continue to not deal with their differences and eventually withdraw from one another. Passive resistance results, and baggage is carried into future conflicts, creating a hopeless situation.
- *Competing* (dominance). One parent's views are expressed at the other parent's expense. Contact becomes confrontational. A power play follows where each party uses position, power, persuasion, and manipulation to win.
- *Accommodating* (smoothing over). If one parent neglects his or her own concerns for those of the other, accommodating results. Differences are played down. Accommodating can cause resentment, defensiveness, passive resistance, or sabotage. The parents are postponing resolution of the problems.
- *Compromising* (negotiating). The goal is to find a solution that will satisfy both parties. Each gives in order to get. Meeting halfway results in neither being happy or committed. Mediocre decisions may result.
- *Collaborating.* The ideal way for the custodial and noncustodial parents to exist is to work together. Differences are valued, and the parties explore what both parents can bring to the lives of their children. The needs of Mom and Dad are expressed and respected. They try to consider the perspectives of both parties at all times and work in the best interests of the children. Collaboration is based on both parties acknowledging that conflict exists, wanting to find

a resolution, communicating effectively, committing to finding a good solution, and determining to take as much time as needed to do it right.

Questions You Ask

Conflict with the Former Mate

How important is it that my ex-husband and I get along?

Research has been done to see if conflict between parents living apart affects the children. Many of those results reinforce the importance of cooperation between the two parents. Of course, both of you being interested in making that happen is the best way to bring it about. But your interest alone in doing what is best for your child can make a difference. Remember the following ABCs:

- Always put the kids first. Set aside your own emotions or feelings of unfairness.
- Be open to changes in plans or opinions.
- Communicate respectfully as appropriate. This may mean phone calls, letters, or face-to-face encounters with an impartial party present.
- Dislike the inappropriate *behavior* of your ex-husband, not the *person*.

If you and your former husband need help in getting along, check with mediation courts in your city to see if classes or counseling services are offered. In some courts, classes are mandated for custody awards and child maintenance. Other courts provide mediation services.

Both you and your ex-husband need to think of the new structure of both households. That means finding new ways of fulfilling your individual parental roles and obligations in ways that are best for the child. If you end up doing all the work alone, however, your sacrifice and pride-swallowing decision will benefit your child in the long run. And that's who counts anyway.

Some problems my ex-husband and I have can never be resolved, or can they?

You should first understand the difference between conflicts and problems. While conflicts are personal and in our minds, problems depend on circumstances and take place outside of each of us. Problems are inevitable when people's lives intersect; conflicts are a result. Conflicts are a state of mind.

In your case, you and your ex-husband have problems over something that both of you care about—your child. These problems may be as minor as where your daughter will go to camp or as major as where she will go to college. The problems are not the conflict. You can control the problems that are inevitable in your relationship before they become conflicts if you work them out together. This will involve compromise and coordination. If only one of you is willing to cooperate, however, it may take a lot of give from the other to make things most peaceful for your child.

I feel like I'm always on the losing end when I deal with my ex-husband. Am I?

You can ignore the conflict and just coexist, continuing to allow the children to live in two separate worlds. This way causes you to think about who's going to win and who's going to lose.

But if you want to resolve conflicts permanently with your ex-husband, you're going to have to forget about who's winning.

One single mom in Iowa, Roxanna, thought with the win-lose mentality for years in raising her son, Daniel. He split his Christmases between his mom's and dad's houses. She decided that one way to work in the best interests of Daniel was to allow him to spend every December 25 with his dad and celebrate his Christmas at home on a different day.

So they started celebrating on the second Sunday of each year. At first, Roxanna felt cheated and the day felt contrived. But over time, that second-Sunday celebration became something really special in Roxanna's and Daniel's home. Roxanna discovered that her decision was a win-win situation. Because she did what was right for her child, it became right for his mom and his dad as well.

How do we get together on our differences?

We forget about each other's separate roles. Instead, each parent focuses on the interests and needs of the children. To do this:

- *Explore your differences and define the problem.* Disclose feelings, express viewpoints, and listen.
- *Agree to a win-win situation for your family.* Focus energy on solving problems, agree to a safe climate, identify common ground, agree on a goal.
- *Achieve consensus.* Brainstorm solutions, choose the best solutions, create an action plan.
- *Learn from conflict.* Reflect on the process and set goals for further improvement. Give each other feedback on how you handled the conflict and set goals for growth.

As a result, you become problem solvers. You work on mutually agreeable outcomes. You let up on each other but press harder on the problem. You focus on the interests of the child and discover solutions that are beneficial to all concerned.

Conflicts with the Children

I want my family to learn from conflicts as we resolve them effectively. How can I make that happen?

Conflict can be used positively to forge a stronger, more united family by venting emotions constructively and allowing for authentic communication. Both parent and child should have a safe forum for expressing his or her concerns. Positive conflict resolution revitalizes relationships and creates a spirit of co-operation. At the same time, it empowers individual members of the family and encourages personal growth.

You can explore differences through communication. Agree to a win-win situation for every member of the family through collaboration. Achieve consensus between both parents by creating options and choices. Finally, learn from the conflict. Reflect on what you gained from dealing with the issues. Let your children take part in this discovery.

A single-parent home that uses conflicts negatively, however, looks much different. It doesn't seek the best solutions. Self-centeredness deepens differences and causes areas of agreement to disappear while prolonging con-flict. Communication breaks down and is replaced by name-calling and fighting. Trust is destroyed and resentment grows. The family becomes polarized as it belittles differences between the parents and seeks a win/lose situation. Manipulation results and negative baggage is gathered and carried into future conflicts.

What's the best way to resolve conflict with children?

Parent-child clashes often become power struggles in win-lose situations and nurturing goes out the window. In such unequal matches, the parent usually wins because he or she has more physical and psychological strength. Children often feel powerless and resort to destructive ways to make their point and influence the outcome.

By contrast, in win-win problem solving, the child participates in a joint search for a solution that both parties can accept. Say you need to generate a chore list so work can be distributed among the family members bearing in mind your time constraints. Get the children together. List the chores, divide them up, assign them, and designate conse-quences for not fulfilling them. When this is accomplished, heavy-handed authority becomes unnec-essary. Advantages of this type of win-win conflict resolution strategy include:

- The child is invited to help find a solution.
- A higher quality solution usually results when both parent and child participate.
- There is a natural motivation to accept the agreement.
- Opportunities arise for the parent to compliment the child for good thinking.
- Less need exists to resort to parental power.
- Children's self-understanding improves as they learn to express their inner feelings.
- Children learn an effective lifetime technique for dealing with difficulties.

How can we solve problems in a way that builds my son's self-esteem?

Believe it or not, you can boost your son's self-esteem by including him in solving family problems:

- Sit with your child and together seek a solution that both can accept. Listen attentively to your child's point of view. Stifle the temptation to interrupt with parental wisdom.
- Before listing possible solutions, take your child's hand and ask God for guidance in the joint effort. Then suggest that a number of possible solutions exist. Encourage your child to share some suggestions

first. At this early point in the process, don't evaluate or put down any idea. Add to the list as long as either of you has more ideas to volunteer.

- Invite your child to indicate which option looks better to her. Frequently the child will recommend a solution that is fair to both. If that does not occur, state clearly in an "I" message why a choice does not seem adequate to you. Request that the child propose another alternative that might be acceptable.
- When agreeing to a solution, avoid implying, "Now we have the final answer." Instead, recommend that both of you test the proposed solution for a week or so. If it works well, then adopt it. If it fails to satisfy, discuss some possible modification or agree to test another alternative.
- Once you have found a good solution, take time to celebrate. Praise your child for his good thinking and cooperation. Take your child's hand once more and pray for God's guidance.

Begin this process when the child is very young. Not every attempt will be flawless. The process is as important as the product. Don't use your authority to subvert the plan.

I've done everything the right way, but my thirteen-year-old son is rebelling. Have I failed?

Of all the things single parents go through, difficulties with their children are among the worst to endure. One of my own children went through a difficult time in her early teens. Thankfully, it was short-lived, and she came out okay.

But I have never known hurt like the hurt I experienced as I watched this child I loved more than my own life walk—even run—down a path to destruction. I, too, felt like a failure as a parent. I wondered, *Should I quit my job? Should we move? Where do I find help?* I didn't know how to help my daughter, and I didn't know if I should relax my standards or hold more firmly than ever to them.

I felt as though I were facing another divorce, this time from my child. Or worse yet, I wondered if this would mean the death of our relationship. I heard horror stories of kids who rebelled and never returned to their parents.

My daughter is okay, and one day your son probably will be, too. Meanwhile, keep several things in mind:

- You probably have done all you could to raise this child the right way. Leave the rest to God.

- Say yes to everything you can, but hold firmly to the things that must be no.
- Always be loving, but allow him to endure necessary consequences.

Is it poor parenting skills that cause children to rebel?

Sometimes yes, usually no. We live in a time when our kids are faced daily with things that would lure them away and destroy their very souls. Peers, TV, and popular music are among the things we as parents have to fight against taking away our kids. When we face rebellious experiences, it's time, more than ever, to bone up on our parenting skills. I read every parenting book I could find, and I talked and listened to other parents I respected who had suffered and then come out okay on the other side.

Whether or not inadequate parenting skills have contributed to your child's rebellion, it is now time to be the best parent you've ever been to help your son or daughter get through this difficult time.

How do I know there is not something physically wrong with my child that makes him act this way?

You don't and won't until you get him checked. Have a doctor examine him for physiological causes. Depression, anxiety, or hyperactivity may be contributing to the difficulty. I know of parents who have discovered outside influences were to blame—drugs or alcohol. Milton Creagh, a speaker to teens about substance abuse, tells parents to continue to stay physically close to their children during these hard times. He even suggests hugging them often and taking a good whiff as you do to see if your senses alert you to possible dangers. Get help for your child as needed.

Be wise about what you suspect. When you can, be certain by having your suspicions checked by a doctor. Once you discover certain information, you can better handle your strategies for helping.

People always say to pick our battles. How do I know which ones to pick? Should I relax my standards for my child to avoid rebellion?

Relaxing our standards will not avoid rebellion. Choosing your battles carefully might. One counselor I know in California was seeing a mother who complained about her child's behavior. The mother was up in arms because her daughter wanted to shave her legs. The counselor's response? "Save your energies for when your son wants to shave *his* legs."

We should let go of the things that don't matter as much (procrastinating, staying on the phone, losing things, forgetting to thank others for gifts, failing to clean their rooms) and concentrate, instead, on the things that will matter more in the long run (failing classes, running with a bad crowd, staying out past curfew). We have a responsibility to prepare our children for the real world. And the real world will not tolerate tantrums, chemical abuse, disrespect, or irresponsibility. When our children do these things, there is a real price to pay, such as lost jobs or relationships or opportunities. One girl I know was heavily into drug use by the time she was in sixth grade. When it came time to graduate from high school and go out on her own to some pretty exciting things, she wanted to change her name and take on a new identity. She had learned about the hardest kinds of consequences from which no parent could protect her.

My son has been hanging with the wrong crowd at school and has been caught shoplifting. But overall, he's a nice kid. What should I do?

Sounds as though you are denying the truth when it comes to your son. If there are no physical reasons for his rebellion, you must face the fact that he is choosing to do wrong. There are consequences for that. Make him face them. He can change, and you should give him every opportunity to allow that to happen. But you can't force him to comply.

My child says he would rather go live with his dad than obey my rules. This scares me, and I cave in. What should I do?

The best choice you can make at this point is to be strong and let your son go. He is manipulating you like crazy now, and that is just reinforcing his rebellion. One single mom I know had her daughter say to her, "I can just go live with dad, you know. He doesn't have all these dumb rules." Though it hurt the mom who had raised this daughter since she was a toddler, she said, "Life is a series of choices. I guess going to live with your dad or abiding by the rules here is one of those choices you must make."

The daughter did go to live with her dad in another state for a time. Then she asked her mom if she could come back and get her driving permit at home since the new state required that she wait another year. The mom held firmly—but lovingly—to the consequences. She told her daughter, "There is nothing I would like more than for you to return home, but not without obeying the rules our home stands for. There are certain advantages you get as a member of this household—including getting your driver's permit when you choose."

How should I respond while we are resolving conflict within the family?

- Learn to clarify. Most problems come out of misunderstandings.
- Hear feelings in addition to words. Show empathy and don't say anything you will regret.
- Be loving, no matter how you are treated.
- Know yourself. Allow your response to line up with who you want to be.
- Avoid "you" messages that put the other person on the defensive. For example, "You lie to me all the time." Instead, use "I" messages such as: "I feel betrayed when you tell me you will do something and then don't."
- Avoid generalizations such as "always" and "never."
- Resolve the problem rather than blaming, placating, or distracting.
- Confront the person with whom you have the conflict. Discuss the issues only with others who can help. If your ex-spouse won't meet with you, involve a referee.
- Avoid cutting remarks. Hitting someone where it hurts is ineffective in resolving the issue.
- Don't try to win. Many situations single parents deal with have no tidy resolution. Deal with each problem as it arises as best you can and move on.
- Don't bring up the past. You are dealing with today's issues.
- Stop when discussion becomes destructive. Set up another time to resume when emotions have cooled.
- Deal with one issue at a time.
- Be responsible for personal change. Don't try to change others.
- Be willing to forgive and ask for forgiveness.
- Focus on the issue, not on the person.
- Accept all perceptions.
- Get in back of positions to identify needs and interests.
- Identify sources of conflict.
- Establish ground rules and brainstorm creative options.
- Analyze your alternatives objectively.

25

Combating Stress

One Friday, the clock in my car said 9:17 P.M. and I was still going strong with my usual daily chores. Exiting off the interstate, I turned right just in time to see a police officer, who also saw me. His light came on as he made a quick U-turn and hurried up behind me. I eased to the side of the road, and he walked to my car.

"Ma'am," he said, "I pulled you over because you didn't come to a dead stop back at that stop sign. I am going to give you a warning this time. But just remember, if you don't start making complete stops, you're going to have to pay a fine later on."

The following day, I was up by four to accomplish my household responsibilities—dinner in the Crock-Pot, instructions to the children on schedules to meet—before heading toward my seminar. I leaned my head back against the headrest in the car and sighed, already tired though the sun was barely up. Then I remembered the words of the officer from the night before, "If you don't start making complete stops, you're going to have to pay ...."

Remembering what the police officer had told me reminded me of the bigger truths his words implied. We need to take time every day to stop, look around, establish our direction, and check for safety. But how does a single parent find a place to stop and rest amid the stress involved in everyday life?

What You Should Know

Stress results when any physical or mental situation upsets us. Doctors estimate that 75 percent of all medical problems are stress related. These include chronic illnesses like flu, colds, high blood pressure, indigestion, vomiting, diarrhea, ulcers, headaches, and muscle aches. Researchers report that at least 50 percent of the population suffer at least one of these stress symptoms regularly.

Symptoms also come out in behavior in areas such as child/spousal abuse, isolation from family and friends, drug/alcohol/nicotine abuse, depression, anxiety, irritability, mood swings, and eating disorders.

Only some of the stress we experience is bad—conflicts with former mates, money problems, unexpected repairs. Much of what we deal with is not negative—soccer games, birthday parties, holidays. But while the mind knows the difference between good stress and bad, the wear and tear on the body is the same. Heart rate and blood pressure go up, brain activity is altered, and adrenaline appears in the bloodstream.

We can respond to physical or mental stress by: resisting its entry into our lives, ignoring it, getting rid of it, or learning how to live with the changes it brings.

Stressors Following Divorce

During and after a divorce, stress reaches an all-time high. Several factors contribute to this condition:

- *Economic stressors.* The economic status for women usually takes a downward spiral following divorce. Many find their pre-divorce job skills insufficient to earn a living for their families. In addition, the Census Bureau tells us that approximately 53 percent of women who are due child support do not receive court-ordered support. As a result, divorced women and their children often experience a sharp decline in their standard of living.
- *Parenting stressors.* The changes in roles challenge both parents. Time with the family is limited, and money must be stretched to accommodate two households.
- *Psycho-social stressors.* Divorced men are sometimes more socially isolated than divorced women, who are often able to draw more on a supportive network.

Questions You Ask

My two children do not live with me. Thinking and worrying about them all the time causes stress such as I have never experienced before. Why?

Many noncustodial parents who have limited contact with their children experience anxiety, depression, and stress-related illnesses. How your children respond to the changes in the family as well as the reduction in influence you have over your children are probably a lot of what concerns you.

The pain of these emotions often causes noncustodial parents to withdraw from the children. Don't do that. They need you now more than ever. Stay involved—physically and emotionally. The closer you live to them, the easier that will be. Read good parenting books and discover new ways to spend with your children. Pray for your children every day. I realized a long time ago that God takes better care of my children than I could if I were constantly with them.

My divorce will be final soon. What steps can my ex-husband and I take to minimize the stress of conflict for ourselves and our three children?

You are wise to give some thought to this now. Three areas you must take into consideration are:

• *Be sensitive to individual needs of the children.* In all you do, consider them first. Try to keep further changes, such as switching schools or places of residence, to a minimum at first.

• *Redefine parental roles.* Your divorce decree will do part of that for you. But you must find ways to make this new arrangement work well emotionally as well as logistically. For best results, both of you must learn

how to function most efficiently under this new arrangement. If you are the custodial parent, you can lead the way.

• *Agree on visitation.* The children should have regular access to both parents if possible. Agree upon routine visits, holidays, and vacations—and put it in writing. The courts can do this for you, but at great cost. Whether they do or do not assist you, this agreement and a determination to uphold it needs to take hold inside of both you and your former mate. Otherwise, conflict will result, and the children will suffer.

Our son has not done well adapting to the divorce. Much of my attention is given to trying to make ends meet, since we do not get child support. What can I do?

Some researchers say that income—even more than the ongoing involvement of the noncustodial father—is the key factor associated with children's adjustment outcomes. Both income and parent involvement are big causes of stress in the ex-partners' co-parenting relationship.

Do all you can to relieve your stressful feelings over financial concerns. For example, cut costs any way possible or have another single parent move in with you to share expenses. With fewer things on your mind, you'll be able to help your son more.

How important is communication to managing stress?

Stress spreads from one person to another (as in bringing stress home from work) mostly because of not talking about what's wrong.

Sometimes what you tell yourself makes matters worse. We lack objectivity, blame others, become victims, rehash the past, focus on unfairness. Try looking more objectively at the issues by identifying your biases that may be contributing to the stress. You also need to admit how you misjudged the person or event that contributed to the stressful situation. Finally, believe that you have the power to change or adapt to the situation by looking at ways you succeeded in the past.

Tell important people in your life how you feel and work hard to identify the real issues involved. Above all, don't respond on an emotional level and end up in a conflict.

I experience my greatest stress after I get home at night. Sometimes I look forward to finding relief at work. Why is this?

Single parents experience stress at home through three general areas: interpersonal relationships, the demands of balancing home and career, and financial difficulties.

A strained relationship with your former mate is almost a given at one time or another. It often results from poor communication, unclear role definitions, or unfulfilled expectations. At times, minor conflicts between you and your children can be equally as stressful. Much of this stress is caused by unrealistic expectations and the disappointment that results when these expectations aren't met. Another important factor is the roles people assume or allow to be placed upon them by others. This is particularly prevalent in single-parent homes.

Money problems can stress me out quicker than anything. It doesn't look like things are going to get better anytime soon. What can I do?

Remember, more than half of single parents make under $15,000 a year. If you are one of the many who experience financial stress, check your priorities and expectations. Are you still trying to live an unaffordable lifestyle? Do your spending habits conflict with your priorities or long-range goals?

Establish a budget. Work out differences in spending habits and priorities. If you can create a balanced budget, it becomes an impartial means for settling future spending disputes with your children. The budget, not individual preferences or impulse, then dictates spending decisions.

Also, create a savings program. It is part of your budget. Payroll deductions are easiest. Having money tucked away is insurance against future financial stress in the case of job loss, emergency illness, or home repair.

How can I help my child manage stress?

First, you should determine the sources of your child's stress: School? Day care? Family? Friends?

Dr. Archibald Hart recommends ways to help your child cope with stress:

- Be a supportive and involved parent. Don't fight unnecessary battles. Talk out your conflicts. Be careful how you criticize your child. Give your child room to grow. Dispense forgiveness generously. Give your child spiritual guidance.
- Tap into extended family. This helps to provide a sense of belonging. Church can take the place of family, too. We did this when we were first a single-parent family. The church we

Connecting Home and Career

The demands of balancing career and family obligations have always been a source of stress for single parents. You can do several things to reduce stress in this area:

- *Choose what's important.* You and your family must decide what the priorities are. Making choices and setting priorities give you a framework so you can make decisions easily and establish a family routine.
- *Know your limits.* You simply cannot do the job of two people. Stop trying! Discuss these limitations with your children and how they can help cover the needed bases, then let the others go.
- *Learn when to say no.* When a request or demand is made that conflicts with your priorities or exceeds your limits, say no.
- *Don't feel guilty.* Setting priorities and saying no can create guilt. But trying to do it all is unrealistic and guarantees a stressful environment. If you define your priorities and limits objectively and are willing to stay flexible, don't feel guilty!

chose embraced us, and we developed lasting friendships.

- Create a safe environment.
- Get teachers and day-care workers on your side.
- Make sure your child gets enough sleep and exercise.[1]

Combating Stress

Since I can't eliminate stress from my life, how can I gain control over it?

You are right. We can't control the amount or kind of stress that enters our lives, but we do have power over our reactions to it, and that happens when we are in the best physical shape to handle it. I seem to handle stress okay if I hold myself accountable to what I call my S-T-R-E-S-S list:

Sleeping, resting

The ability to relax helps counteract the negative effects of stress. Relaxation stimulates the body's parasympathetic nervous system, which controls stress responses—respiration, heart rate, and digestion. When you relax these areas, you feel more calm. The most basic components of relaxing include:

- *Focusing.* Get your mind off of petty problems and worries and onto something soothing like music or prayer.
- *Deep breathing.* You need to reduce the flow of adrenaline and cortisol into your body.

Regular deep breathing helps you concentrate on the relaxation process.

- *Relaxing muscles.* Tense then relax certain muscles. This helps you become aware of tensions so you can consciously reduce them.
- *Getting good sleep.* Elementary school children need ten to eleven hours; junior high, nine to ten hours; high-school students, eight to nine hours. Only the elderly need less than eight hours. We need to come to regular stops. You and I require a solid night's sleep per night in addition to rest breaks during the day.

Tending time management

- *Take an inventory of your usage of time.* Find out how you are using your hours and what you can do better. Schedule. Plan. Allow time for interruptions. Beware of time bandits that intrude on schedules.
- *Concentrate on the task at hand.* Screen out distractions. Distinguish between essentials and nonessentials.
- *Grasp the big picture.* Major on the majors. Establish long-range as well as short-term goals. Relate daily tasks to your long-range goals.
- *Work at being decisive.* Get all information available and then make a decision. Avoid procrastination.

- *Learn to delegate*, especially those things that can be efficiently done by others. Don't spread yourself too thin.
- *Prioritize*. Some wise person said, the main thing is to keep the main thing the main thing.

Routinely exercising

When you exercise, you get two benefits: You reduce the immediate negative mental and physical effects of stress, and you improve your overall physical capacity to handle future stress. Even if you aren't experiencing stress, routine exercise will improve both your physical and mental state. Exercise counters the negative effects of stress by:

- Limiting the increase in adrenaline that stress triggers, allowing your body to react to the fight-or-flight alarm more efficiently.
- Increasing the amount of beta-endorphin in your system. This morphine-like chemical produces a sense of well-being, reduces the sensation of physical pain, and counters the effects of negative stress hormones. The more you exercise, the longer this "good" chemical lingers in your body.

To reap the stress-reduction benefits of exercise, you need to find an aerobic activity you can engage in for thirty to forty minutes, at least three times a week. This can include walking, bicycling, running, or swimming. You get an aerobic workout if your pulse is at 70 to 85 percent of your maximum heart rate. You can figure your maximum heart rate by subtracting your age from 220. A person who is forty years old would have a maximum heart rate of 180 and an aerobic heartbeat range from 126 to 153. A twenty-year-old would have a maximum of 200 and an aerobic range of 140 to 170.

For longevity and good health, consistent, moderate exercise at least three times a week strengthens the heart, improves circulation, lowers cholesterol, controls weight, reduces conditions associated with hypertension, and helps to handle stress.

Eating healthy

When you are under stress, your body uses up important vitamins and minerals faster than normal. When these are depleted, you feel run down mentally and physically. This makes it hard to concentrate and to remain objective. In addition, your immune system is adversely affected, making you more susceptible to illness. When you eat poorly—junk food with empty calories, foods high in salt or sugar, highly refined foods—you make it hard for your body to withstand the chemical demands of stress. You also put yourself at risk for illnesses and disease.

To combat stress, eat plenty of foods containing vitamin B (whole grains, eggs, nuts, lean meats) and vitamin C (citrus fruits, green leafy vegetables). Vitamin C helps balance the negative effects of stress. For combating ongoing, pervasive stress, supply your body with plenty of protein (lean meat, fish, chicken, nuts), calcium (milk, yogurt, cheese), and potassium (fruits, vegetables). If you need to settle your nerves when under stress, reach for carbohydrates (sugars, starches). It's easy to reach for candy and cookies during stressful times like the holidays, but these can take your metabolism on a roller-coaster ride that goes from boundless energy to exhaustion. Better choices are foods such as pasta, yogurt, popcorn, and nuts.

Some foods can make stress worse by making you too sluggish to respond effectively or by increasing your anxiety. Foods high in fat such as french fries, potato chips, and other fried foods are hard to digest and can make you feel tired. That's why you feel sleepy after a heavy meal. The body has diverted its resources to digest the food.

Depressants and stimulants such as alcohol, nicotine, and caffeine affect your central nervous system. Nicotine produces an artificial stress response in your system. Alcohol creates a chemical imbalance leading to higher levels of tension and anxiety. Five or more drinks a week can create an artificial, chemically induced state of stress. While alcohol may provide a temporary numbing effect that makes stress more bearable, it does nothing to help overcome the cause. It can also lead to mental depression. Too much alcohol dehydrates you and depletes your body of important vitamins and minerals. Substitute going for a walk or listening to soothing music.

Caffeine increases susceptibility to stress, irritability, and nervousness, and can disrupt your sleep and digestion. It can increase your level of tension and anxiety, making it difficult to objectively analyze a stressful situation. Eliminate caffeine if possible or at least reduce the amount.

Socializing

Research shows that people who regularly give and receive affection live longer, are healthier, and report a higher quality of life than those who do not. Greet your loved ones with hugs and undivided attention at some point through the day. Resolve daily hassles with your family. Teamwork makes chores easier, and sound communication will avoid and resolve many problems. Stay in touch with relatives for emotional and practical support.

Friends can help in times of crisis. Maintain your social network and make new friends whenever possible. Reciprocate invitations, return calls, schedule regular get-togethers. Let your friends know how important they are. Clubs and churches provide organized ways to get together with people who share your interests, goals, and beliefs. These friends can provide a support network in times of need. You might also join sports, professional, political, or charitable organizations. Do something fun at least once a week. As single parents, it is easy to neglect fun time with other adults. But we each need to find our laughing spots—doing things and being with people we really enjoy.

Strengthening spiritual commitment

Researchers Frank Furstenberg and Graham Spanier say religious affiliation and social participation are correlated with lower distress and better post-divorce adjustment.[2] Spiritual beliefs can be a powerful resource during times of stress. Having trust in God decreases feelings of isolation and abandonment and gives life a sense of meaning and purpose. Developing a source of guidance in your life will help put stressful events into perspective. Take time each day to be still, pray, and reflect on God's Word, the Bible.

Not long ago, I realized it was as essential for me to get dressed in the morning with prayer as it was for me to get dressed with my clothes. Then at the end of the day, I have found it refreshing to lie on my bed and talk to God. I ask him what we should do about a bill I can't pay and to help me be more patient with the children. It is during the most difficult times of my life that I have drawn the closest to him and he to me. The Bible says, "Ask and it will be given to you; seek and you will find; knock and the door will be opened to you. For everyone who asks receives; he who seeks finds; and to him who knocks, the door will be opened."[3]

Twenty-Nine Stress Reducers for Single Parents

- Believe in yourself. You can handle what life dishes out.
- Don't take stress from others personally. If your daughter lights into you as you walk in the door at night, remember, you probably were a convenient scapegoat. Remove yourself briefly from the situation, then go back to her and receive the respect you deserve.
- Accept the things you can't change. Remember that life has its ups and downs. Look

ahead to when things will improve.

- Acknowledge your feelings to yourself and those affected by them.
- Stay busy. Changing your environment for a day may give you a fresh perspective or strength. Pamper yourself with a hot bath, a good book, or a visit with a friend.
- Get support. Stress is not external, but instead it's how you react to people, situations, and threats to your family's security. Because you don't have a spouse to bounce things off, it is especially important to find one or more persons with common values to become your sounding board. They may be a friend, family member, or counselor. Allow them to provide valuable insight.
- Find creative solutions. Look at the stress from a different angle instead of becoming immobilized by your fears. Find ways to use your existing skills to deal with the stress. Break it down into workable steps. Change your focus from seeing difficult situations as stressful to seeing problem solving as a new challenge.
- Accept and adapt. Even the darkest cloud has a silver lining. Discover the silver lining and then dwell on some of the good things about being a single parent—closeness you

develop with your child, fewer relationship demands, and you don't have to fix a formal dinner or iron shirts. You need to take charge. Use your coping strategies and keep moving. Take an active approach by pursuing a new direction for your family.

- Begin your day fifteen minutes early and do something you enjoy.
- If you usually take thirty minutes for a task, allow forty-five. It will decrease stress and increase quality.
- Strategize. Identify specific steps toward a solution to the situation. Evaluate the problem, examine the options, and develop a method for changing or coping with the situation.
- Kill guilt. You are a single parent. Period. There is nothing you can do about it now. You cannot go back and rechoose, redo, or relive. Guilt is unproductive, self-destructive, and a major source of stress. Let it go and make the best of life now for your sake and for the sake of your family.
- Don't hassle over the small things. Acknowledge your feelings of aggravation, then look beyond them to specific solutions or the future when things will change. Also, keep your perspective. Small stressors look large for the present but fade as you let them. See

them for what they are: small irritants, not earthshaking crises.

- Break down big jobs into small components. This strategy prevents a task from becoming overwhelming to you. Make a list of the work you want to accomplish each day. This will give you a sense of control over your workload. It can include weekly chores like cleaning the house or unusual tasks like cleaning the basement.
- Recognize the signals of stress your body gives you. These physical manifestations of tension tell you something is wrong in your environment or in your response to it.
- Take breaks throughout the day to stretch, rest your eyes, do neck rolls. These activities relieve tension for the moment.
- Become more aware of your surroundings. Slow your walk and conversation. This will help you absorb more of your surroundings and reorient yourself to a slower pace.
- Avoid being a perfectionist. Put your best effort into whatever you are doing. Then relax and don't worry about the results. By continually striving for perfection, you create tension for yourself.
- When problems overwhelm you, remove yourself temporarily from them. When your mind is rested, you will be able to find better solutions.
- Ask: Will completing this task matter three to five years from now?
- Reevaluate your need for recognition.
- Read books and articles that have nothing to do with your vocation.
- Play soft background music.
- Drive in the slow lane of traffic.
- Occasionally leave your watch at home.
- Tape record a phone conversation. Do you talk, ask, or listen most? Do you look for something else to do? Do you supply endings for others' sentences?
- Recall past enjoyable experiences for a few minutes each day, not how much you have accomplished or acquired.
- Recognize what your values are. Where do they come from?

All living creatures experience stress, but we are equipped to stand up under these challenges, and we can even become better through them.

God created an oyster with a special product called "nacre" that goes to work when an invading substance, such as sand, enters the shell. The foreign substance is coated with thin sheets of nacre in successive circular layers until it is completely enclosed, forming a pearl. The pearl takes on the same luster and color as the lining of the shell. If that lining is dull, the pearl that is developed will also be without luster and have no value.

Stress invades our lives much the same way the sand invades the oyster—it pushes us out of our love affair with comfort. We cling to comfortable living until something disrupts our equilibrium and propels us into some other journey.

Stress is a necessary by-product of our everyday living and plays a role in our learning and growth. We do not want to eliminate it from our lives because it causes us to develop maturity and character. But we *do* need to manage stress better, to handle the stressful grains of sand that enter our shells. Who knows, we just may watch those invaders grow into something of beauty and maturity in us—lustrous pearls that we might not otherwise have known.

26

Coping with Change

The day my husband walked out began a series of ongoing, unwanted changes for me and my family. By the spring of 1988, the divorce was final, we lived in a different state, we had moved from our house to an apartment, the children were placed in day care while I worked, and my dad had died. What more could a family take?

One day when I was a freshman in high school, I saw an unusual sight. It was winter and the ground was covered with snow. We lived in Ohio. The school bus had just dropped me off at our home and, as I was walking toward the house, I looked up. There in one of the honey locust trees was a clump of locust blossoms. They bloom profusely in late spring in Ohio, but to find them in the dead of winter was impossible. I got my dad's ladder and clippers from the garage. I cut the delicate flowers and took them to my English class the next day and wrote about them.

Twenty years later, in May, I was deeply involved in my divorce proceedings. The sadness was more than I could bear. One day, driving in the early afternoon to the attorney's office, I stopped at a traffic signal and rolled down my window. Suddenly I got a whiff of something. What was that familiar smell? Honey locusts.

I looked around and saw a whole grove beside me. And then I remembered my discovery all those years ago. This memory gave me new strength to find another clump of locust blossoms amid all the death and bleakness around me.

There is a time for everything, and a season

*for every activity
under heaven:
a time to be born and a time
to die,
a time to plant and a time
to uproot,
a time to kill and a time
to heal,
a time to tear down and
a time to build,
a time to weep and a time
to laugh,
a time to mourn and a time
to dance,
a time to scatter stones and
a time to gather them,
a time to embrace and a
time to refrain,
a time to search and a time
to give up,
a time to keep and a time
to throw away,
a time to tear and a time
to mend,
a time to be silent and
a time to speak,
a time to love and a time
to hate,
a time for war and a time
for peace.[1]*

Change—something Solomon in all his wisdom understood. Change, the one thing that will never change. As single parents, we have discovered that change is an unchangeable part of our lives. So how do we deal with it?

What You Should Know

We talked about the stages of loss earlier (see chapter 8, "Grief"). Those stages—denial, anger, bargaining, depression, acceptance—also apply in dealing with change. I said good-bye to that which I lost in the change. I entered the stage of hope and into acceptance of my new way of life. I no longer grieved the loss of our life before the change, but was greeting a new day and a new way of life.

I knew I was on my way when I realized the change wasn't so bad after all and that things could be okay. Though I still wished my children were growing up with their father in the home, continued observation of him and the process caused me to see that we would have had other problems down the way. Our values and priorities had grown worlds apart. I realized one day when my children were happily playing in our home that my mother had been right when she told me there were worse things than divorce, such as living in a really bad situation. The losses were beginning to pale, and our new life was taking root. I felt renewed enthusiasm for life and for the good things taking place.

A couple of years ago, I flew from Colorado back to Ohio. I had several appointments to keep. I drove through the town where I had grown up and had made special memories, but I was glad I didn't live there anymore. I stopped in the town where we began our new lives after the divorce and saw many of the people we love from there. But I was glad I didn't live there any longer either. And then I found myself in the town where I had lived while married. How freeing it was to not want to go back to the things I had fought so hard to keep. How liberating it was to turn the car in the direction that had become a new life for my children and me.

Questions You Ask

But I liked things the way they were. I don't want them to change. How do I cope?

Knowing that change is a normal part of life and coping with it when it comes can be two different things. Even changes for the better can feel threatening and scary. Newton's law of motion dealing with inertia says: A body at rest will remain at rest if it is not acted upon by an outside force.

When my divorce took place, all I wanted to do was return to my former sense of well-being. My restful state had been acted upon by an outside force, and I fought hard to resist. But that part of my life was over, and I took steps to move on.

Today, life is good once again, but sometimes I want to go back to the warm nesting place where my family and I retreated and found healing. I often long to be with the people, places, and church that made us feel safe following the divorce. But when we go back, I realize once again that this chapter in our lives is closed, though the relationships we developed are not. Circumstances and people are different now, and so are we. We have moved on. Things have changed.

Why is change so hard to accept?

Whenever things change, we lose something. We can lose tangible things, such as possessions and relationships, or intangible things, such as hopes and dreams. Even happy changes involve loss and must be grieved. Since the grieving process hurts and can take a long time, we resist change.

Change upsets our sense of routine, security, and order and causes us to adapt to new ways of living. Human beings like predictability and set scheduling. Significant changes—losing a mate, a job change, or moving—disrupt our sense of order and force us to adapt to living in new ways.

How are we supposed to handle change?

Managing change is a two-step process.

- *Say good-bye to the old.* This happens by grieving whatever we lost in the change. Saying good-bye means letting go emotionally as well as physically of past relationships, possessions, and locations. The only way to do that is to grieve the loss.

When I was married, we lived in southeastern Indiana on our horse farm in a spectacular, refurbished 1817 farmhouse. Antique brass hardware adorned the interior doors. Old beveled glass was built into the front door. Original hardwood floors with square-head nails planked our study. Our kitchen was tiled and decorated to perfection, and the greenhouse outside the French doors spoke of one more reason for its uniqueness. The envy of the town, the farmhouse received newspaper coverage and even one award.

Eighteen months after my husband left, the day came for the kids and me to leave. The morning the movers came, I walked through the house for one last look. Everything had been divided, though the divorce was not final. I turned the lock and closed the door quietly, securely, permanently. As I drove down the long tree-lined drive, the rearview mirror turned upward, tears fell. I didn't look back.

One of the professors at the university later told me of her own painful, final departure after her divorce. It made me laugh. She, too, had moved to Ohio. As she had pulled away from the house, her only daughter beside her, the woman had cried. Lost in the depths of emotion, loss, despair, and sadness—all the things that come with change—she knew they were leaving their former life behind. Suddenly her daughter said, "Mom, you look like a frog when you cry."

So much for tender moments.

- *Greet the new.* This is especially hard if we are dealing with a change we did not want in the first place. Adapting to life without a person who has died, adjusting to life after a relationship breakup, or fitting into a new neighborhood after a job transfer involves a difficult time of transition. It may take some time before we can move through the grief stages and get to the place where we can emotionally say hello to our new way of life.

We lived in Ohio for a year before I purchased a home. My children were three, five, and seven years old. One Friday night during my fifth quarter at the university, I took the kids by their new house. We picked up the keys from the sellers and looked around at its empty rooms. Then I took them to meet their dad for the weekend.

Sunday night, I picked them up and brought them back to the house, now filled with our things, including curtains at the windows. That night we had snacks on the floor of the kitchen as we started saying hello to the new. The children squealed with delight as they put their things in their rooms where they wanted them. Ashley was on the phone before long telling a friend about this wonderful change. That house became home for us for the next seven years.

But what about the old traditions that also went with the change? How can I justify the loss of those to my kids?

You can't. Try to keep as many things the same as you can. Maintain as many traditions as your life will allow, then create new ones.

In the backyard of our new home, we had a damp spot where nothing grew. Water pooled there after each Ohio downpour, and it killed the grass and other vegetation. I called a landscape architect who came in and studied the conditions. He brought in some dirt, built up the mound, and planted iris bulbs, pussy willows, Shasta daisies, and hemlock. Every year as I clipped branches to make a spring bouquet or picked the strawberries from the mound under the trees, I was reminded to also measure our family's growth. We had taken the conditions that existed and planted new things there—things that actually thrived on the environment we offered. We established new memories and traditions, and home became a special place once again.

I know the divorce is not the only change my family and I will have to endure. How can we remain flexible to the unforeseeable?

Your survival and that of your children is directly related to your ability to adapt to change. Here are some healthy ways to adapt:

- See change as an opportunity, not a problem. Celebrate it with your kids. Look for the opportunities it offers and take advantage of them. If, for example, your job necessitates a relocation to the South, point out how much closer you will be to the beach.
- Don't let fear paralyze you. Sometimes we ignore or avoid change, but it doesn't go away. You make the choice. Take charge. Look for opportunities to make change work for you.
- Accept change as normal and positive. Reevaluate your goals regularly. Don't be afraid to change them. Fine-tune your plans for action so they fit your goals, values, and needs.

During the past year, my husband left, my father died, we moved to a new town, and I changed jobs. No wonder our home is disrupted. How can I know how these changes have affected us?

Researchers Holmes and Rahe studied how different changes affect us:

If you score less than 150 points, you have one chance in three of getting a serious illness

The Impact of Life Changes (over a two-year period)[2]

Life Event	Number of Occurrences	Value Score
Death of a spouse		100
Divorce		73
Marital separation		65
Detention in jail or other institution		63
Death of a close family member		63
Major personal injury or illness		53
Marriage		50
Being fired at work		47
Marital reconciliation		45
Retirement from work		45
Major change in the health or behavior of a family member		44
Pregnancy		40
Sexual difficulties		39
Gaining a new family member		39
Major business readjustment		39
Major change in financial state		38
Death of a close friend		37
Changing to a different line of work		36
Major change in the number of arguments with spouse		35
Taking on a mortgage greater than $10,000		31
Foreclosure on a mortgage or loan		30
Major change in responsibilities at work		29
Son or daughter leaving home		29
In-law trouble		29
Outstanding personal achievement		28
Wife beginning or ceasing work outside the home		26
Beginning or ceasing formal schooling		26
Major change in living conditions		25
Revision of personal habits		24
Troubles with boss		23
Major change in working hours or conditions		20
Change in residence		20
Changing to a new school		20
Major change in usual type or amount of recreation		19
Major change in church activities		19
Major change in social activities		18
Taking on a mortgage or loan less than $10,000		17
Major change in sleeping habits		16
Major change in the number of family get-togethers		15
Major change in eating habits		15
Vacation		13
Christmas		12
Minor violations of the law		11
TOTAL		

in the next two years. If you score between 150 and 300, your chances are 50–50. If you score more than 300 points, your chance of serious illness is almost 90 percent.

How much stress is associated with change?

When confronting change, you have three options:

- *Resist and fight to maintain status quo.* This produces only temporary results. Eventually the change will happen, regardless of what you do.
- *Avoid change.* You fail to acknowledge the change. You behave as if no change occurred. You develop unhealthy coping mechanisms, which cloud the real issues. This creates continual stress because you are engaged in continual conflict within yourself.
- *Confront and adapt to change.* This is a healthy response that minimizes stress. People who roll with the punches during change experience less stress. If you resist change, you can create stress that causes greater harm than the change itself.

Once the change is in place, what can I do to adapt?

- *Commit to change.* Alter the way you handle daily obligations and schedules and the things you allow to accumulate.

- *Solve problems.* Problems can control you, sending you into paralyzing depression or producing nonproductive anxiety.
- *Improve communication.* Realize the impact of your words so those words can contribute to your life rather than complicate it.
- *Reevaluate possessions.* Rather than being tied to the world of things, eliminate some of them by recognizing the true value of everything in your life.
- *Control perfectionism.* Excellence is not the same as being perfect. Rethink the need to have everything perfect.
- *Stop procrastinating.*
- *Pray.* Ask God to help you and your family to adapt.

How will these things help me accept change?

Change the way you look at change.

- *Always expect the unexpected.* Factor in some flexibility in your plans. Opportunities occur when you least expect them, and some flexibility in your thinking and scheduling will let you take advantage of those delights that pop up from time to time.
- *Anticipate change.* Embrace it—things and people, jobs and marriages. They all change. Change often represents an opportunity to move on to

new and more exciting times in your life.

- *Make a commitment to change.* Rather than waiting for change to sock it to you, why not anticipate it? If you think you might be laid off from work, find out what the job market is like. If you are in a relationship that is not fulfilling, end it now! Don't wait for events to happen to you.

- *Change a habit that is slowing you down.* Studies show that most habits can be changed in twenty-one days. Decide today to change something about your life and stick with it for twenty-one days. Chances are excellent that you will have changed for good.

How do I solve the problems that come?

Problems can throw a nasty curve into the game of life.

- Confront issues. Delayed action prolongs the agony and complicates matters.
- If a problem is yours, own it. Seek solutions until you resolve the issue.
- Ask others for advice.
- Don't waste precious time worrying.
- Concentrate on one problem at a time.
- Don't postpone decisions.
- Put the problem behind you. Everyone makes mistakes. The only person who doesn't make

them is the one who doesn't do anything.

- Realize that bounding in and out of the grief stages is normal. Don't be discouraged if you find yourself moving from depression to anger, acceptance to bargaining, depression to denial. You will feel like you are regressing when that happens, but you are not. Rather, each time you reenter a stage, it will have less intensity and will last a shorter time than it did the time before. You are moving forward, and the process will end.

Your Kids and Change

How can I help my son adapt to his new neighborhood?

Author Gary Sprague recommends the following:

- Help him talk or draw a picture about what he remembers about the old house, neighborhood, school, and friends.
- Give him a camera. Show him how to take pictures of his new house, neighborhood, school, and friends. Help him put them together into a scrapbook and maybe even write a story or comments about each photo. Take it to a copy shop and duplicate the pages to send to important people in your lives. Work hard at preserving old traditions with fondness while

establishing new ones with enthusiasm.[3]

Can I suffer the consequences of change for my child? I don't want him to hurt like I do.

I sometimes look to God's creation for important life lessons. There is one I have learned much from:

Before a chrysalis can become a butterfly, it must remain in a tightly wrapped cocoon. It squeezes, grows, and convulses while inside. Onlookers decide they might like to help it gain its freedom.

But it is during this time in the cocoon that the butterfly undergoes a metamorphosis. This time of change and growth provides color to the butterfly's wings and strength to its body. If the process is cut short, the butterfly will never be able to fly.

Your child will face inevitable changes throughout life. Let him get good at it now. After all, like the butterfly, he is adding strength and color to his character. And before you know it, he will be flying on his own.

27

Enhancing Communication

My oldest daughter, Ashley, was at a basketball game with her friend. Her friend's younger sister, Lindsey, came up to them and said something, then walked away.

At the end of the game, their dad told them they would have to wait to leave because Lindsey had dropped her coat behind the bleachers. "Oh," said Lindsey's sister, "I thought she said she spilled her Coke on the bleachers."

It's all in the communication.

What You Should Know

A survey of three thousand high-school students showed that the message they want to convey most to their parents is, "Please communicate and listen to us more." When parents neglect their children's communication needs, parents function as little more than robots, mechanically furnishing food, clothing, and shelter. Kids retaliate in devious ways, often by sabotaging whatever the parents try to do.

Sometimes we jump to a guilty verdict before our children are finished speaking. Attentive listening is required for any two-way communication. A friend admitted he had a habit of browsing through the newspaper while his son talked. He has now stopped fake-listening. A child needs active, not passive, attention.

"Inactive listening" is what single parents have gotten so good at—letting the words go in one ear and out the other. "Selective listening" is when you hear only what you want to hear. "Reflective listening" is the most effective kind. It listens to the whole message and then clarifies what is being said and communicates understanding.

Questions You Ask

My son overheard me say while on the phone with a single girlfriend that I envied her lack of responsibility with no kids to look after. While the idea was okay, what my son heard wasn't, and it made him cry. What else has he heard me say?

Often when we are around our children, our guard from work is down. We can relax and be ourselves. As a result, we present those we love the most with the least we have.

Writer and single parent Patti Townsley Covert tells us that it takes forty positive messages to counteract a single negative one.[1]

The best thing all single parents can do is to be aware of what they are saying and be sure they are conveying the right message. Have your son help you be accountable. When one of you says something that causes confusion, call "ding ding" or some such word or phrase. Ask the other to elaborate. This will allow for clarification to avoid misunderstanding and cause each of you to think before you speak that way in the future. After all, it's not just the words we speak but the messages they convey that are important.

How can I keep up with my growing child's language? Doesn't communication become more difficult then?

Single parent D. Erdmann of Illinois wrote this note:

> While trying to teach my six-year-old the importance of verbal communication versus a nod, shrug, or shake of the head, I realized how computer literate he was becoming.
>
> After receiving no response to a question, I said, "No one can read your mind." Then I added a twist, "No one, except God."
>
> After thinking a minute, he asked, "You mean God can download my brain?"

Our kids, starting at the earliest ages, speak a different language than the one you and I are accustomed to. With the easy accessibility to the different media, including computers and print material, they have much more to stimulate this than we did.

Stay close to your child. Listen carefully. Talk openly. Develop all the trust you can handle when he's young. Then when he's older, he'll know who to come to for direction.

My teen is hard to talk to. What's the single most important rule I should remember in communicating with him?

Don't put him on the defensive. It is easy to send "you" messages and put the blame on someone else when something goes wrong. "I" messages eliminate the accusatory tone and foster goodwill. "I get nervous and jumpy when someone sneaks up behind me and yells." "When I'm driving, I get distracted when there's so much commotion in the backseat."

This is less damaging than suggesting that the child is to blame for your actions. If you assign blame, the child immediately tries to shift it elsewhere and the battle is on. By contrast, "I" messages prompt a more honest response from the child about his feelings. They also help the child consider other people's feelings.

Listening

The other day my daughter said, "You never listen to anything, Mom! You didn't hear a word I said, did you?" What can I do about this?

Single parents don't have the luxury of explaining all the valid reasons they have for not listening carefully. In most instances, if good listening does not occur, the chance is gone. Listening effectively is difficult, and most of us were never taught how to listen. Instead, many parents have worked hard to master one significant coping mechanism—tuning out. We often hear what is being said but do not listen. Hearing is a physical act, but listening is intellectual and emotional. Hearing only recognizes sounds; listening requires understanding.

Why is it necessary that single parents become good listeners?

Our kids need someone to talk to who knows, loves, and understands them. If not us, they'll turn to someone else. They need to be able to share their joys and their frustrations. Good listening improves communication between us and our children. It allows

---

What communication habits do I have that are turnoffs to my kids?

A group of teachers identified certain communication practices adults should avoid:

- Interrupting during a conversation.
- Minimal listening, letting your mind wander.
- Being judgmental, unwilling to see another person's point of view.
- Making up your mind before you hear all the facts.
- Belittling another person's remarks.
- Criticizing individuals publicly.
- Failing to express any appreciation or to give credit.

them to talk from their perspective and from what's important to them as we begin to better understand their world. It also prepares us to adapt to changes in maturation.

Our job? To listen. Not only is listening important in how we interact with our children now, but we are teaching them how to apply these valuable skills to their own lives later on. Our listening says, "I care about you."

Listening carefully to former mates who are interested in engaging in an argument puts us in control of the conversation and dissipates any heated discussion. Listening makes us better moms, dads, employees, friends, and former mates.

How can I listen better to my daughter when I have so many things going on?

You begin by listening to what your daughter says—the "words." Words comprise only about 10 percent of what she says, but they are an important part of her message. Understand her words and ask for clarification when necessary.

Next, listen to the "reasons" your daughter says what she says. This will be easier since you know her so well. When you listen for her intent, you combine her words, body language, prior experience, and biases she has on each subject. What is the emo-tional meaning of her words? Understand *why* she is saying it rather than merely *what* she is saying.

Then, assess your daughter's "nonverbal communication"— body language and voice tone. What is she saying with her body? You are concentrating on *how* she is saying something rather than just *what* she is saying.

Meanwhile, be aware of the messages you are conveying with your nonverbal signals—a frown, furrow, tapping on the steering wheel. These nonverbal signals will inhibit what your daughter is saying to you.

Finally, put yourself in your daughter's shoes and understand what is shaping her feelings. She needs to hear your empathetic and nonjudgmental reactions. Suspend your judgment of what your daughter is saying. You are listening with an open mind— not necessarily agreeing with her.

How should I listen to my child when he is angry?

Don't use the words "should," "would," "ought," or "must" ("You should never say things like that."). Also, don't use the words "never" or "always" ("You never act right in public!").

Instead, try reflective, active listening. It involves repeating, paraphrasing, and summarizing your child's words so that both of you know you are connecting:

"Am I hearing you say you think I didn't handle this situation well?" Your response can make all the difference in how he expresses his emotions.

How do I ask questions that won't make my daughter defensive?

Once again, use "I" messages such as: "When you talk like that, I feel disrespected because of your words and tone of voice." This keeps her from having to defend herself and puts the emphasis, instead, on you. You can also ask clarification questions:

• What's an example of that?
• What will happen if . . . ?
• What do you want?
• What can you do about it?

Keep your conversations confidential. Your daughter will build trust in you when you do, and she will come to you later with more important things.

Sometimes I get so emotional about things when my son and I are talking. Can these emotions keep me from listening as I should?

Once when my children were two, four, and six, we were in the apartment where we had moved following the divorce. The children's father had done much to break up our family and destroy the trust I had in him. My emotions ran pretty high. But one night in the kitchen, my four-year-old daughter was on the phone with her dad saying how much she loved him. She hung up and talked incessantly about her dad. I thought I would burst. I was tired, overwhelmed, and stretched beyond belief doing this single-parenting thing. I wanted to stop that little girl and describe all the things he had done to hurt me and our family.

But suddenly I remembered that she loved me whether I made a good dinner for her or a lousy one. She loved me for no reason, and she loved her father the same way. I had no business interfering with that. If I had, this small girl would have remembered not to talk when she felt like it in the future because of Mom's response.

Emotions that stem from things that have happened, how tired you are, or what just happened at work act like filters that affect your understanding of what is being said. Your mind-set will be influenced by your current emotions, the situation, and your expectations for your son. By simply identifying and controlling the filters that impede good communication, you can become a better listener.

What kinds of distractions to listening should I be aware of?

In most cases, both external and internal distracters can be controlled, but it will take some work. Physical distractions distance you from the speaker. To minimize physical distracters, maintain eye contact with your child, watch body language, don't move around or fiddle, and summarize what the speaker says so you can be sure you are hearing what she is saying.

Noise and movement can be serious barriers to good listening. Eliminate all the noise you can—TV, telephone, radio—from the setting where you are trying to listen.

Mental distractions—anger, worry, fear, fatigue—are internal distracters. You can minimize the effects of distractions by identifying what is the distraction (e.g., having a bad day at work). Then tell yourself you will deal with it after the children's needs are met in the evening. If you are angry or worried about something, tell God about it. He wants to do the things you need that you cannot do.

How do I show understanding for my child's concern without agreeing with everything he says?

When you show you are trying to understand him, you tell your child you care about him and care about his situation, not that you agree with what he is saying. This puts you in a nonadversarial position. Say things like "I see your point . . . ," "I've been there before myself. . . ." Use nonverbal signals by nodding, touching, maintaining eye contact, or moving toward your son. Your son will know, *Hey, Mom's trackin' with me.*

But how do I refrain from being judgmental? For me, that's the hardest part.

Don't go into a listening situation thinking it is a battle you must win. Being a good listener asks that you set aside your own ideas and opinions. Your teen might say, "I hate school. I have to do so much homework and get no time with my friends." There are several ways you can respond:

- *Use "I" messages.* Say something such as: "I get the impression you've got a lot going on right now." It's your teen's turn to respond, and you have been nonjudgmental without agreeing with him. You might also say, "I'm concerned because I think you are overloading yourself with extra activities."
- *Understand your child's feelings.* Ask yourself, *What is my son feeling? Why is he feeling this way?* Then say, "You feel angry because your teacher treated you unfairly." You are reflecting your son's feelings and reasons for the feelings as you understand them.
- *Ask questions.* These questions should have no right or wrong answers and should not be

able to be answered with yes or no. They force your child to rethink what he is saying. "What makes you feel so overwhelmed with school?"

To help you with your decision to leave out judgmental reactions, be sure you are responding to the idea or situation, not the person who is talking. Also, respond to the present, not the past. Describing and not evaluating will help you hear and not judge what is being said.

Are there things I can do to help my son listen better to me as well?

Begin by what you are doing—modeling and teaching good listening skills. If your son is open, teach him some good listening skills. Be creative. Make a list of instructions he needs to listen to in order to find a special present. You can tell him several chores you want him to do before he goes outside to play. Send non-verbal messages to your son when he is not listening. Ask questions he needs to answer to help him stay focused. Phrase what you say so that your son's emotions are working for him and not against his reception. Above all, don't become the adversary. If you feel an argument coming on with your son, try one of the following:

- Don't respond immediately. Ask yourself, *What are the real*
issues? Or *Whose problem is this?* Change the subject. Repeat the key points.
- Show lots of empathy and little judgment. Keep calm and don't take what he says so personally.

Can good listening keep me from getting into fights with my ex-wife, too?

Yes. Good listening can help you defuse conflicts and enhance effective communication with anyone.

- Don't respond out of emotion. Your goal is to turn a conflict into a discussion. Ask yourself, *What skills do I have that can help solve this problem?* Control your emotions for the sake of settling the issue in a nonjudgmental way.
- Criticize the issue or the behavior, not your ex-wife. This is not the time to dredge up past mistakes.
- Remember that your ex-wife has worth. Conflicts are power struggles, which are no-win situations. The more you argue, the more frustrated you will both become. You don't have to agree with her, but respect her right to have a different opinion. Try to understand what she is saying and why she feels that way.
- Avoid generalizations such as "you always" or "you never." They polarize a conflict and

shift the focus away from solving the problem at hand.

What kinds of nonverbals can I use to improve my listening skills?

You can concentrate on two areas of nonverbals:

- *Facial expressions*. Be sure they are consistent with your body language. Don't, for example, smile while crossing your arms and legs. Make your facial response spontaneous and not contrived. Neutral faces show you are being non-judgmental. Smile if you agree with what the speaker is saying, and indicate with your face that you don't understand when something is confusing.

Above all, use effective eye contact.

- *Gestures*. Be sure you are sitting or standing erect. Don't cross arms and legs or show restlessness. Avoid nervous gestures like biting your lip. Mirroring the speaker's body language shows that you agree with what he is saying.

How do I know when my four-year-old daughter needs me to listen if she doesn't say so?

Watch her nonverbal communication. A crying four-year-old needs someone to take time with her. An acting-out fourteen-year-old needs the same thing.

The younger your children are, the more you will have to read

What do I need to keep in mind while developing better listening skills?

A good listener believes:

- I want to listen.
- My goal is to respect the speaker.
- I will use all my physical tools to show I am listening.
- I will watch for clues in body language.
- I will strive for accuracy.
- I will listen with an open mind.
- I am in control. I will look for things to agree with and build from there.
- I will make others feel important by remembering things they say.
- The more I practice good listening, the better I will be.
- I will listen to myself and stop negative words from hurting others.

body language. Listen empathetically and nonjudgmentally, and you will get more information from your child. Be sure your nonverbals don't turn your child off. Sometimes young children will talk about a fantasy friend that will tell you much about their own fears and concerns.

As your daughter gets older, listening becomes even more important. It builds her self-esteem and teaches her your values and expectations. As you listen to her when she is older, you help her talk her way through difficulties and find solutions based on your family values. Meanwhile, she realizes she and her problems are important enough for you to take time for.

Remember to listen to your children with empathy and without judgment. They are trying to decide who they are apart from you. Many things they say are

Ten Steps Toward Better Listening

- Eliminate external (radio, others talking, TV) and internal (your own agenda) distractions.

- Do not listen to a conversation with your mind already made up. Listen with an open mind.

- Listen with your mind for accuracy, inaccuracies, facts and figures, words and ideas.

- Move your body toward the speaker to take in more of what he is saying. At the same time, don't crowd. You can move toward a speaker without crowding him.

- Don't react only to what the speaker implies. Also consider the content, intent, and nonverbal message.

- Hear the whole message through eye contact, body language, facial expressions, and voice tone.

- Decide why certain words evoke a certain response in you and do something about it.

- Do not decide how you will answer while the other person is still talking.

- Don't give judgmental answers. "That was wrong," or "You shouldn't have done that." Instead, hand them back the responsibility to think: "Why do you think your words were offensive?" or "What could you have done differently?"

- Take initiative to be a better listener. Set a new goal each week for improving in this area. Then assess how you did.

not really what they believe, but instead are spoken to evoke a reaction. If you are empathetic, you are saying you love them no matter what they say or do. If you suspend judgment, you are saying, "I want to listen to how you feel."

Once you have shown them the empathy and nonjudgmental qualities they seek, help them understand what they are saying. Ask clarifying questions such as, "How did that make you feel?" or "Why do you think she said that?" They need to come to grips with their ideas more than they need you to explain or judge them. This equips them for making decisions, takes the burden off you, makes them feel loved, and keeps communication lines open. One single mom in California sits down on the floor with her teen where there is nothing that can distract either of them. The mom looks Kathi in the eye, and Kathi talks. It has worked them through many rough spots.

Whether you are talking to your kids whom you love or your ex-mate whom you do not, miscommunication is guaranteed to complicate even the most sensible lifestyle. Things said poorly or left unsaid altogether can create interpersonal problems in every area of your life.

Think before you speak and then think again before you act. Ask God to help you know what to do. The Bible says, "If any of you lacks wisdom, he should ask God, who gives generously to all without finding fault, and it will be given to him."[2]

Twelve Tips to Better Communication

- Express in your own words what you think your child is saying. "I want to understand what you are saying. Is this what you are thinking?" and then offer your paraphrase of the child's message. Simple feedback requires that you say very little, but such questions will foster more accurate understanding.

- Use brief, noncommittal responses that encourage your child to say more. For example, "I see. I'd like to hear more about it." "Then what happened?" "That was really important, wasn't it?"

- Be alert to what your child says nonverbally. Watch for physical cues that may be more significant than the words shared.

- Look a child in the eye while listening. To avoid eye contact is to appear uninterested in what the child says. She soon gets the feeling that her words aren't worth your attention.

- Compliment a child for every evidence of good thinking. Tell how much you appreciate opportunities for the two of you to share thoughts.

- Take time to communicate with a child who comes to you with questions. The child will never be more ready to listen.

- Resist the temptation to interrupt a child's sharing with moralizing "you" messages. This sabotages genuine communication. Trust your children to work through many of their own problems as you listen to them.

- Get down on the same eye level for one-on-one communication. Consider how insignificant you would feel attempting to talk with someone ten feet tall.

- Make daily opportunities to listen to each child. Some parents schedule a longer weekly "talk-time" on the calendar. Then a child can look forward to a special time just with you.

- Say such things as: "How are things with you today?" "How did you feel about what happened?"

- On a birthday or other celebration, give a coupon good for a gift of time together. Then make that time a notable experience shared by just the two of you.

- Realize what an inadequate substitute a TV set is for a parent. The TV talks but never listens to your child. Neither can it hold your child's hand or say, "I love you."

28

Finding Time

Single mom Laura Sydnam of Washington wrote:

> My seven-year-old daughter and four-year-old son had been pleading for months to get a pet. I was concerned about the expense and time involved in caring for one, so I said no. But their persistence caused me to compromise and get a goldfish.
>
> Following a trip to the pet store for the big purchase, we stopped for groceries. I was hurrying down the aisle trying to gather what I needed so I could get home. My son was trying to keep up while holding his bag of goldfish. Suddenly he stopped. "Hey, Mom. Would you slow down? I don't want these fish to think we're having an earthquake!"

Such is the life of the single parent. But how do we control our time with all we have to do?

What You Should Know

The month before I graduated from high school, my baby brother was born. I started college in the fall, and four years looked like an eternity. But one day I decided not to measure my four years in classes, but to measure it in terms of my little brother growing up. It wouldn't be any time before he was four. I was right, and I got to enjoy his growth along the way. That's how valuable our time should be.

The average person's day looks something like this:

An Average Person's Day

Activity	Hours Spent
Sleeping	8
Personal hygiene	1
Preparing and eating meals	3
Commuting	2
Working	8
Total:	**22**

This leaves about two hours each day to do all of the other things that make life work. Most people, however, waste at least two hours a day.

Questions You Ask

I have always had a terrible time managing my time. Now that I'm a single parent, is there any hope for me?

Most people fritter their time away—a little here, a little there. To start on the road of time management, note where these fritter critters are lurking. Consider the following:

- Start each day by getting out of bed on time and making a to-do list on paper that you can refer to all day long.
- Set priorities. Concentrate your time and energy on the things that matter.
- Know what is expected of you. Is it the science fair at school or cupcakes you need to bake? Is it a meeting at the church? What do you need to accomplish? What can be omitted?
- Eliminate time wasters—waiting for an appointment, making two trips when one will do, doing tasks separately when they can be combined.
- Keep track of how you spend your time each day.
- Have the correct tools, ingredients, and materials and know

where they are—it saves time and energy.

Once I take care of the family and work, there's nothing left for me. How do I squeeze that in, too?

- *Budget and schedule your time.* Make an appointment with yourself on your calendar.
- *Schedule quiet time.* Ask family members to respect the time you schedule for yourself. You may choose to do it first thing in the morning, when you first get home from work, or the last thing at night. Just do it.
- *Prioritize.* Do this daily as well as on a long-term basis. Concentrate on your family and those who really matter to you.
- *Learn to say no.* Say yes only if you have the time or if you need to be involved for the sake of your family.
- *Reduce your standards.* Your house doesn't always have to be clean. I've learned this lesson well.
- *Delegate.* Stop thinking, if you want something done right, do it yourself. Let the kids help with housework. Teach them how to do the basics: dusting, running the sweeper, doing laundry. Resist the urge to do it over yourself.
- *Consolidate.* Keep a list of errands and do those that are in the same area at the same

time. Cook two meat loaves and freeze the extra one.

When I take time for myself away from the children, I am better when I am with them. I feel guilty about it sometimes. Is this selfish of me?

The purpose of time by yourself is to replenish your body and spirit and equip you for what lies ahead. I manage my quiet time in the morning, and it is the most essential part of my day. What do I find to do?

- *I exercise.* I walk or run outside when possible. Other times I exercise to a tape or on a couple of pieces of equipment I have in my bedroom.
- *I read.* A couple of books beside my bed provide much enjoyment or relaxation. Other books provide an opportunity for me to learn new skills for my work.
- *I write.* Gathering my thoughts on paper is something I do best in the morning. Most of this material comes from notes I jot down during busier times of my days—driving, cleaning, or traveling.
- *I study a couple of chapters from the Bible.* The books of Psalms and Isaiah in the Old Testament provide quick, direct application to me when my time is limited. The Gospels— Matthew, Mark, Luke, and John—offer the words of Je-

sus on topics that are equally relevant to my day as to individuals in the Bible. Other times, I read whole books of the Bible—Genesis, Exodus, Deuteronomy, Joshua, and so on. The stories told on these pages endear each of the characters to me.

- *I pray.* I keep a simple formula in mind that helps to keep my prayers balanced. One I use is:

A—Adoration (praising God for who he is).

C—Confession (asking him to forgive my sins).

T—Thanksgiving (giving thanks for what he's done).

S—Supplication (praying for others from a list I make of people in need).

Many individuals I know are not morning people. Instead, they find time for themselves during their lunch break or before bed. The time of day doesn't matter. Just be sure you do it. Your dedication to this time will enhance the rest of what you have to do.

How can I make a schedule for myself that I can stick to?

Prepare realistic to-do lists. Decide how much time you will need, then allow for those minutes in your day. Use an appointment book that you keep close. Mark everything from home and work and church in the same book.

Put a family schedule on a large wall calendar that everybody can see and use. Once a week, enter upcoming obligations onto the calendar and insist that everybody keep up with the schedule.

Make lunches for the whole week on Saturday. Create and freeze meals for unexpected guests. You can freeze sandwiches that will be thawed by lunchtime each day. Put a weekly dinner menu on your refrigerator based on what you have on hand and what you have found on sale. This will save having to make the decision each day. Shop ahead and have your children help with daily chores.

Schedule time to do laundry, housework, yard work, and paperwork on a regular basis rather than letting it pile up. Do big projects such as cleaning out the basement a little bit at a time so it doesn't overwhelm you. Write and mail checks to pay bills twice a month. Be sure to note when bigger bills such as insurance and taxes are coming due. Mark birthdays and anniversaries. Keep cards and stamps on hand. Check your calendar at the beginning of the week and get the appropriate cards in the mail.

Provide a place for family members to list what they need the next time you shop. We have a white marker board in our kitchen that shows grocery lists, chore instructions, and phone messages. Schedule all repairs or checkups for the first appointment of the day. This will minimize your waits.

Schedule your time and let others know you are booked. One friend of mine calls and is able to talk for hours, but I cannot afford to stay on the phone for long. One way I've found to handle this dilemma is to instruct my children to say I will call her back. When I do, I am in control of the time and length of the call. This isn't always easy to arrange, but it is necessary if I am to continue with relationships I have developed and still keep on schedule.

In all this planning and scheduling, be sure to allow for some fun. If you're doing the other things right, you should have time for it.

Time at Work

I've been a single parent for two years. I need to get all my work done at work so I can concentrate on the children when I get home. How can I stop people from interrupting me at work?

- If possible, get to work thirty minutes before others arrive. You'll be amazed at how much you can get done.

- If you work in an office, arrange your work space so your back is toward the door. Other people are less likely to interrupt you without eye contact.
- Close your door, if you have one. If not, be creative. My editor works in an open office without a door, but she has a red ribbon she stretches across the opening with velcro. It reads. "Editorial Deadline: Please do not disturb."
- If someone stops in and talks too long, stand up and take a short trip or ask that person what time it is. You can also remove extra chairs from your office so the one interrupting you doesn't make herself at home. If appropriate, just tell the visitor you are busy.

I put things off till the last minute. This stresses me out with the kids and often makes us late for appointments. What can I do?

Everyone procrastinates. But if you do it all the time, you've got reason to be concerned. For procrastinators, "one of these days" eventually becomes "none of these days," and procrastination turns into attitudes guaranteed to get in the way of personal and professional success. These will help:

- Do the mundane tasks. The more exciting things will wait.

- Don't just sit around. Make things happen.
- Take ownership. Your bills weren't paid on time because you didn't pay them.
- Stop wondering where you will start. Just start cleaning out those drawers.
- Set deadlines and meet them.
- Make your work and home environment pleasant. I never liked to play in a messy room when I was little. That got me to cleaning up lots of places before I got busy playing.
- Have a friend hold you accountable to finish a project by a certain date.
- Do first things first. You might start with the yuckiest. The others will be a breeze.
- Break large jobs into small segments. If you have a basement that will take a week to do, work on it for one hour a day till it's done.
- Reward yourself for completing tasks.

I need to put the kids first and then prioritize the other things in my life. Besides my kids, how do I know what's most important?

Get a plain notebook and a pen and set aside some quiet time to start applying the plan of your life.

- *Mission.* Ask yourself how you want to be remembered. Consider your family as you do this. Let them help you create a mission statement. For example: "Our time and work is devoted first to our faith in God and then to our commitment to each other as a family."

- *Goals.* These are the tangible things we want out of life—getting our bills paid, buying a new couch, developing more lasting relationships. Force yourself to write down your goals on separate pages, giving each a realistic deadline. Make at least one one-year goal, one five-year goal, and one lifetime goal. For each goal, list all the steps required to make that goal happen. Prioritize your goals by numbering them in order of importance. A goal is a dream with a deadline. "Eat evening meals together at least three times every week." In her book *Women Who Do Too Much* (Zondervan, 1992), Patti Sprinkle suggests setting goals as seasons of your life, (i.e., while Nick is still at home, until the kids are in school, and the like).

- *Plans.* Write incremental steps that will get you to each of your goals. Determine how much time each will take and what resources you will need. "The calendar located in the kitchen will mark the time for dinner we reserve together."

You should see my basement. I keep holding on to junk. How can I talk myself into getting rid of it?

When you are tempted to say, "I might need that someday," or "It will come back in style if I wait long enough," or "It just needs a little fixing up," throw it out or give it away. If you don't need it now, get rid of it. Resist acquiring new things. Have a garage sale.

To help you organize, you might try tackling a problem closet or basement with three piles: give-away, throw-aways, store-aways. Everything should find homes in one of these places. Then give, throw, or store.

The telephone will be my undoing. I find it hard to hurt people's feelings by cutting them off the phone too abruptly. But I can't take proper care of my kids and still stay on the phone. What can I do?

I came to this same realization when my children were very young. I would be polite and attentive to those who called me, and grumpy and demanding to my children. It didn't compute. My children were getting the subtle message that many other things were more important than they were. You are wise to try to nip this in the bud. Try the following:

- Screen out unimportant calls with an answering machine.

- Return phone calls at a good time for you when you can control how long you talk, for example, by saying, "I have to fix dinner now."
- Politely but firmly tell callers you can't talk right now.
- Get right to the point when you make a call: "I wanted to get back to you, but I only have a couple of minutes."
- Get an unlisted telephone number.
- Spend your time like your money—carefully.

I drive one hour to and from work each day. How can I productively use this time?

First, consider getting something closer to home. That hour costs you two hours each day, ten hours each week, forty hours each month, and so on. In addition, it takes you too far away from your children. What if you have to get home for an emergency?

While you are commuting, however, you can make productive use of your time. Pray or have quiet time, organize your day, prepare a to-do list, plan meals, create shopping lists, tape-record letters and memos, listen to educational tapes or books on tape.

You can also plan your lunch time productively: buy gas, make personal phone calls, shop for groceries, take a nap, stop at the dry cleaner's, schedule a doctor's appointment, go holiday shopping, think about how to improve your balance, get your car washed, write a letter, take a walk, read a book.

One more thought on time. My baby brother grew up long ago. He even served in Desert Storm. I've passed through many four-year chunks since my college days: gray hairs and wrinkles chronicle each one.

But every time I consider an undertaking, I remember the babies still in my home. It won't be any time till they are grown. Four years is just a drop in the bucket. Too soon they will be gone, and I will have all the time in the world to do those other things I want to do.

The Bible tells us to make the most of every opportunity and to take charge of our lives: "Make level paths for your feet and take only ways that are firm."[1] I hope I'm doing that, and I trust you are, too.

29

Managing Money

Most of those raising children alone—moms or dads, divorced, never-married, or widowed, teen or grandparent—have run into money problems. No matter how much we have, we seem to need more. Of course the frequency and severity of these difficulties depends upon the circumstances within each home. But having money problems and being a single parent just seem to go together.

One single mom from British Columbia wrote:

> I raised my two children without a car, so we used buses. We often had to take more than one bus to arrive at our destination. My children often asked me how many buses it would take to get to wherever we were going.
>
> One day her four-year-old daughter asked, "Mommy, how many buses does it take to get to heaven?"

What You Should Know

Besides the lack of parental involvement with children, financial problems pose the most serious threat to single-parent families. The Census Bureau reports that in single-parent homes, 46 percent live at or below the poverty income level. In two-parent homes, only 8 percent live in poverty. Expenses go up as two households are set up (child care, health care, and so on) and the income usually drops by about 21 percent per adult.[1]

Mothers typically earn less than fathers, and many children cannot rely on the noncustodial parent to pay full child support regularly. About half of divorced mothers receive no child support at all, and for those who do receive it, both the reliability and the amount of the payments drop over time.

Questions You Ask

The more I make, the more I spend. Why doesn't there ever seem to be enough money?

I heard a married woman say once that it didn't matter if she brought in an income to the house or not, the family was never better or worse off. The more they made the more they spent.

You and I should remember that single parents aren't the only ones with money problems. Nearly everyone lacks financially to some degree or another. Do the very best you can in this area, then what you lack in money in your home, make up for in love and commitment.

Our finances were a mess when we divorced. My ex-husband continues to have poor spending habits. How can I be sure his habits will no longer affect me?

Notify all banks, credit card companies, and other financial institutions that you want your name removed from all accounts. Then establish bank and credit card accounts in your own name.

I am paying both alimony and child support to my ex-wife. It's breaking me financially. What can I do?

Structure as much money as you can to go as alimony payments. They are tax deductible to you and taxable to your ex-wife. This will give you at least some break. You might also have the amount of child support you pay reviewed. If either you or your ex-wife has had a substantial change in income, you may be able to adjust the amount you pay.

How do I cover my health insurance since the divorce?

If you were covered on your husband's policy, it is possible to remain on the plan for up to thirty-six months following the divorce per the Congressional Omnibus Budget Reconciliation Act, or COBRA. But you may have to pay group health rates. The company you work for may offer a better deal. Check it out thoroughly.

If neither of these work and an individual policy is too expensive, shop around for a major-medical coverage, which takes care of only accidents and major illnesses. You can get a $1,000 deductible to keep your premiums low.

What scholarship resources are available for sending my son to college?

Talk to the high-school guidance counselor. They have scores of books, lists, and applications available. Some will even assist you in completing these forms.

Your library is full of resources similar to the following:

How to Put Your Children Through College Without Going

Broke (New York: The Research Institute of America, Inc.).

Daniel Cassidy and Michael J. Alves, *The Scholarship Book* (Englewood Cliffs, N.J.: Prentice Hall).

Directory of Financial Aid for Minorities, ed. Dr. Gail Ann Schlacter (Redwood City, Calif.: Reference Service Press).

Directory of Financial Aid for Women, ed. Dr. Gail Ann Schlachter (Redwood City, Calif.: Reference Service Press).

Paying Less for College (Princeton, N.J.: Peterson's Guides).

Alan Deutschman, *Winning Money for College* (Princeton, N.J.: Peterson's Guides).

Need a Lift? (Indianapolis: The American Legion).

Also try the Internet for further information.

For information on federal aid programs, call the Student Aid Information Center at (800) 433-3243.

For information on cooperative education, write to: The National Commission for Cooperative Education, 360 Huntington Ave., Boston, MA 02115.

For information on the AmeriCorp program, call (800) 942-2677.

I'm a single mom. What about college for me? I want to begin a new life and make more money

besides. Are there scholarships available?

Writer Elizabeth Watson lists the following resources for scholarships[2]:

- Orville Redenbacher's Second Start Scholarship Program, P.O. Box 4137, Blair, NE 68009. Several $1,000 scholarships are available to undergraduates enrolled in an accredited degree program who are over the age of thirty.
- Business and Professional Women's Foundation, Clairol Loving Care Scholarship Program, 2012 Massachusetts Ave. N.W., Washington, DC 20056. Phone (202) 293-1200. Scholarships worth $1,000 are available to women over thirty who seek to upgrade their skills or complete their education.
- Business & Professional Women's Foundation, Florence Morese Scholarship, 2012 Massachusetts Avenue, N.W., Washington, DC 20056. Phone (202) 293-1200. Scholarships worth $1,000 are available to women who are at least twenty-five years old and who have spent five or more years in full-time homemaking. Must be seeking employment due to death of a spouse or dissolution of a marriage.
- Brookhaven Women in Science, Renate W. Chasman Scholarship, P.O. Box 183, Upton, NY 11973. Phone (516) 282-7226.

Scholarships worth $1,000 are available to junior or senior undergraduates or first-year graduate students pursuing a career in science, engineering, or mathematics, but whose education was interrupted because of family, financial, or other problems.

- National League of American Pen Women, Inc., Scholarships Grants for Mature Women, 1300 Seventeenth Street, N.W., Washington, DC 20036. Phone (202) 785-1997. Scholarship grants worth $1,000 are available to women who are at least thirty-five years old.

Because I don't have much financially, I haven't bothered to draw up a will. I'm wondering, now that I'm on my own, is this wise?

It's wise to start thinking about doing something soon. Without a will, the courts can make choices that will affect your heirs in a major way:

- They can choose your child's guardian.
- Stepchildren will get nothing.
- No trust will be set up to take care of your young children.
- You can't leave special things to special people.
- A handicapped child may inherit your money and disqualify himself from government aid.

How can I tell the difference between what I need and what I want?

Author Larry Burkett suggests that you determine the difference between your needs, wants, and wishes. Burkett defines them as follows:

- *Needs.* Food, clothes, housing, health care, job.
- *Wants.* Comforts, conveniences, things nicer than you have.
- *Wishes.* Luxuries, items you can get along without.[3]

He recommends filling in a chart like the one below:

Needs	Wants	Wishes
Transportation		
Food		
Clothes		
Housing		
Recreation		

Money and My Kids

I am newly divorced, and we don't have the money we used to have. How do I get my child accustomed to what we can and cannot afford?

Go over with your child what you have coming in and what you have going out. Get the child's input on ways you can cut back in one area (food) to provide more for other areas (clothes, entertainment). Whatever you do, include your child every way possible to enhance success.

I'm afraid that if I cut back too much financially, my child will resent me. What can I do?

Syndicated columnist Ann Landers says, "Kids who have everything they want soon lose respect for money—and for their parents."[4] Don't be afraid to set limits. You will save a lot of hassles for yourself and your kids if they know how to set up and live by a budget, balance a checkbook, save, and avoid the pitfalls of credit.

How can I teach my kids to function on a budget?

Larry Burkett recommends doing the following activity with your kids:

- Choose a job with a certain salary. Explain how twice-monthly paychecks are determined.

- Determine net spendable income by subtracting taxes and charitable contributions. Show them a copy of your pay stub to see how this is figured in the salary you get.

- Estimate budget percentages. Allow them to set the amount they want to spend in each category—prioritizing what they value most. Total should equal 100 percent:

_____ Housing (mortgage, insurance, taxes, electricity, natural gas, water, sanitation, telephone, maintenance).

_____ Food.

_____ Automobile (payments, gas and oil, insurance, license, taxes, maintenance, repair, replacement).

_____ Insurance (life and medical).

_____ Debts (credit cards, loans, notes).

_____ Entertainment and recreation (eating out, trips, baby-sitting, vacations).

_____ Clothing.

_____ Savings.

_____ Medical expenses (doctor, dental, drugs).

_____ Miscellaneous (cosmetics, cleaning supplies, allowances, subscriptions, gifts, and so on).[5]

My children and I have started going to church regularly. We have heard for the first time about tithing our money. What is tithing? Do we all need to give even if we have so little?

The Bible teaches to give to God before anything else. Ten percent is the amount talked about in the Old Testament. Say your net income is $800 bimonthly. God instructs us to give $80 to the church of which we have become a part. That amount given to God through your church acknowledges that all good things come from him.

"'Bring the whole tithe into the storehouse, that there may be food in my house. Test me in this,' says the LORD Almighty, 'and see if I will not throw open the floodgates of heaven and pour out so much blessing that you will not have room enough for it. I will prevent pests from devouring your crops, and the vines in your fields will not cast their fruit,' says the LORD Almighty."[6]

The amount you give back to God is not set in stone—but that you do is. Let your children see you giving to God. They will see a mom or dad who is taking care of some bigger issues, regardless of how things look on the surface. This will reinforce values you want to instill and deter your children from the egocentric world in which they live.

I've tried to pay my tithes, but I resent putting money in an offering plate at church when my family needs so much. Why not let others do the giving?

If you let others do the giving, you let others get the blessings from God. I know it doesn't make sense, but you can't outgive God. The more you give to him, the more he gives back to you.

There is an important key, however, to receiving from God: He wants you to give without begrudging it. "Each man should give what he has decided in his heart to give, not reluctantly or under compulsion, for God loves a cheerful giver."[7]

If you give cheerfully, God gives back to you. It's that simple.

Are there general guidelines about what percentages of our money should be going where?

Larry Burkett suggests the following for each budget category:[8]

Housing	30–36 percent
Food	12–17 percent
Auto	15–20 percent
Insurance	3–7 percent
Debts	5–6 percent
Entertainment	5–8 percent
Clothing	5–6 percent
Savings	5 percent
Medical Expenses	4–8 percent
Miscellaneous	5–10 percent

How much allowance should I give my children?

Money columnist Mary Hunt tells how she put her kids on a

monthly cash salary. Mary and her husband required the boys to give 10 percent of this salary to their church and save another 10 percent. They generated lists that described everything the children would be responsible to pay. While Mary required that the boys do chores, their salary was not dependent on their performance, much as salaries in real life are not slashed for a mistake.

This plan, according to Hunt, takes the bad-guy image from the parents. It eliminates the stress that money can cause between parent and child. The kids spend what they have and do not ask for loans. They saved more than the required minimum. Finally, they developed their own financial skills.[9]

How early should I start teaching my daughter about money?

When your daughter is as young as three, you can start teaching her about money. She should be receiving a weekly allowance. As she gets older, she should be responsible for saving 20 to 25 percent of her money for bigger ticket items. Acclimate her early to making charitable contributions and giving money to your church. The earlier you educate her about a budget, the earlier its importance will kick in.

By the middle school years, your child should be able to do extensive comparison shopping. Teach her how to select the best deals.

No quick answers exist for the money woes of a single parent. However, many good books have been published to help you in this area. Be sure you know your financial limits, then spend within them. If you don't have money for it, don't buy it. In the meantime, read all you can about managing money.

30

Developing
Safe Relationships

When I was eighteen, I spent the summer with my parents in Arizona. During that stay I dated a young man a little older than I was. He had experienced a lot more than I had and knew what he wanted, including getting married. I had just won a one-year scholarship to the university in our hometown and was getting an opportunity to do something that had not yet been done in my family—get a college degree. I was excited about what the fall would bring, and the last thing I was thinking about was finding a person to marry.

One night we hiked to the top of a nearby mountain overlooking the city, and we sat and talked. David asked me what my definition of a perfect husband would be. I opened my mouth to respond, but nothing came out. I had never thought about the question or its answer. He pressed me for a response.

"Well," I began, "if you asked me for my definition of a perfect mom, I would know. Based on my acquaintance with my own mother, I have some criteria on which to build my expectations for all moms. But until I know someone to fit the role of husband in my life, I don't know how to define him now."

Needless to say, my romance with David ended that night, but I have often thought of my lack of response to that question. I find it frightening to realize that nine years later when I actually married my husband, I had no more idea of what it was I wanted from a mate than I did that warm Arizona evening.

What You Should Know

As single parents, we need to be equipped with the right relationship radar when it comes to finding friends and romantic relationships. Psychologists and authors Henry Cloud and John Townsend say we need to find safe people to:

- *Help heal the hurt from past relationships.* In a healthy way, good friends can help you heal—especially if there is a good balance in what you are giving and receiving. Giving always helps make one healthier.
- *Change the patterns that led you into trouble.* The more you expand, the greater will be your vision. You can understand more truths and realize more options.
- *Assist in childrearing.* Many people have helped me to raise my children—the members of the church we attended, youth leaders, coaches, and some teachers.
- *Build a spiritual growth system.* Find a friend who is on a similar plane as you are emotionally, spiritually, and intellectually. Make it a time of growth for both of you.
- *Reenter the world of dating* and not repeat the same mistakes.[1]

Questions You Ask

Victimization

I have had so much happen to me, I don't trust anyone and think everyone is out to get me. How can I get over this?

It sounds as though you have stopped believing in your own power in life, and you see people and circumstances as controlling you. In essence, you think life stinks and there's nothing you can do about it. Read on to find out how to change that belief.

My mother was married four times, and she still feels powerless to change the direction of her life. I am now divorced and afraid I have inherited her victim mentality. Is this possible?

You may have learned this way of responding from your mother, but you didn't inherit it. And you have the power to change it.

The powerlessness that we feel as victims is a response learned from someone who treated us in an inappropriate way at some point in our lives. This treatment often comes from the mate in the never-married or divorced situation. Single moms who feel victimized often glorify the troubles they go through rather than learning from them or altering what needs to be

changed. They often find themselves saying, "But I'm a single
parent," as if that gives a blanket
explanation for the struggles
they face.

Many single-mom victims
assume they can never be happy
like other people. They act as
though they are always on the
short end of the stick. They
appear vulnerable and in pain.
They become martyrs and do not
have relationships where they
can express their needs, let alone
get them satisfied. These women
hold on to past pains, and this
immobilizes them to effectively
handle the present. What's worse,
their kids watch and learn the
fine art of victimization in their
own lives.

Deciding you have allowed
yourself to feel victimized is the
first step toward fixing things.
Then, to free yourself from victimization, try the following:

- *Take responsibility for yourself.* Set boundaries to keep
  hurtful circumstances and
  people away from you. They
  can only go to this point and
  no further.
- *Redefine your relationships.*
  Look more closely at yourself
  and others to decide what kind
  of distance to put between
  you and the danger.
- *Do not blame yourself.* Blame
  only reinforces your own sense
  of powerlessness.

How can I choose relationships that do not feed my victimization?

Berry and Baker say the
answers can be found through
exploring your feelings and
honestly facing the characteristics of your relationships—
either casual or romantic—by
doing the following:

- Notice how power is negoti-
  ated between the two of you.
  If you treat the powerless person as powerful, the relationship may become dangerous
  to both of you.
- Observe how pain is handled
  in your relationship. When you
  get hurt, the hurt rarely stops
  with the event that caused it.
  Human pain doesn't stay frozen
  in a moment in time but
  echoes far beyond instances
  of mistreatment.
- Watch for the blame game.
  Victims can be consumed with
  assigning blame rather than
  taking responsibility for their
  own pain.
- Look at how you deal with
  control in your relationship.
  Victims have an excessive need
  for control that is rooted in
  their feelings of powerlessness over their own emotions.
- Watch for evidence of revenge.
  It is often mistaken for justice.
- Judge the health of your relationships by paying attention
  to your own feelings.[2]

Friendships

After my divorce, I lost most of the friends I had as a married person. How can I develop new friendships in this phase of my life?

Help your friends feel comfortable around you. Don't be so depressed. Let them know the new things going on. Don't force them to choose between you and your former mate. No matter what direction you choose to go, you are in for some changes—especially regarding your relationships. Seek out those individuals who are good for you and your children. Try the following:

- *Church.* Get involved in youth groups, Sunday school classes, small groups, and outside activities.
- *Work.* Go to lunch, take a break, arrange an after-hours outing with someone you enjoy being with.
- *Kids.* As you get involved in those activities that interest your children, you can also get involved with the other adults who participate (coaches, leaders, parents, friends).

You might also move someplace new and get a different job. I relocated about eighty miles away to begin a doctoral program. We found new friends, a new church, and new surroundings. Because of the busyness involved with my schooling, I didn't have time to wallow in my miseries. As a result, I began to heal from my heartache. Then when I visited old friends, I was more fun and comfortable to be around.

What kind of friendships should I look for to benefit both my kids and me?

Friendships involve lots of work. Making friends is a conscious choice by the two people involved. Each person should be able to nurture the other and accept one another as he or she is and overlook weaknesses.

Different friends fill different needs. What we want from a friendship we need to bring to that friendship. The Bible says to have friends, show yourself friendly.[3] Most of the really good friendships we have came as a result of involving ourselves with things we like to do. We don't usually find our closest friends by looking for them.

I feel in such need of adult companionship that I tend to tell too much to friends when they come around. What can I do?

Spread out your interaction so you manage it better as it comes. If you have a prolonged friendship with another person, that person will get to know plenty about you. Don't try to tell it all in the first week. Many try to force a friendship instead of letting it evolve naturally. Then when something happens to break the union that never should have been in the first place, too many secrets have been told.

A friend who dumps her secret thoughts too quickly puts the other person in the position of a counselor rather than a friend. The give-and-take of the relationship never happens, and you become too cumbersome a burden for that person to bear. Be transparent, but only as appropriate. Be wise about when you say what and let your friend *see* the qualities in you rather than *hear* all your descriptions.

One friend is going through a divorce and calls me all the time, since I experienced the same thing several years ago. I've gotten so I dread her calls. Is this wrong?

When one person looks to someone else to solve their problems, that person becomes dependent and the friendship becomes need-driven. Your friend sounds very needy and is becoming too dependent on you. This will not help your friend, and it will wear you out. A friend who depends on you too much for her emotional support often has a victim orientation to life.

Determine the difference between a person in need and a needy person. An emotionally healthy person who is going through a tough time might need your help to regain her perspective. She is honestly seeking solutions and is willing to work toward these solutions. A needy person continually talks about her problems yet never takes steps toward resolving them. Suggest counseling to your friend and explain that you can't do anything else to help.

Also, be aware of other unhealthy friendships, such as the person who wants to be your friend because of your position, status, money, or inclusion in a particular group. Others want a friend for the sake of having a friend.

You need to keep in mind the importance of balance, the fact that your needs must be cared for in the relationship as well. You may need to allow the other person to struggle for the sake of her personal growth as you did.

Assess your friendships periodically to make sure they are healthy. You should teach this skill to your children as well. My daughter currently has a friend who is very needy and possessive and who has influenced my daughter to make some wrong choices. It has been an opportunity for me to not forbid my daughter to see the girl, but to let her work through her own decision.

Though I am almost forty-five, I want to learn how to find the best

people to have in my life. How do I begin?

Henry Cloud and John Townsend, authors of the book *Safe People*, say, "While there are different kinds of unsafe people, many of them fall under three categories:

- *Abandoners* start relationships they can't finish;
- *Critics* take a parental role with everyone;
- *Irresponsibles* are people who don't take care of themselves or others."[4]

You might start by recognizing these three types and which one you have been attracting. Then, read a book such as *Safe People* to find ways to plug the information into your own circumstances.

Romantic Relationships

The first time I married, I chose someone just like my dad. Besides our own parents, who else influences our decisions about relationships?

The other factors that contribute to our selection of mates are outside people who affect us in a specific way: coaches, relatives, friends, teachers, acquaintances. Individuals who enter the lives of children play a role—either positively or negatively—that influences the kind of person they long to spend their lives with.

These factors—parents, friends, teachers, acquaintances—each make their stroke onto the canvas that paints the image of the person we choose. That image includes character, parenting skills, appearance, ambition, interests, chemistry, spirituality, personality, and intelligence.

Do I search for someone like me, or do opposites really attract?

Opposites do attract, but they don't stay stuck as a rule. If you want the possibility of something permanent, similarity is of paramount importance. Every place your lives can match will be an asset in your upcoming relationship. The essential similarities vary somewhat. But generally, you can search for such things as intellect, values, interests, and role expectations. Neil Clark Warren provides a fifty-item list of helpful marriage similarities.[5]

Many times we look for people who fill the empty places in our lives or will compensate for weaknesses we feel we have. The Bible warns us against being unequally yoked[6] with another person. That means finding someone a lot like ourselves in several ways: intelligence, values, intimacy, interests, beliefs, and expectations about roles.

Certain differences, including personal habits, use of money, skills, interests, values, and spiritual beliefs, can spell trouble down the line.

I'm crazy about a guy I just met. How do I know if he's the one I should marry?

Myles Munroe writes, "If the person you love can tell you why he loves you, get rid of him."[7] What he means is, if that person's love is based on loving your long blond hair or athletic prowess, what happens when the hair falls out in chemotherapy or sports activity is placed on the back burner to give attention to more demanding things in life?

Let passionate love mature before you decide to marry. Time gives a clearer perspective. Most relationships don't survive when passions fade or reasons for loving disappear. Take this time to get to know yourself. Learn more about who you are, what your interests are, and where you want to go. As you discover the answers, you have something more distinct to offer someone else. If your relationship withstands all this discovery, it's probably worth pursuing.

What are some major reasons why we choose wrong mates?

Many times, we single parents think nothing could be worse than being alone. We decide we need someone to help our emotions, finances, parenting, and schedules. Sometimes one or both individuals are too anxious to get married. A surprising few of us know what we are looking for. Many times we don't give ourselves enough time to know potential mates and our expectations become unrealistic. Other times, we haven't taken enough time to heal from our first disappointing relationship, and we find someone on the rebound. When the other person is not observed in lots of different settings for an extended period of time, we don't learn personality traits, and we ignore problems.

Much time spent with this person while keeping an open mind will help you make the right decision.

I have been dating a Christian man for several months. We have much in common and care deeply for each other. My ten-year-old son, however, resists my association with this man. He makes negative comments and gets angry when my friend comes around. What should I do?

I believe our number one priority is our children. First you must decide if this is a person you could marry and if he could make your family better. Be sensitive and honest about answering those questions within yourself. If the answer to either of these questions is no, end the relationship. Then delve more deeply into why you answered no. If you can answer yes to these questions, you need to move forward while handling your son carefully.

Take your son alone to a neutral, nondistracting location where you can do something the two of you enjoy: fishing, walking, wading. Allow him to say all that is on his mind without rebuttal from you. It might help to give him a pencil and paper to organize his thoughts before he begins.

Then address each issue, one by one. Brainstorm ways this person can enrich your life as a family and not take away from it. Uncover valid reasons your son may have for developing his dislike. He may be able to see characteristics in your friend that you are too close to observe.

Agree on places you can both compromise. Two nights a week, for example, can be devoted to just family without your friend around. But your son must be prepared for your once-a-week date with this person. Let your son see your willingness to work with him.

Then pray together. By allowing your son to see you take this issue to God in a vulnerable, open-minded way, you are modeling a technique for him to use for his own problems. Assure your son that your role as his mom is the most awesome privilege of your life. He needs to hear that often

now that he is sharing your affections with someone else.

I want to be in a relationship more than anything. I've been a single parent now for six years, my children are almost grown, and my new career is well under way. What can I do?

It sounds as though you have taken care of some of the most important things during the last few years and have made the most of being single—grieving in healthy ways, caring for the children, finding fulfilling employment. But you cannot make a love relationship happen. It either does or it doesn't. You can only place yourself in a strategic position to attract the kind of person you want. But be aware of the following:

- You are still vulnerable. Go into each potential relationship with your eyes wide open. One single mom I know says she would rather want what she doesn't have than have what she doesn't want.

- Don't spend so much time focusing on a potential mate that you fail to develop wonderful friendships. Many life mates are found among the friends a person has. But whether you find a life mate or not, you need friends for accountability, support, and help through challenging times.

- Don't stop growing personally. Keep reading, improving,
  and growing in all the areas
  that interest you most. Then if
  you find that special someone,
  you will be decked out in your
  Sunday best.

Sex Outside of Marriage

**Do I have to live the rest of my life
deprived of physical intimacy?**

At a university in Ohio, I
taught a class on current issues
to 120 students. I was responsible for bringing in various speak-
ers to present one side of different issues, and allowing the
students to observe. A nurse
gave a presentation I will never
forget.

This nurse brought in a
garbage bag and dumped its
contents on the front desk. She
explained how when she goes
into an operating room, she must
protect herself. She proceeded to
dress in all the required garb—
gown, hat, gloves, pants, and so
on—till she was completely covered except for her eyes. Then
she put on her glasses.

"And you are told to use *this*
to protect yourself," she said as
she held up a condom. "This little
device fails about 2–3 percent of
the time due to method failures
—breakage, slippage and manu-
facturer defects. User failures—
failure to wear, hold in place
upon withdrawal of penis, or

poking holes—makes the number even higher.[8]"

Next, she had several students
hold different colors of Play-Doh
in front of the class. The nurse
had two students touch the red
to the yellow Play-Doh as she
described that Mary dates John
and they have sex, but then they
break up. The two pieces of clay
pull away, but traces of their
colors are left on each other.
Other combinations are made
down the line till all the colors
are mixed. "When you have sex,
you are sleeping with all the
other partners that person has
had," the nurse said.

Intimacy can be found in other
ways, however. Find a relationship with God. Develop deep
friendships. Spend time with
family. These associations will
fill many of your empty places.

**"No sex outside of marriage" is a
religious thing. What if I am not a
religious person?**

All religions and philosophies,
no matter how different the beliefs, have some fundamental
codes of conduct and values that
are largely the same—rules they
follow for the perpetuation of
mankind.

Whether our source is religion
or philosophy or plain personal
logic, the basics are similar. These
basics are directions of cleanli-
ness, honesty, respect for life,
commitment to marriage, disci-

pline, and personal responsibility. From generations of humans who have lived before us, we have learned ways of behaving that work best. It's called "morality." An immoral lifestyle ultimately leads to hurt, heartache, and misery for all concerned.

We are passionate people. We must teach our kids to control their passions. We cannot teach our kids until we have mastered them ourselves and given our children reasons to do the same.

31

Getting Remarried

In the late 1960s, a popular TV program appeared entitled "The Brady Bunch." For several successful years, the episodes centered around a man with three boys who had married a woman with three girls. Instead of financial problems, viewers observed a stay-at-home mother with a full-time maid and a loving husband who earned a generous living for his newly combined family. I don't know that any of us knew whether ex-mates were deceased or merely absent, but neither of them seemed to present challenges. Child support was not discussed, and the biggest problems the children handled were whether or not to make cheerleading or the school football team. Past decisions never haunted either husband or wife, and the families seemed to blend without a hitch

Many watched the show assuming that was all there was to creating a Brady-like bunch. Two people brought together eight people, and they all lived happily ever after.

No one apparently informed the Bradys that remarriage is difficult, and the parties have to work hard to not be among the 80 percent of second marriages that fail. So what can we do to prepare ourselves for trying it again?

What You Should Know

American Demographics gives the following profile for those who remarry:

- The average divorced woman who gets remarried is 35 years old and has been divorced for 3.9 years.
- The average divorced man is 39 and has waited 3.6 years.

- The interval between marriages lengthens with age.
- Grooms aged 20 to 24 wait an average of only 1.3 years before remarrying.
- Grooms aged 65 and older wait 7.1 years.
- Remarriage rates for the divorced are highest among young adults.
- The number of remarriages peaks among older age groups.
- In 1988, 20 to 30 percent of divorced young adults (aged 20 to 24) married again. The rate of remarriage for young women is slightly higher than for men. After age 24, however, marriage rates are higher for men. Among divorced aged 45 to 54, 10 percent of men remarried in 1988, compared with 5 percent of women. Remarriages involving older adults are usually the second time for both partners. Young adults usually remarry a never-married person.[1]

Marriages	1970	1988
Both single	68.8%	54.5%
Wife previously married	7.3%	11.4%
Husband previously married	7.6%	11.1%
Both previously married	16.3%	23%

American Demographics also reports that in 1970 about one in three marriages was a remarriage for at least one of the partners. Today, that share is approaching half.

American Demographics tells us that the United States leads the world in its belief in romantic love. Eighty-six percent of American college students say they would not marry without love. Brazil comes in a close second, and more than three-quarters of students can't do without love in Mexico, England, Australia, and Hong Kong. College students in India are the most likely to marry without love; only 24 percent say no to marriage without love. Arranged marriages are still common in India. Japan and the Philippines fall in between, with 62 and 64 percent saying no to marriage without love.[2]

Questions You Ask

My wife died three years ago when our children were nine and eleven. I have been remarried now for just over a month, and my children are acting much as they did when they lost their mother. Why?

All members of your family had to take time to adjust to the changes the death of your wife brought. For your remarriage, a whole new set of adjustments is necessary. Stepchildren will add still other adjustments.

Your children, now twelve and fourteen, are at the most difficult age for accepting a stepmother. They will need to adapt to everything new in their home situation while also balancing their own adolescent concerns. They will learn most by seeing appropriate balance, efficient conflict resolution, and good decision making modeled by you. Be patient, kind, loving, and wise. Know everything you can about adolescents and teens. Understand that they are not weird and neither are you. You all just need lots of love and understanding and patience.

I was a single dad for five years. What can I do now to help all of us adjust to remarriage?

Humans were created for calm, solid, and secure settings. Losing stability can be upsetting to everyone. You need to keep as many things the same as you can. Establish new traditions that work well for all family members. Respect each other's responsibilities, rights, and importance to your family unit. Allow each to have a voice.

Remarriage is going to be lots of hard work, but you have some very good reasons to hang in there. Here are some things that might help:

- Attend all special activities in which other family members are involved. Let your wife do this by herself at times so she can establish her own rapport with the children.

- Make courtesy and respect a standard in your home. This includes privacy and freedom to express feelings in a constructive way.

- Keep extended family and the other parents as involved as possible. If you can introduce your children to your wife's family, let them establish their own traditions with the children. Don't force them to follow in the steps of those who came before. Help them understand where your kids are in their transitions, preferences, and dispositions.

My ex-husband remarried almost three years ago. Since that time, he has had little time to spend with our children. Why?

After separation, fathers normally maintain contact with their children. But as time goes on, many fathers invest less and less time in the relationship. Reasons could include:

- Fathers are more likely to remarry and become involved in a union that introduces stepchildren. Contact with their own biological children often decreases because of time and financial constraints as well as additional responsibilities imposed by the new family.

- Emotional needs once met by the biological children are often met by stepchildren, and the parent's contact with biological children may not be as crucial.

- Increased geographical distance because of remarriage or job changes can create emotional distance.
- Custodial mothers often become more vigilant gatekeepers once the father establishes a new family.

I need to know why so many second marriages fail so I can know what to watch out for in my own. Can you help?

The biggest reason for failed second marriages may be our expectations. We plan to have our second marriage be just like a nuclear family when it is not. We also often enter a second marriage in hopes of making up for mistakes in the first. Closeness, bonding, and trust are expected to develop too soon. A class is taken or a book is read, and the new couple expect rejection, anger, guilt, and jealousy problems to be erased.

Several reasons may contribute to your discomfort:

- *If you have two people* who have both been married and been single parents. You both have a history from other relationships and your losses. This creates a lot of baggage under one roof.
- *You have no history.* All that the children remember does not include your wife or the combination of the two of you. Your wife was not present (even though biological parents were divorced, they were there somewhere) for important events in their lives such as Christmases, birthdays, and firsts at school. You are strangers suddenly living together, and the little experience you have together inhibits the building of a common identity. When the many connections within the stepfamily and the intricate connections outside the family combine, it makes for much complexity.
- *You have no model.* No scripts are written for how to build a stepfamily. Every couple who forms a new marriage has to wing it just like all the others before them.
- *Loyalties are divided.* Children are often afraid that if they love their stepparent, they will betray their biological parent. Parents are afraid that loving their stepchildren will prevent them from drawing closer to their biological children.
- *"Where do I belong?"* Physical space is sometimes rearranged to combine the two households. A shortage of time, money, and bathrooms is a result. Attention from the biological parent inevitably changes. Chores and responsibilities are newly defined.

- *"We're broke."* Although the combining of two incomes often alleviates many of the financial strains, it doesn't eliminate them. In fact, remarriage often complicates money issues even more. There are more people who need the resources, and two people now have to decide how the money is spent. The division may make for more strain than ever before.
- *The roles change.* Some children have functioned as surrogate spouses, confidants, and decision makers for some time. Then enters the stepparent, who assumes those roles.
- *Bonds are already formed.* The closeness between the parent and child before the marriage is often stronger than the marriage itself—and certainly has more foundation. This is different from the nuclear family where the strongest bond grows between the married couple. Children in nuclear families gain security when the marital relationship is strong and satisfying. Children in a stepfamily may feel threatened by a biological parent's alliance with someone who is not emotionally bonded to them. This insecurity and the children's responses to it may undermine the happiness of the family.

- *Different needs.* The new couple needs a honeymoon to help adapt to the change. The children need extra attention at the same time. The sexual relationship between the mom and dad may add to the confusion of the children and their own emerging sexuality. Add to that the varying stages in the grief cycle that all of you are in.
- *Lack of support.* A gross lack of support exists from schools, churches, and communities for the stepparent family.

Should We or Shouldn't We?

A wonderful woman and I have decided to get married. How do we prepare the kids?

There's much you can do to prepare everyone, and you'll be glad you took the time.

- Talk to your children, but don't give them the responsibility for making the final decision. Remarriage is an adult choice.
- Include the children from both sides in your wedding.
- Eliminate as many unknowns as possible, such as how each parent parents, what changes will be involved, and so on.
- Watch your kids. Stay close to them. Observe their reactions. Talk to them often and help them feel free to express their feelings without being shot down. They desperately need

to feel loved, included, and assured that you are not replacing them with someone else. Then be sure you don't.

Understand that all the preparations in the world will not eliminate some difficulties that lie ahead.

It's been a difficult year. I married a woman with two children last year, and I have two children of my own. Can you suggest ways for helping to blend our families?

Remember that all change takes time to assimilate. Allow that time for the benefit of all concerned. Then try these suggestions for blending:

- Have regular dates alone with your spouse.
- Don't attribute every problem to being a blended family. Most problems are similar to those in intact families.
- Don't assume the worst. If your husband is late picking up your child, maybe it was a flat tire.
- Turn lose-lose situations into win-win situations. For example, together you can talk through conflict resolutions so that everyone wins. If two siblings want to watch different TV programs at the same time, together work out an arrangement where each gets a turn to choose the show.
- Don't turn issue issues into people issues. If one of *your*

children responds negatively to one of *her* children, walk back through the problem and generate ideas for doing it better. Don't attack the individuals.
- Don't ever side with yours against hers. Blend together in every way possible.

I am a single mom who wants to remarry more than anything. Will this take my son away from his father?

Nearly three-fourths of all mothers remarry; half of those within five years. Remarriage brings some advantages but often comes with a price tag of emotional rivalries between parents and children.

Remarriage does not have to affect the amount of contact the children have with their noncustodial, biological father unless you move away. If relocation does become necessary, work together with your former mate to keep the relationship close. That connection needs to be kept strong, no matter what other demands are placed upon you. And your children need to be assured of that.

Where can I find help with the transitions of remarriage?

The integration of a new family member is not easy. Seek help with remarriage difficulties before marrying. Seek out a church in your area that provides remarriage counseling. Find a support group—both formal and informal—that can help you with the transitions. These and other forums should allow you to discuss items such as:

- Combining different family cultures and identities.
- Distribution of family resources (money, time, and affection).
- Loyalty conflicts.
- Feelings about the prior relationships.
- Roles and responsibilities.
- Visitation by nonresident children.

Such programs and groups can help parents in stepfamilies develop realistic expectations, arrive at a clearer understanding of their new roles and feelings, and help them deal more effectively with the problems of everyday life.

Should I fill the role of father to my stepchildren?

Few children want anyone to waltz into their lives and take the place of their biological father. But most children have a longing for a father that needs to be satisfied. Your supportive involvement with the children will likely make an important difference in their lives. Your role, however, should not be to fill another's shoes, but to bring shoes of your own. Build something with each child that belongs to just the two of you.

Keep in mind that you may never get it together with your stepchild, but you will always be ahead for trying.

Can you suggest some reading material to help us through the process?

For children:
Berman, Claire. *What Am I Doing in a Stepfamily?* Secaucus, N.J.: Lyle Stuart,1982.

For parents:
Einstein, Elizabeth. *The Stepfamily: Living, Loving, and Learning.* New York: Macmillan, 1982.

Visher, Emily B. and John S. Visher. *Stepfamilies: A Guide to Working with Stepparents and Stepchildren.* New York: Bruner/Mazel, 1979.

Visher, Emily B. and John S. Visher. *How to Win as a Stepfamily.* New York: Dembner Books, 1982.

Palmer, Nancy S., William D. Palmer, and Kay Marshall Strom. *The Family Puzzle.* Colorado Springs: Pinon Press, 1996.

Resources for stepfamily weddings may be obtained by writing: Clergy Services of Greater Kansas City, 706 West 42nd Street, Kansas City, MO 64111.

Moving Ahead With It

- One woman I know who works with single moms recommends that they begin all decisions with intense prayer—for months if necessary.

- Don't give up, even on the worst of days. You've made a decision to be married, now commit to the long haul.

- Don't control. It will cost you dearly.

- From your earliest decisions to proceed, include the children with your plans.

- Maintain reasonable goals.

- Be sensitive to the feelings of all family members, even if those feelings are irritating.

- Provide neutral territory so that all family members have special places of their own.

- Don't let finances become a problem. Live within your means.

- Develop good communication with your mate's ex.

- Avoid trying to fit a preconceived role.

- Be kind, patient, and a good sport.

- Don't wear your feelings on your sleeve.

- Set limits and enforce them, work out rules ahead of time with the children, and support each other when the rules have to be enforced.

- Let the children express their feelings for the natural parent.

- Expect ambivalence. It's normal.

- Don't expect instant love. Bonding takes time.

- Don't take all the responsibility. The children need some, too.

- Maintain the primacy of the marital relationship. Some stepparents spend too much time and energy trying to work out their stepparent roles and neglect their own relationship.

- Stay positive.

- Attend church together and have regular family devotions with prayer and Bible reading.

The Children and Remarriage

What can I expect from the children after our remarriage?

You will now be responsible for helping to nurture someone else's children. Adults select their new mates, but the children have no say in who they get as a stepparent or as new siblings. In such marriages, siblings probably will not love each other or even get along automatically. Children often resist a new stepparent's expectations for behavior. Former single parent and attorney Nancy Palmer suggests the following:

- Go slowly. Developing good relationships takes time.
- Listen with your whole self. Say little. Attend carefully to what a child may be saying between the lines of conversation.
- Understand what life must be like for the children, both your own and your spouse's. Neither may have been stepchildren before. Listen to them, talk with them. Let your attitude communicate to each one, "I care about you. Tell me what you are feeling."
- Always expect good behavior. Act surprised at any evidence of misbehavior. Avoid saddling a child with reminders of former misdeeds.
- Never ridicule or laugh at a child's ideas. Search for posi- tive values in what the young- ster has shared.
- Probe for overlooked areas of expertise or talent in each child. Once discovered, acknowledge that child as your "resident expert" in that specialty.
- Recognize each child's positive qualities and traits. Be particu- larly alert to this when focus- ing attention on a quiet child.[3]

What emotions is my son having regarding my remarriage?

The only way you can find out is to get him to talk. Author Gary Sprague describes the following concerns expressed by kids in stepfamilies:

"I keep comparing my step- parent to my birth parent."

"I can't get along very well with my stepparent."

"I don't get along with my stepbrothers and sisters."

"I am jealous of my new half brother or sister."

"I feel sorry for my parent who is still single."

"My stepparent plays favorites with her own children."

"I spend less time now with my birth parent."

"I am jealous of my step- parent."

"My parents continue to put me in the middle."

"My parents are too busy to spend time with me."

"My stepparent competes with my birth parent."

"I don't know what to call my stepparent."

"My parent's last name is different from mine."

"I don't feel safe or secure in my family anymore."

"My parents fight about visitation."[4]

Remarriage should be one of the most carefully thought-out decisions you will ever make. The changes it brings will reverberate through you and your new mate and all the children involved. This choice affects all future choices you will make. Proceed with care, go slow, and be wise.

Some single parents will marry for the first time, others remarry following death or divorce. Whether you marry or not, be well informed. You have too much to lose to do otherwise.

Today's Journey:
Vaya Con Dios

Shortly after moving to Colorado, I passed an interstate sign that indicated the exit to Grand Junction. *Oh*, I thought, *it's been more than ten years since I was there. Maybe I'll just buzz over and visit.*

Many months passed before I actually got an opportunity to go to Grand Junction. I found out quickly, however, that it was not just a "buzz" away. Instead, it was several hundred miles.

I often think the same way in my single-parenting life. I have determined I am on the right road, and I expect to get to my destination quickly and without trouble. But the journey seems difficult and endless at times, and it causes me to forget to see the beauty along the way. Sometimes I doubt that I'm the best person to make the trip or that I'm even heading in the right direction.

If we are committed to our families and have asked God to join us in making the journey, we will never be alone. It might take longer than we had planned and more troubles may occur than we ever expected. But if we follow the map and drive carefully, we're going to make it safely. We're on the right road, so let's sit back and enjoy the ride.

Notes

Part 1: What Route Brings You Here?

Marital Status

[1]Romans 5:5.

Chapter 1: The Divorced

[1]Census Bureau, 1995.

[2]American Demographics, 1995.

[3]Leslie N. Richards and Cynthia J. Schmiege, "Problems and Strengths of Single-Parent Families: Implications for Practice as Policy," *Family Relation*, (July 1993).

[4]Barb Schiller, "A Grip on Grief," *Single-Parent Family* (August 1995).

Chapter 2: The Never-Married

[1]Census Bureau, 1995.

[2]Census Bureau, 1995.

[3]1 John 1:9.

[4]Barbara Dafoe Whitehead, "Dan Quayle Was Right," *Atlantic* (April 1993).

[5]Gary Sprague, "Breaking the Cycle," *Single-Parent Family* (January 1996).

[6]Henry Cloud and John Townsend, *Safe People: How to Find Relationships That Are Good for You and Avoid Those That Aren't* (Grand Rapids: Zondervan, 1995).

[7]Neil Clark Warren, *Finding the Love of Your Life* (Colorado Springs: Focus on the Family, 1992).

[8]Kelly Martindale, "How to Tell Your Kids Not to Even Though You Did," *Single-Parent Family* (February 1996).

Chapter 3: The Widowed

[1]Ephesians 4:26.

[2]Ephesians 4:31–32; Romans 12:17.

[3]Elisabeth Kubler-Ross, *On Death and Dying* (New York: MacMillan, 1969).

[4]Ecclesiastes 3:1–2.

[5]Hebrews 9:27.

[6]Jeremiah 29:11.

Part 2: What Legalities Are Involved?

Issues

[1]Matthew 10:16.

Chapter 4: Custody

[1]1 Chronicles 28:10 AMPLIFIED.

[2]G. Newman, *101 Ways To Be a Long-Distance Super Dad . . . or Mom, Too* (Saratoga, Calif.: R. & E. Publishers, 1996).

Chapter 5: Visitation

[1]J. Flippen, "Two Bedrooms," *Single-Parent Family* (May 1995).

Chapter 6: Child Support

[1]Census Bureau, 1995.

[2]Nancy Palmer and Ana Rodriguez, *When Your Ex Won't Pay* (Colorado Springs: Pinon Press, 1995).

Part 3: How Do You Feel?

Emotions

[1]C. S. Lewis, *A Grief Observed*, (San Francisco: HarperCollins, 1961).

[2]Lewis, *A Grief Observed*.

Chapter 8: Grief

[1]John 11:35.

[2]Elisabeth Kubler-Ross, *On Death and Dying* (New York: Macmillan, 1969).

[3]Barbara Schiller, *Just Me and the Kids* (Elgin, Ill.: David C. Cook, 1995).

[4]Barbara Schiller, "A Grip on Grief," *Single-Parent Family* (June 1995).

[5]Claudia Jewett, *Helping Children Cope with Separation and Loss* (Boston: Harvard Common Press, 1982).

[6]Greg Cynaumon, *Single Parents with Troubled Kids* (Colorado Springs: Nav-Press, 1992).

Chapter 9: Fear

[1]D. Gackenbush, *Harry and the Terrible Watzit.* (New York: Clarion Books, 1977).

[2]Proverbs 1:7.

[3]Carol Kent, *Tame Your Fears* (Colorado Springs: NavPress, 1993 in No. 5).

[4]C. S. Lewis, *A Grief Observed* (San Francisco: HarperCollins, 1961).

[5]Kent, *Tame Your Fears*.

[6]Psalm 37:23 KJV.

[7]Karen Randau, *Conquering Fear* (Waco, Tex.: Word, 1991).

[8]Gary Oliver, *Good Women Get Angry* (Ann Arbor, Mich.: Servant, 1995).

[9]Edmund J. Bourne, Ph.D., *The Anxiety and Phobia Workbook* (Oakland, Calif.: New Harbinger, 1995).

[10]Philippians 4:6–7.

Chapter 10: Anger

[1]Neil Clark Warren, *Make Anger Your Ally* (Colorado Springs: Focus on the Family Publishing, 1990).

[2]Frederick Buechner, *Wishful Thinking* (San Francisco: Harper & Row, 1973).
[3]Ephesians 4:26 NKJV.
[4]Albert Ellis, *Anger: How to Live With and Without It* (Flushing, N.Y.: Asia Book Corp., 1994)
[5]Ephesians 4:31–32.
[6]Warren, *Make Anger Your Ally*.

Chapter 11: Guilt

[1]James Dobson, *Emotions: Can You Trust Them?* (Ventura, Calif.: Regal, 1980).
[2]Ty C. Colbert, *Why Do I Feel Guilty When I've Done Nothing Wrong?* (Nashville: Nelson, 1993).
[3]Les Parrott III, *Love's Unseen Enemy* (Grand Rapids: Zondervan, 1994).
[4]Carmen R. Berry and Mark W. Baker, *Who's to Blame?* (Colorado Springs: Pinon, 1996).
[5]Colbert, *Why Do I Feel Guilty?*

Chapter 12: Forgiveness

[1]Lewis B. Smedes, *Forgive and Forget* (San Francisco: Harper & Row, 1984).
[2]Smedes, *Forgive and Forget*, 1984.
[3]Smedes, *Forgive and Forget*, 1984.
[4]Smedes, *Forgive and Forget*, 1984.
[5]Jay Carty, "Have Your Nostrils Flared Lately?" *Single-Parent Family* (September 1996).
[6]C. S. Lewis, *A Grief Observed* (San Francisco: HarperCollins, 1961).
[7]Matthew 6:12 NEB.

Chapter 13: Sadness or Joy?

[1]Siang-Yang Tan and John Ortherg Jr., *Understanding Depression* (Grand Rapids: Baker, 1995).
[2]Archibald Hart, *Counseling the Depressed* (Waco, Tex.: Word, 1987).
[3]Brenda Poinsett, *Why Do I Feel This Way?* (Colorado Springs: NavPress, 1996).
[4]Poinsett, *Why Do I Feel This Way?*
[5]Ella Wheeler Wilcox, *The Best Loved Poems of the American People* (Garden City, N.Y.: Garden City Books, 1936).
[6]David Popenoe, "A World without Fathers," *WQ* (Spring 1996).
[7]Popenoe, "A World without Fathers."

Part 4: Who's Riding Along?

Chapter 15: Elementary Schoolers

[1]Ken Canfield, *The Heart of a Father* (Chicago: Northfield, 1996).
[2]Gary Sprague, *Kids Caught in the Middle* (Nashville: Nelson, 1993).
[3]David Popenoe, "A World without Fathers," *WQ* (Spring 1996).

[4]Sprague, *Kids Caught in the Middle.*

[5]Doug Easterday, "Child or Companion?" *Single-Parent Family* (June 1996).

Chapter 16: Adolescents

[1]James Dobson, *Parenting Isn't for Cowards* (Waco, Tex.: Word, 1987).

[2]Jeenie Gordon, "Parents Taking Action," *Single-Parent Family* (September 1996).

Chapter 17: Older Teens

[1]James Dobson, *Parenting Isn't for Cowards* (Waco, Tex.: Word, 1987).

[2]K. Huggins, *Parenting Adolescents* (Colorado Springs: NavPress, 1989).

[3]D. Veerman, *Parenting Passages* (Wheaton, Ill.: Tyndale House, 1994).

[4]David Popenoe, "A World without Fathers," *WQ* (Spring 1996).

[5]Gary Sprague, *Kids Caught in the Middle* (Nashville: Nelson, 1993).

Chapter 18: Boy or Girl?

[1]William Beausay II, *Boys! Shaping Ordinary Boys into Extraordinary Men* (Nashville: Nelson, 1994).

[2]2 Corinthians 12:10.

[3]Twila Paris, "The Warrior Is a Child," (Nashville: Benson Company, Inc., 1988). Used by permission.

[4]Susie Shellenberger and Greg Johnson, *258 Dates While You Wait* (Nashville: Broadman and Holman, 1995).

Part 5: What Roadblocks Do You Face?

Chapter 19: Discipline

[1]Proverbs 13:24 NASB.

[2]Proverbs 22:15 NKJV.

[3]Proverbs 23:13.

[4]Proverbs 19:18 LB.

[5]Revelation 3:19.

[6]D. Baumrind, "Some Thoughts about Childrearing," *Influences on Human Development*, eds. U. Bronfenbrenner and M. Mahoney (Hinsdale, Ill.: Dryden, 1975).

Chapter 20: Self-Esteem

[1]D. Baumrind, "Some Thoughts about Childrearing," *Influences on Human Development*, eds. U. Bronfenbrenner and M. Mahoney (Hinsdale, Ill.: Dryden, 1975).

[2]Philippians 4:8.

Chapter 21: Preparing the Kids

[1]Proverbs 22:6.

[2]1 Timothy 6:6.

Part 6: What Are You Learning?

Chapter 21: Preparing the Kids

[1]Centerwall, "Television and Violence," p. 3060 and George Will, "Turning Into an Aggressive Society," *Rocky Mountain News*, April 11, 1993.

[2]Robert S. Lichter, Daniel Amundso, "A Day of TV Voiolence: 1992–1994," Center for Media and Public Affairs (1994).

Chapter 22: Setting Goals

[1]Myles Munroe, *In Pursuit of Purpose* (Shippensburg, Penn.: Destiny, 1992).

[2]Habakkuk 2:2–3 NASB.

[3]Florence Littauer, *Silver Boxes* (Waco, Tex.: Word, 1991). Used by permission

Chapter 23: Finding Balance

[1]William and Nancie Carmichael, *Lord Bless My Child* (Wheaton, Ill.: Tyndale House, 1995).

[2]Kathy Peel, *How to Simplify Your Life* (Waco, Tex.: Word, 1994). Used by permission.

[3]Luke 2:52.

[4]Matthew 6:20.

Chapter 25: Combating Stress

[1]Archibald Hart, *Stress and Your Child* (Waco, Tex.: Word, 1992).

[2]Frank F. Furstenberg Jr. and Graham B. Spanier, *Recycling the Family: Remarriage after Divorce* (Newbury Park, Calif.: Sage, 1984).

[3]Matthew 7:7–8.

Chapter 26: Coping with Change

[1]Ecclesiastes 3:1–8.

[2]Thomas Holmes and Richard H. Rahe, "The Impact of Life Changes," "Social Readjustment Scale," *Journal of Psychosomatic Research* 11 (2) (New York: Pergamon, 1967).

[3]Gary Sprague, *Kids Caught in the Middle* (Nashville: Nelson, 1993).

Chapter 27: Enhancing Communication

[1]Patti Townsley Covert, "Hidden Messages," *Single-Parent Family* (May 1996).

[2]James 1:5.

Chapter 28: Finding Time

[1]Proverbs 4:26.

Chapter 29: Managing Money

[1]Census Bureau, 1995.

[2]Elizabeth Watson, "College Just May Be the Answer," *Single-Parent Family* (November 1994).

[3]Larry Burkett, *Surviving the Money Jungle* (Gainesville, Georg.: Christian Financial Concepts, 1995).

[4]Larry Burkett, *Surviving the Money Jungle*, 1995.

[5]Larry Burkett, *Get a Grip on Your Money* (Colorado Springs: Focus on the Family, 1990).

[6]Malachi 3:10–11.

[7]2 Corinthians 9:7.

[8]Larry Burkett, *The Financial Guide for the Single Parent* (Chicago: Moody Press, 1997). Used by permission. Both a book and a workbook are available.

[9]Mary Hunt, *The Complete Cheapskate Monthly* (Colorado Springs: Focus on the Family Publishing, 1996).

Chapter 30: Developing Safe Relationships

[1]Henry Cloud and John Townsend, *Safe People* (Grand Rapids: Zondervan, 1995).

[2]C. R. Berry and M. W. Baker, *Who's to Blame?* (Colorado Springs: Pinon, 1996).

[3]Proverbs 18:24 KJV.

[4]Cloud and Townsend, *Safe People*.

[5]Neil Clark Warren, *Finding the Love of Your Life* (Colorado Springs: Focus on the Family, 1992).

[6]2 Corinthians 6:14 KJV.

[7]Myles Munroe, *Single, Married, Separated, and Life after Divorce* (Shippensburg, Penn.: Destiny Image, 1992).

[8]Trussell and Hatcher as published in *Contraception*, January 1992, Vol 45, No. 1.

Chapter 31: Getting Remarried

[1]American Demographics, 1995.

[2]American Demographics, 1995.

[3]Nancy S. Palmer, William D. Palmer, and Kay Marshall Strom, *The Family Puzzle* (Colorado Springs: Pinon, 1996).

[4]Gary Sprague, *Kids Caught in the Middle* (Nashville: Nelson, 1993).

Resources

Part 1: What Route Brings You Here?

Aldrich, Sandra. *Living Through the Loss of Someone You Love*. Ventura: Regal, 1990.

Burns, Bob and Tom Whiteman. *The Fresh Start Divorce Recovery Workbook*. Nashville: Nelson, 1992.

Gordon, Jeenie. *There's Hope After Divorce*. Grand Rapids: Spire, 1991.

Hart, Archibald D. *Helping Children Survive Divorce*. Dallas: Word, 1996.

Newman, George. *101 Ways to Be a Long-Distance Super Dad . . . or Mom, Too*. Saratoga, CA: R & E, 1996.

Richmond, Gary. *Successful Single Parenting*. Eugene, OR: Harvest House, 1990.

Taylor, Rick. *When Life Is Changed Forever*. Eugene, OR: Harvest House, 1992.

Part 2: What Legalities Are Involved?

Blankenhorn, David. *Fatherless America*. New York: Basic Books, 1995.

Collins, Gary R. *Family Shock*. Wheaton, IL: Tyndale, 1995.

Palmer, Nancy and Ana Rodriguez. *When Your Ex Won't Pay*. Colorado Springs: Pinon, 1995.

Part 3: How Do You Feel?

Grief

Becton, Randy. *Everyday Comfort*. Grand Rapids: Baker, 1993.

Davis, Verdell. *Let Me Grieve, But Not Forever*. Dallas: Word, 1997.

Fitzpatrick, Barol. *A Time to Grieve*. Uhrichsville, OH: Barbour, 1995.

Kubler-Ross, Elisabeth. *On Death and Dying*. New York: McMillan, 1969.

Les Strang, Barbara. *After-Loss*. Summerland, CA: Harbor House, 1992.

Robinson, Haddon W. *Comfort Those Who Grieve and Those Who Want Help*. Grand Rapids: Discovery House, 1996.

Sisson, Ruth. *Moving Beyond Grief*. Grand Rapids: Discovery House, 1994.

Soder-Alderfer. *With Those Who Grieve*. Scarsdale, NY: Lion, 1994.

Taylor, Rick. *When Life Is Changed Forever*. Eugene, OR: Harvest House, 1992.

Fear

Kent, Carol. *Tame Your Fears*. Colorado Springs: NavPress, 1994.

Randau, Karen. *Conquering Fear*. Nashville: Ralpah/Word, 1991.

Warren, Paul and Frank Minirth. *Things That Go Bump in the Night: How to Help Children Resolve Their Natural Fears*. Nashville: Nelson, 1992.

Anger

Campbell, Ross. *Kids in Danger*. Wheaton, IL: Victor, 1995.

Carter, Les and Frank Minirth. *The Anger Workbook*. Nashville: Nelson, 1993.

Oliver, Gary J. and H. Norman Wright. *Good Women Get Angry*. Ann Arbor: Servant, 1993.

Warren, Neil Clark. *Make Anger Your Ally*. Colorado Springs: Focus on the Family, 1990.

Guilt

Colbert, Ty C. *Why Do I Feel Guilty When I've Done Nothing Wrong?* Nashville: Nelson, 1993.

Johnson, Becca C. *Good Guilt, Bad Guilt*. Downers Grove, IL: InterVarsity Press, 1996.

Parrott III, Les. *Love's Unseen Enemy*. Grand Rapids: Zondervan, 1994.

Wilson, Sandra. *Released From Shame*. Downers Grove, IL: InterVarsity Press, 1990.

Forgiveness

Berry, Carmen Renee and Mark W. Baker. *Who's to Blame? Escape the Victim Tray and Gain Personal Power in Your Relationships*. Colorado Springs: Pinon, 1996.

Haney, Joy. *How to Forgive When It's Hard to Forget*. Green Forest, AK: New Leaf, 1996.

Harvy, Robert and David M. Benner. *Choosing the Gift of Forgiving*. Grand Rapids: Baker, 1996.

Smedes, Lewis. *Forgive and Forget*. New York: Harper and Row, 1984.

Sadness

Hulme, William and Lucy. *Wrestling With Depression*. Minneapolis: Augsburg, 1995.

Poinsett, Brenda. *Why Do I Feel This Way? What Every Woman Needs to Know About Depression*. Colorado Springs: NavPress, 1996.

Joy

Clairmont, Patsy, Barbara Johnson, Marilyn Melberg, and Lucy Swindoll. *The Joyful Journey*. Grand Rapids: Zondervan, 1994.

Leavill, Jo Ann Paris. *Joy in the Journey*. Gretna, LA: Pelican, 1994.

Other Emotions

Berry, Carmen R. and Mark W. Baker. *Who's to Blame?* Colorado Springs: Pinon, 1996.

Carney, Glandion and William Long. *Trusting God Again*. Ann Arbor: Servant, 1994.

Fryling, Alice. *Reshaping the Jealous Heart*. Downers Grove, IL: InterVarsity Press, 1994.

Mains, Karen Burton. *Lonely No More*. Dallas: Word, 1993.

Rankin, Peg. *Yet Will I Trust Him*. Ventura: Regal, 1980.

Sprinkle, Pat. *Learning Who and How to Trust Again*. Ann Arbor: Servant, 1994.

Varick, Lori A. *Designed for Dependency*. Lynnwood, Wash.: Emerald, 1994.

White, Jerry. *The Power of Commitment*. Colorado Springs: NavPress, 1985.

Part 4: Who's Riding Along?

Beausay, William II. *Boys! Shaping Ordinary Boys into Extraordinary Men*. Nashville: Nelson, 1994.

Beausay, William II and Kathryn. *Girls! Helping Your Little Girl Become an Extraordinary Woman*. Old Tappan, NJ: Revell, 1996.

Cline, Foster and Jim Fay. *Parenting Teens With Love and Logic*. Colorado Springs: Pinon, 1992.

Groseclose, Kel. *This Too Shall Pass*. Nashville: Dimensions, 1995.

Huggins, Kevin. *Parenting Adolescents*. Colorado Springs: NavPress, 1989.

Kuykendall, Carol. *Give Them Wings*. Colorado Springs: Focus on the Family, 1994.

Neff, Miriam. *Helping Teens in Crisis*. Wheaton, IL: Tyndale House, 1994.

Pipher, Mary. *Reviving Ophelia*. New York: Ballantine Books, 1994.

Rutter,Virginia Beane. *Celebrating Girls: Nurturing and Empowering Our Daughters*. Berkeley: Conari Press, 1996.

Simon, Mary Manz. *How to Parent Your Teenager: Understanding the In-Between Years of Your 8–12-Year-Old*. Nashville: Nelson, 1995.

Stinnett, Nick and Michael O'Donnell. *Good Kids: How You and Your Kids Can Successfully Navigate the Teen Years*. New York: Doubleday, 1996.

Part 5: What Roadblocks Do You Face?

Barnes Jr., Robert G. *Who's in Charge Here? Overcoming Power Struggles With Your Kids*. Grand Rapids: Zondervan, 1990.

Canfield, Ken. *The Heart of a Father*. Chicago: Northfield, 1996.

Chase, Betty. *Discipline Them Love Them*. Elgin, IL: David C. Cook, 1982.

Cline, Foster and Jim Fay. *Parenting With Love and Logic: Teaching Children Responsibility*. Colorado Springs: Pinon, 1990.

Dobson, James. *Dare to Discipline*. New York: Bantam, 1970.

Greenfield, Guy. *The Wounded Parent: Hope for Discouraged Parents*. Grand Rapids: Baker, 1990.

Kimmel, Tim. *Little House on the Freeway*. Portland: Multnomah Press, 1994.

Langston, Teresa A. *Parenting Without Pressure*. Colorado Springs: Nav-Press, 1994.

Leman, Kevin. *Bringing Up Kids Without Tearing Them Down*. Nashville: Nelson, 1995.

Moore, June Hines. *You Can Raise a Well-Mannered Child*. Nashville: Broadman, 1996.

Peel, Kathy and Joy Mahaffey. *A Mother's Manual for Summer Survival*. Colorado Springs: Focus on the Family, 1989.

Phelan, Thomas W. *1-2-3 Magic: Effective Discipline for Children 2–12*. Glen Ellyn, IL: Child Managment, Inc., 1995.

Phelan, Thomas W. *Self-Esteem Revolutions in Children: Understanding and Managing the Critical Transitions in Your Child's Life*. Glen Ellyn, IL: Child Managment, Inc., 1996.

Scott, Buddy. *Relief for Hurting Parents*. Lake Jackson, TX: Allon Publishing, 1989.

Smith, Tim. *The Relaxed Parent*. Chicago: Northfield, 1996.

Sprinkle, Patricia. *Children Who Do Too Little*. Grand Rapids: Zondervan, 1996.

Sprinkle, Patricia. *Women Who Do Too Much*. Grand Rapids: Zondervan, 1992.

Veerman, David. *Parenting Passages*. Wheaton, IL: Tyndale House, 1994.

Part 6: What Are You Learning?

Dealing with Conflict

Crary, Elizabeth. *Help! The Kids Are at It Again: Using Kid's Quarrels to Teach "People Skills."* Seattle: Parenting Press, Inc., 1997.

Maloney, H. Newton. *Win-Win Relationships*. Nashville: Broadman, 1995.

Coping with Change

Cloud, Henry. *Changes That Heal*. Grand Rapids: Zondervan, 1995.

Coyle, Neva and Zane Anderson. *Living By Change or By Choice*. Minneapolis: Bethany House, 1994.

Kondracki, Linda. *Going Through Change Together*. Old Tappan, NJ: Revell, 1996.

Managing Money

Briles, Judith. *Raising Money-Wise Kids*. Chicago: Northfield, 1996.

Burkett, Larry. *The Financial Guide for the Single Parent*. Chicago: Moody Press, 1997.

Paris, James L. *Living Financially Free*. Eugene, OR: Harvest House, 1995.

Developing Safe Relationships

Cloud, Henry and John Townsend. *Safe People*. Grand Rapids: Zondervan, 1995.

Hawkins, Don. *Friends in Deed*. Chicago: Moody Press, 1995.

Getting Remarried

Aranza, Jacob. *Making a Love That Lasts: How to Find Love Without Settling for Sex*. Ann Arbor: Servant, 1996.

Palmer, Nancy and William D. *The Family Puzzle*. Colorado Springs: Pinon, 1996.

INDEX